Regent Hotel – Kowloon

1) Go to "museum next to hotel "The Peak"

2) Ocean Park (on The Peak) Ocean Park

HONG KONG

<u>Linens</u> Fang's Sheets and Linen Co.
   55-57 Stanley, main street
   HK   813 0337-8
   FAX: 813 2292

<u>HandBags</u> Ashneil (Designer Look A Like)
   Shop 114, Far East mansion, 1/F
   (opp. Sheraton Hotel)
   5-6 middle Road - Kowloon
   Tel 3660509, 7220173
   T.S.T.P.O Box 95501, HK
   FAX: 7210170

<u>coats, suits, etc Tailor</u>
   Pete' Fashions & Optical
   57 Peking Rd., 3/F1.
            Metropole Bldg.
   Opp. Hyatt
   FAX: 24 368-8818
   Tel. 2 368-8818
   above Spag. House

<u>Antiques</u> Charlotte, Horstmann
   Ocean Terminal - Kowloon
   Gerald Godfrey, Ltd.
   Tel 2735-7167
   Fax: 2730 9412

✱ <u>Wah Tung China Co., Ltd (ceramics)</u>
   See folder, enclosed - fabulous

HONG KONG

Caroline Courtauld and Jill Hunt
revised by Nicola J A Saunter

Copyright © 1993 The Guidebook Company Ltd, Hong Kong

Distribution in the United Kingdom, Ireland, Europe and certain Commonwealth countries by
Hodder & Stoughton, Mill Road, Dunton Green, Sevenoaks, Kent TW13 2YA

British Library Cataloguing-in-Publication Data
A catalogue record for this book is available from the British Library

Grateful acknowledgment is made to the following authors and publishers for permissions granted:

Alfred A Knopf Inc and Bloomsbury Publishing Ltd for
Video Night in Kathmandu and Other Reports from the Not-So-Far East © 1988 Pico Iyer

Jonathan Cape Ltd for
A Many-Splendoured Thing © 1952 Han Suyin

William Morrow & Co and André Deutsch Ltd for
The Monkey King © 1978 Timothy Mo

Viking Penguin Inc and A P Watt Ltd for
Hong Kong © 1988 Jan Morris

Deborah Rogers Ltd for
'Good or Bad Chih' by Bruce Chatwin, originally published by the New York Times in 1987

HarperCollins Publishers and Oxford University Press for
The Road © 1959 Austin Coates

Faber & Faber Ltd for
Foreign Mud © 1946 by Maurice Collis

Editor: Peter Fredenburg
Series Editor: Anna Claridge
Illustrations Editor: Caroline Robertson
Map Design: Bai Yiliang

Front and back cover photography by Nigel Hicks
Photography courtesy of Airphoto International 9, 16–17, 92–93, 204; Altfield Gallery 20, 21; Patrick
Van den Berg 148; Rex A Butcher 123 (below); David Chappell 25; Ray Cranbourne 77, 98, 192;
Richard Dobson 54, 152, 172–173, 185; Peter Fredenburg 59, 212; Greg Girard 68–69; The Guide-
book Company 88–89, 106–107, 110, 123 (above), 180; Nigel Hicks 5, 38, 39, 43, 65, 118, 132, 136,
149, 157, 197; Hong Kong Museum of Art 115, 127, 216 (below); Public Records Office, Hong Kong
30, 31, 37, 145; Kate E Schermerhorn 189; Wattis Fine Art 216 (above); Martin Williams 103;
Rainbow Chiu 129

Production House: Twin Age Limited, Hong Kong
Printed in Hong Kong by Sing Cheong Printing Co Ltd

Central looking towards Causeway Bay

Contents

Introduction

—David Dodwell

With your nose pressed to the window of the jumbo descending into Hong Kong, you can be forgiven for serious alarm as you watch the chopsticks of the family at supper in the tenement block pass below the aircraft's poised wheels.

Just when you are sure the undercarriage is going to rip nests of television aerials from the rooftops, the jumbo banks judderingly right, hits the runway, roars into reverse thrust—and all you can see is water on all sides. You would not be human if the adrenalin were not rushing, and it is quite likely that the adrenalin will keep running for the duration of the stay. Whether it is the teeming streets, the Manhattan skylines, the maritime hubbub, the night-time neon spectacles, or joss-scented Taoist temples, even locals often walk Hong Kong wide-eyed.

Beneath Hong Kong's wholly cosmopolitan veneer beats a proud and self-assured Cantonese heart. It has its own heroes and icons; its own vibrant film industry; stars of stage and screen like Anita Mui and Jackie Chan, who may not be known outside the Territory, but who have wealth and cult status within to match Michael Jackson; a cuisine so particular that many Hong Kong Chinese are at best mildly tolerant of other cuisines; a language so vivid and fertile that many say they can only swear, or talk about sex, in English. This is a confidence born out of knowing you can succeed if you work hard, and seeing evidence of the fruits of hard labour all around: Hong Kong has more Rolls Royces per capita than anywhere in the world; it is the world's largest market for cognac; it boasts 130,000 millionaires in a population of 5.5 million, and 1,300 with fortunes over HK$125 million. Gone is the ragamuffin colony of shanty huts and sweatshops. In its place is a global force in world trade and finance in which Italy has become a leading exporter due to the sheer weight of demand for marble, which envelops the inside and outside of buildings, covers many floors, and even lines public fountains.

Richard Hughes, one of Hong Kong's most perceptive journalist-historians, said in his now-classic book *Borrowed Place, Borrowed Time* that Hong Kong 'is a rambunctious, freebooting colony, naked and unashamed, devoid of self-pity, regrets, or fear of the future'. Even today his image holds true—except for the fear of the future. Because it is perhaps this anxiety—recognized specifically since the 1984 signing of the Sino-British Joint Declaration on the future of the Territory as the certain return of Beijing as sovereign ruler—that explains the extraordinary energy that drives its 5.5 million people. Wags have often commented that Hong Kong is driven at any one time by fear or greed—and often both.

It is perhaps then a combination of this apprehension and greed that has transformed Hong Kong from the 'barren rock, with hardly a house upon it' so sneered at by Lord Palmerston, Britain's Foreign Minister in 1840, into the world's 11th greatest trading

Kai Tak Airport, with Hong Kong Island in the background

power with wealth (as measured by gross national product per capita) surpassing that of Ireland and Spain, and creeping close up on Italy and Holland.

The voyage from 1840 through the next 150 years was set to be a roller-coaster ride, as early settlers were amply warned. Within a month of the first land sale on the island a typhoon apparently unroofed every new building on the waterfront, passed on into China, and then returned with a vengeance to wreak havoc on repair work barely begun. The colony's steadily growing population has been given frequent cause to remember they are living on borrowed time—in particular over the past 50 years. Whether it was occupation by the Japanese army as it swept across China and Southeast Asia during the Second World War, or Mao's communist revolution in 1949, the Cultural Revolution in 1967 or the Tiananmen Square massacre in 1989, Hong Kong has never been allowed to forget that it is, was and will always be part of China.

For the floods of refugees fleeing the turmoil that has so often blighted China over the past century, the storm clouds over the motherland have cast a shadow of insecurity across the tiny British colony and prompted many to view Hong Kong as little more than a way-station *en route* to greater stability in the United States, Canada or Australia. For an administration privately alarmed by the rate of emigration since 1984, there has been relief that recipient countries can handle applications from no more than 40,000 emigrants a year. A relief too that worldwide recession has persuaded many to return to a still-buoyant Hong Kong once foreign passports have been secured.

But as more have settled to make Hong Kong their home, and a middle class of professionals has taken root, so worries about China's control have focused on whether Beijing will allow them the political freedoms they have come to take for granted under colonialism's dispassionate meritocracy. The Tiananmen massacre, which brought more than one-fifth of the Hong Kong population onto the streets in candle-lit processions of protest, was but the latest chilling reminder that Beijing sees democracy and anarchy as very much the same thing, and plans to have no truck with either. Hong Kong's embryo democrats, recognizing that their borrowed time runs out in under five years, have been given cause to wonder how China's cloak will fall once the protective shelter of Britain's colonial rule is withdrawn.

But if China has cast dark shadows over Hong Kong, it has also given the Territory its silver lining. The astonishing growth that has been traced over four decades has largely been facilitated by China—for both negative and positive reasons. Hong Kong would never have given birth to its world-beating cloth and garment industries if Shanghai's textile magnates had not fled China for Hong Kong between 1949 and 1952 along with any equipment they could salvage. Even in the darkest days of Maoist xenophobia during the 1950s and 1960s, Hong Kong gained by being China's only window to the outside world. The 13 'sister banks' clustered around the Bank of China in Hong Kong never stopped operations as exclusive conduits for China trade.

But it is since 1978, when Deng Xiaoping, China's wily and pragmatic successor to Mao, launched the policy of 'opening up to the outside world', that China has made Hong Kong's economic miracle possible. Hong Kong industrialists, chronically short of space and manpower, leapt at the chance to shift operations onto the mainland, enriching at a stroke both themselves and millions of mainlanders who had been force-fed a diet of Maoist pie-in-the-sky for 30 years. Today, an estimated 25,000 factories operating in China are either owned by, or are producing exclusively for, Hong Kong companies. They employ over 3 million people—three times Hong Kong's own manufacturing workforce. If they are in any way anxious now about Hong Kong, it is not because of concern about what China might do after 1997, but because their fates are already in the hands of Beijing.

The rate at which trade has grown between Hong Kong and China is simply breathtaking. Hong Kong's exports to China in 1979 were a mere HK$2 billion. By 1992, they amounted to HK$208 billion. China's re-exports through Hong Kong have grown at a similar pace—from HK$7 billion in 1979 to HK$153 billion in 1991.

While Hong Kong has continued to prosper as China's window to the world—and as the focal point for much of the hectic economic growth throughout the Pacific region— so it has managed to continue expansion unscathed through a world recession more severe than any since the 1930s. Governor Chris Patten, expected to be the 28th and last British governor of the Territory, has forecast average growth for the next five years of five per cent a year. His advisors say per capita GDP will have risen to US$30,500 a year by 1997—on a par with Italy and Holland today, and within 12 per cent of France. They say foreign trade will total US$548 billion—up from HK$99 billion in 1991, putting the Territory in the world's top ten trading powers. It is expected to have one of the world's largest container ports at Kwai Chung, capable of handling 9.2 million containers a year, and a new airport north of Lantau island channelling 35 million people a year along its runways.

As Hong Kong's economic and commercial roots have spread deeper into China, so China's presence in Hong Kong's domestic economy has burgeoned. It is difficult to calculate how much of the economy is now controlled by, or owned by, mainland Chinese because very few of China's most powerful companies have any need or inclination to divulge their activities to the outside world. Most of the Territory's water comes from China, as does the lion's share of its fresh food. Huge Beijing-controlled conglomerates like China Resources, China Merchant Steam Navigation, China International Trust and Investment and China Travel manage much of the trade through the Territory, own an increasing proportion of the property and hold who knows what stake in companies on the Hong Kong Stock Exchange. They are matched by provincially owned giants like Guangdong Enterprises. All are served by the Bank of China or its 'sister banks'.

All in all, if it were not apparent a decade ago, it certainly is now: Hong Kong is inextricably part of China—or as Richard Hughes would have had it, 'an impudent capitalist survival on China's communist *derrière*'. As it is absorbed as part of Deng's idea of 'one country, two systems', an increasing number in the Territory recognize that the most promising future lies not in cocooning itself in the 'high degree of autonomy' promised under the 1984 Joint Declaration, but in powering growth in southern China so strongly that Hong Kong becomes the *de facto* capital of the country south of the Yangzi. Already it is the principal dynamo for the 120 million people of Guangdong and Fujian provinces to its immediate north. This would be a fitting role for Richard Hughes' 'rambunctious, freebooting colony', whether before or after 1997—and a fitting epitaph on 150 years of borrowed time—for Hong Kong is living proof that borrowed time is as good as any.

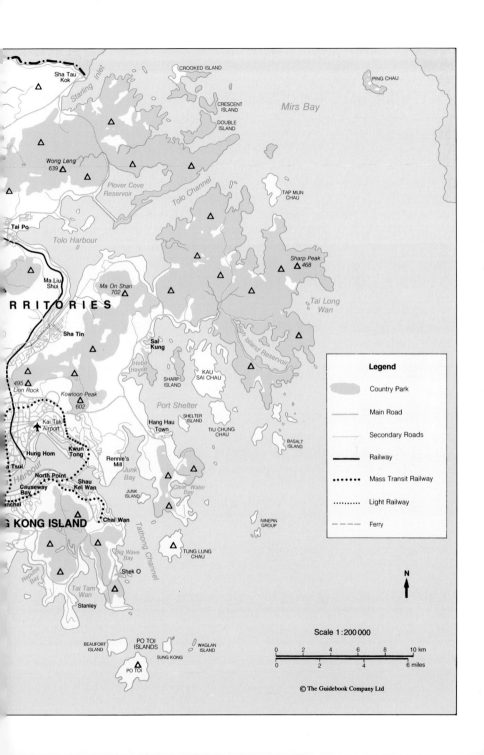

Sha Tau Kok

Starling Inlet

CROOKED ISLAND

PING CHAU

CRESCENT ISLAND

DOUBLE ISLAND

Mirs Bay

Wong Leng 639

Plover Cove Reservoir

Tolo Channel

TAP MUN CHAU

Tai Po

Tolo Harbour

Sharp Peak 468

Ma Liu Shui

Ma On Shan 702

Tai Long Wan

R R I T O R I E S

Sha Tin

Sai Kung

High Island Reservoir

Hebe Haven

KAU SAI CHAU

SHARP ISLAND

Port Shelter

495 Lion Rock

Kowloon Peak 602

Kai Tak Airport

Hang Hau Town

SHELTER ISLAND

TIU CHUNG CHAU

BASALT ISLAND

Hung Hom

Kwun Tong

Rennie's Mill

a Tsui

Harbour

North Point

Causeway Bay

Shau Kei Wan

Junk Bay

JUNK ISLAND

Clear Water Bay

nchai

G KONG ISLAND

Chai Wan

Tathong Channel

NINEPIN GROUP

Big Wave Bay

TUNG LUNG CHAU

Repulse Bay

Shek O

Tai Tam Wan

Stanley

BEAUFORT ISLAND

PO TOI ISLANDS

WAGLAN ISLAND

SUNG KONG

PO TOI

Legend

Country Park

Main Road

Secondary Roads

Railway

Mass Transit Railway

Light Railway

Ferry

N

Scale 1 : 200 000

0   2   4   6   8   10 km

0   2   4   6 miles

© The Guidebook Company Ltd

Arriving in Hong Kong

THE AIRPORT

Like many of Hong Kong's public facilities, Kai Tak Airport has barely been able to keep up with the increasing number of users. Massive expansion is underway, and a new airport on Lantau will be built by the end of the century. But for the moment, arriving passengers should expect a minimum of half an hour to come through Customs and Immigration, and at peak times formalities may take an hour or more.

The terminal building, with its busy concourses and minimum of seating, is designed for efficient passenger handling. In the pre-departure areas you must keep an eye on the computerized departure boards because there are no public announcements of flight departures. An airport tax of HK$150 (free for children under 12 years old) is charged when leaving Hong Kong.

For the benefit of arriving passengers, helpful information counters are run by the Hong Kong Tourist Association (HKTA), the Hong Kong Hotels Association (which will book rooms for you), and the Hong Kong Association of Travel Agents. No matter what your budget, it is always sensible to reserve accommodation in advance, as Hong Kong's increasing importance as a base for doing business with China means many hotels are full virtually all year round.

TRANSPORT TO AND FROM THE AIRPORT

Taxis can be hired just beyond the arrivals hall at two well-disciplined queues (make sure the driver uses the meter). Regular **airport bus** services running about every 15 minutes provide an economical way to get to most major hotels. Route A1 goes along Nathan Road, serving 19 hotels and the YMCA in Tsimshatsui for a flat HK$8.00; A2 stops at eight hotels in Central and Wanchai for HK$12; A3 serves four hotels in Causeway Bay for HK$12; and A4 runs a service to Taikoo Shing. The earliest departure is 7 am and the latest midnight. Put the correct amount in the driver's box as you enter—no change is given on the bus. Many hotels have their own airport buses. Contact a hotel representative outside the customs hall, or ask at the Hong Kong Hotels Association desk.

Although Kai Tak is very near the city centre, roads can be congested and you should allow at least half an hour to get to the airport from Tsimshatsui and an hour from Central during morning and evening rush hours. At other times it takes less than 20 minutes from either area.

Facts for the Traveller

Visas

Visa requirements differ, depending upon nationality. Visitors from most countries can enter Hong Kong without a visa for periods varying from seven days to one year. US citizens can stay for a month without a visa, while Commonwealth citizens can stay up to three months. Visitors from Western European countries fall either into the three-months or one-month category. UK citizens with passports issued in Britain do not need visas at all—when they first arrive a stay of one year is normally granted, and an extension is usually easily obtained.

All visitors must hold valid travel documents and an onward or return ticket and should be able to show they have enough funds to cover their stay in Hong Kong. Residents must register for an identity card and must carry the card or some other proof of identity at all times. Visitors are technically exempt from this regulation, but in your own interests you would be well advised to carry your passport or other similar documents wherever you go in Hong Kong.

Customs

As a free trade centre, Hong Kong allows most items to be carried in duty free. The only dutiable items are tobacco, alcohol, cosmetics and petroleum products. Duty-free allowances for visitors are: 200 cigarettes, 50 cigars or 250 grams (half a pound) of tobacco; one quart of alcohol; perfume in reasonable quantities. Firearms (that is, personal property such as rifles and revolvers) must be declared and handed into custody until departure.

Vaccinations

No vaccinations are required unless you have been in a cholera- or smallpox-infected area within the preceding 14 days.

(following pages) View of Hong Kong and Kowloon from the Peak

Safety

Hong Kong is undoubtedly one of the world's safest cities, and women travelling alone are unlikely to encounter problems, whether eating out, shopping or going to bars. Some of the major hotels offer women-only floors or sections, but few people deem this necessary. The streets are well lit and the level of random street crime is minimal—and even more unlikely in the case of a foreigner. Pickpockets are active in tourist areas, however, so hold onto your belongings in crowded places such as the MTR and Tsimshatsui main streets. Hong Kong is also a safe place to bring children and there is a surprising amount for them to do. However, watch out for the traffic—Hong Kong's streets are very crowded and vehicles often mingle rather too closely with pedestrians.

Climate

Hong Kong has a climate with distinct seasons. A long, hot and humid summer with heavy rain contrasts with a drier and cooler (occasionally chilly) winter. Autumn varies from a few weeks to three or four months, and spring may be no more than a few days. By far the most pleasant weather is during autumn and early winter, from October to the end of December. Skies are clear and blue, the humidity is relatively low (around 70 per cent) and there is little rain. Temperatures during the day reach the mid-20s °C (high 70s °F) and rarely fall below 10°C (50°F) in the evening. March and April are the most unpleasant times of the year, often damp and depressing, with low clouds and mist obscuring even the lower hills. There is little sunshine and increasingly higher temperatures. This is the season when residents complain of mildewed leather, soggy newspapers and walls running with condensation. August is typhoon season (tropical storms with winds of hurricane force), although direct hits on Hong Kong are rare. The public receives plenty of warning via the Observatory's series of signals, hoisted at various points throughout the colony and announced at frequent intervals on television and radio.

What to Wear

Visitors usually find the Hong Kong Chinese well dressed and fashion conscious. Air-conditioning is virtually universal in hotels, restaurants and the larger shops; nonetheless, lightweight clothes are essential for summer. It can be a good idea to take a jacket if you are going to eat in an air-conditioned restaurant—some of them are freezing! You will need an umbrella in the summer, but these are cheap and plentiful locally. Men can wear light trousers and shirts on most occasions during summer, but jackets and ties are advisable for some business appointments and are mandatory in a few smart restaurants. They are also required in the evening in some hotel bars, such as the Mandarin's Captain's Bar. Central heating is rare in winter. Bring some warm clothes—sweaters, jackets and a light overcoat—if you are visiting between December and March.

Money

CURRENCY
As the financial centre of Asia, Hong Kong has over 156 licensed banks from 11 countries. Bank of America, Citibank, Chase Manhattan, Banque Nationale de Paris, Barclays International, Bank of Tokyo—to name a few—all have several branches. A comprehensive network of local banks, including the Bank of China, covers the Territory. Banking hours are from 9 or 10 am to 4.30 pm, with some banks staying open as late as 6 pm.

There is no central bank in Hong Kong. The local Hongkong and Shanghai Banking Corporation Ltd, established in 1864 by Hong Kong-based merchants, and the London-based Standard Chartered Bank issue the territory's banknotes in denominations of $1,000, $500, $100, $50, $20 and $10; in addition there are coins worth $5, $2, $1, 50 cents, 20 cents and 10 cents. Hong Kong currency can be freely imported or exported.

EXCHANGE
Currencies and traveller's cheques can be changed at any bank or at hotels (where the rate tends to be less favourable) and at the many money changers in the business district. Most shops frequented by tourists will also accept payment in hard foreign currencies. Since October 1983, the Hong Kong dollar has been pegged to the US dollar at a rate of HK$7.80 to US$1. The rate at banks fluctuates very slightly from the peg. Sample rates for the other major currencies in February 1993 were:

| £1 | HK$11.25 | 1DM | HK$4.75 | Can$1 | HK$6.15 | S$1 | HK$4.70 |
| 1FFr | HK$1.40 | A$1 | HK$5.30 | 1SFr | HK$5.15 | J¥100 | HK$6.40 |

CREDIT CARDS
Credit cards are widely accepted, but shops are more likely to offer a discount for payment by cash or local personal cheque.

TIPPING
Restaurants, bars and hotels generally add a 10 per cent service charge to bills, but it is customary to leave small change for the waiters. For short trips within the city, taxi

Quick off the Mark

The wonderful progress of our settlement at Hong-Kong, at the first outset, affords perhaps one of the most striking instances that has ever been recorded of the astonishing energy and enterprise of the British character. Great as were the early strides made even by some of the Australian colonies, situated too at the opposite end of the globe, their progress, compared with that of Hong-Kong, was slow and difficult. When our forces were assembled in the harbour of Hong-Kong, on their return from Canton, in June, 1841, there was not a single regularly built house fit for the habitation of Europeans upon the island; for the Chinese villages can hardly be taken into account. When the expedition set sail for Amoy, about two months afterwards, a few mat sheds and temporary huts were all that indicated the future site of the town of Victoria, or pointed out what was soon to become the centre of British commerce in that part of the world, and the seat of British power upon the threshold of the most populous empire the world ever saw.

Within one year from the completion of the first house, not only were regular streets and bazaars for the Chinese erected, but numerous large substantial warehouses were built, mostly of stone, some already

Fort Victoria Kowloon, 1843 (left); Hong Kong Harbour, 1843 (right), T. Allom

finished, and others in progress. Wharfs and jetties were constructed of the most substantial kind; the sound of the stone-mason's hammer was heard in every direction, and a good road was in progress, and an admirable market was established in English style, under covered sheds, and well-regulated by the police. The Chinese willingly resorted to it, and brought abundant supplies of every kind, readily submitting themselves to all the regulations. Large commissariat stores and other public buildings, including barracks at either end of the town, were finished. The road, which was carried along the foot of the hills, extended already to a distance of nearly four miles, and a cut was making through a high sand-hill, in order to continue it further; and at intervals, along the whole of the distance, substantial and even elegant buildings were already erected. The numerous conical hills which distinguish this part of the island were nearly all levelled at the top, in readiness to commence building new houses: stone bridges were in progress, and the road was rapidly proceeding over the hills at the eastern end of Victoria Bay, leading down to Tytam Bay, and the picturesque village of Chek-chu.

The Chinese inhabitants seemed to fall readily into our ways and habits; their labourers and mechanics worked well and willingly for moderate pay, and came over in crowds from the opposite coast to seek work; tradesmen thronged in to occupy the little shops in the bazaars; two European hotels and billiardrooms were completed; and, in short, every necessary, and most luxuries, could be obtained with facility at Hong-Kong, within the first year of permanent settlement. Even the Portuguese missionaries came over and built a sort of convent and a chapel; the Morrison Education Society and the Missionary Hospital Society commenced their buildings; more than one missionary society made it their head-quarters, and the Anglo-Chinese College, at Malacca, was about to be removed to this more favourable spot. A small Roman Catholic chapel was nearly finished, and a neat little American Baptist chapel had been opened for divine service, being the first Protestant place of public worship ever established in that part of the world—of course, with the exception of the old company's chapel, in the factory at Canton. There was, however, no church of England service performed at that time on the island—a deficiency which happily has since been remedied.

Foreign merchants had also commenced building, and it was a curious sight to see the hundreds of Chinese labourers working upon the construction of our houses and roads, and flocking from all quarters to furnish us with supplies, and seeking their living by serving us in every way, at the very time when we were at war with their government, and carrying on hostile operations against their country-men to the northward. At the same time, also, Chinese tailors and shoemakers were busy in their little shops making clothes for us, and Chinese stewards superintended our establishments, while Chinese servants (in their native costume, tails and all) were cheerfully waiting upon us at table: and all this within little more than one year after the first land-sale at Hong-Kong, and while we were still at war.

William Dallas Bernard, *The Nemesis in China*, 1847

drivers do not expect a tip, elsewhere five to 10 per cent is normal. The going rate for porters at the airport is HK$5 per piece of luggage. Hotel bellboys expect HK$5 per bag carried. At barber shops and hairdressers a reasonable tip is 10 per cent of the bill.

Language

For all its veneer of Western sophistication, Hong Kong is unequivocally Chinese where language is concerned. The main Chinese dialect is Cantonese, which is as different from Mandarin, generally spoken throughout mainland China, as French is from Italian. Minority dialects include Shanghainese, Chiu Chow and Hakka.

Officially, English has equal status with Chinese, as reflected in bilingual road signs, public notices, and business and government documents. However, comprehension of English is limited among people you will encounter on public transport or in shops and restaurants other than those accustomed to catering to the local expatriate community. Taxi drivers can be relied on to recognize English names for obvious tourist destinations, but if directed anywhere off the beaten track they may take you to the nearest police station for help or simply ask you to try another taxi. The adventurous tourist would be well advised to ask a hotel receptionist to write out intended destinations in Chinese characters or to carry a street index with English and Chinese place names.

Hong Kong Tourist Association

Tourism is big business in Hong Kong and responsibility for its smooth running rests with the Hong Kong Tourist Association (HKTA), a statutory body 90 per cent subsidized by the government, which co-ordinates the activities of the city and advises on development. If you need advice or information, it is always worth trying the HKTA first, as its staff are helpful and polite. Facilities include a telephone information service (tel 801 7177 Monday–Friday and public holidays 8 am–6 pm; Saturday and Sunday 8 am–1 pm) and several information centres: Star Ferry Concourse in Kowloon, by the ferry entrance (daily 8 am–6 pm); Shop 8, Basement, Jardine House, 1 Connaught Place, Central (Monday–Friday, 8 am–6 pm, Saturdays 8 am–1 pm); Kai Tak Airport, Buffer Hall for arriving passengers (daily 8 am–10.30 pm). There are also representative offices in the US, Europe and Australia. Cathay Pacific Airways represents the association in other areas.

The HKTA publishes a great deal of literature, including a useful tourist map and a frequently updated series of leaflets on shopping, hotels, beaches, museums, walks and other tourist topics. Their free pocket *Official Hong Kong Guide* is disappointingly padded out with advertisements, but the *Dining and Nightlife Guide* and the *Shopping Guide* contain indispensable lists of all the HKTA-approved shops (some 1,300 of them) and restaurants, together with a selected directory of services visitors may need and some useful maps. They also publish a weekly newspaper, *Hong Kong This Week*, mostly useful for its practical information and 'What's On' column.

The familiar HKTA sign—a red junk enclosed in a white circle—indicates that the member is nominally bound to 'maintain ethical standards' and to 'discourage malpractices contrary to the best interests of visitors'. The HKTA investigates any complaints against their members (which should be made by telephoning 524 4191 ext 278) and can terminate membership if appropriate. They will also initiate legal action against a member who has cheated visitors.

Telephones

Hong Kong's subscribers do not pay for local calls, so phones are free in most shops and many hotel lobbies and restaurants. A visitor need only ask to use one. Public call boxes exist in many places, and it costs HK$1 to phone anywhere in the Territory. All numbers are seven-digit and no area codes are necessary.

Getting around Hong Kong

The transport system of the world's most densely populated metropolis is, predictably, highly complex and in a state of perpetual modernization and expansion. A fast-growing population, the engineering problems caused by steep mountain slopes, a bedrock of decomposed granite and a harbour dividing the two main urban centres all conspire to create a transport planner's nightmare.

For the visitor, these problems have resulted in a delightfully wide range of transport. However, in a Territory where there are too many cars for the meagre 693 miles of road, traffic congestion is a perennial problem. Just about all forms of public transport are packed during rush hours (8–9.30 am and 5–6.30 pm). On fine Sundays or public holidays, ferries to outlying islands and all means of getting to the New Territories and to the beaches are equally crowded. If you want to be comfortable, avoid travelling at these times.

Taxis

Hong Kong taxis are cheap by international standards, and in most places they can be easily hailed in the street. In the rush hour, it is best to head for a taxi rank. These can be found outside most hotels, MTR stations, and bus and ferry terminals. In the urban-based red cabs, flagfall is HK$9 for the first two kilometres, with an additional charge of HK90 cents for every 200 metres thereafter. An additional HK$20 is charged if either cross-harbour tunnel is used. Green cabs, which are restricted to rural areas in the New Territories, have a flagfall of HK$8 for the first two kilometres and 90 cents per 200 metres thereafter.

Most drivers understand enough English to get you to the better-known destinations, but Kowloon drivers tend to be vague about Hong Kong Island and vice versa. Taxi drivers are all licensed, and the cars are metered. If you have a problem with an unco-operative driver, note the time and number of the taxi and contact the HKTA or the police, who will pass on your complaint to a special centre.

Ferries

Ferries are a major form of transport in Hong Kong. Services go from Hong Kong to all the major outlying islands; others link different points on both sides of Victoria Harbour (see the map on page 12). Hoverferry services run to Cheung Chau Island and to Tsuen Wan in the New Territories, as well as to Macau.

The most famous service is offered by the Star Ferry Company, whose chunky green-and-white boats have been plying between Central and Tsimshatsui since the end of the last century. For atmosphere and value for money, this seven-minute journey would be hard to beat anywhere in the world. Passengers pay at a turnstile—HK$1.50 for first

The Star Ferry makes its way across Victoria Harbour

class (top deck), HK$1.20 for second class (lower deck). The Star Ferry operates between 6.30 am and 11.30 pm. Passengers never have to wait more than a few minutes, except in the early morning and late at night on Sundays, when departures are at 20-minute intervals. The company also plies a route between Central and Hunghom—a very convenient way to reach the Coliseum and Hunghom Railway Terminus—as well as Wanchai to Tsimshatsui and Hunghom, and Central to Jordan in Kowloon.

Ferries to the largest of Hong Kong's outlying islands, run by the Hong Kong and Yaumatei Ferry Company, leave from the bustling, shabby Outlying Districts Ferry Pier in Central. Tickets are on sale about half an hour before departure from different ticket offices for each route. Queues form early at weekends (when many fares double, so it is best to travel mid-week). Once on the boat to Lantau or Cheung Chau, it is very pleasant to sit out on the deluxe class sun deck. Both Hong Kong Island and the mainland look magnificent from the sea, at night as well as in the daytime. And there is a wealth of other craft to look at—huge passenger liners, cargo vessels, jetfoils to Macau, fishing junks at work and, if you are lucky, a deep-sea fishing junk with batwing sails spread wide.

Fares are HK$12 for deluxe class on a weekday trip to Lantau (55 minutes direct) and HK$7 for the lower second class deck, which has no air-conditioning or sun deck. There are toilet facilities and a small snack bar on board.

Buses

Hong Kong's heavily used bus network reaches most corners of the Territory. First-time visitors to Hong Kong are likely to have difficulty working out the route of any one bus, since only the terminus is displayed on the front. The best solution is to call the HKTA, which gives excellent up-to-date information on the best route to take. Although some of the major tourist and commuter routes are now running air-conditioned vehicles, most buses are cramped, dirty and driven at terrifyingly high speeds.

They are, however, cheap as fares range from HK50 cents to HK$22. Drop the money into the coin box (the amount is usually displayed beside the box) as you get on; no change is given. There are no conductors on board, and you should not rely on any help from the driver in recognizing your destination. To signal that you want to get off at the next stop, push the black rubber strip on the ceiling.

Minibuses

Once you work out how to use them, the cream-coloured minibuses with a red stripe, which weave in and out of traffic stopping virtually anywhere, provide a quick, convenient way of getting about. These 14-seater privately owned vehicles run mostly on major routes in direct competition with double-decker buses or trams, and thanks to their total disregard for safety and common sense, their drivers cover distances considerably more quickly than their rivals. The minibus can stop just about anywhere (except in certain restricted zones); hold out your hand to hail a bus, and simply shout at the driver when you want to get out. Choosing the right minibus is sometimes difficult; although the final destination is displayed on the front, the sign is sometimes too small to see until the bus has whizzed past. Fares (shown in the front window and paid when you get on) are a little higher than ordinary buses and fluctuate according to demand, sometimes tripling when it rains or on race days.

Minibuses with a green stripe are known as maxicabs and are under tighter government control than the others. They are designed to serve areas which do not have a full bus service. Fares (usually paid when you get on), frequency and stopping places are all fixed. Many of the most useful routes for tourists have their terminus on either side of City Hall in Central.

TRAINS

Hong Kong has only one railway line—a section of the old Canton–Kowloon Railway, which first opened in 1911. The line has seen grander days, when it formed the last leg of the London–Hong Kong run, terminating in a splendid granite and red brick railway station on the Tsimshatsui waterfront (only the Clock Tower remains).

Today, double-tracked, streamlined high-speed cars with a passenger capacity of 775 run to China from Kowloon station at Hunghom (right beside the cross-harbour tunnel) from about 6 am until 11 pm. Check with the HKTA or at the station for up-to-date timetable information. Tickets (HK$7 standard) must be bought at the station prior to departure. Children under three ride free, and children 12 and under pay half fare. Stored-value tickets are available, which can also be used on the MTR.

If you have the appropriate travel documents for China, you can stay on the train until the final stop at the border, where Canton-bound passengers climb down and walk across Lowu Bridge into China. There are also four direct express trains a day between Kowloon and Canton.

The train passes through Mongkok, Shatin, the Chinese University, Tai Po Kau, Tai Po and Fanling and Sheung Shui—an interesting journey with picturesque views across Tolo Harbour and glimpses of New Territories rural life. Avoid trains during the statutory holiday breaks, such as Chinese New Year and Easter, when thousands of people visit friends and relations in China, or on sunny Sundays when campers, walkers and barbecuers swarm to the New Territories.

RICKSHAWS

A rickshaw in the traffic chaos of Central or Tsimshatsui looks as incongruous as it would in New York or London. Nevertheless, a few old rickshaw operators lurk by the Star Ferry concourses on both sides of the harbour seeking out tourist business. If you don't mind seeing an old man huff and puff, you can pay between HK$50 and HK$100 for a slow trip around the block. No new licences have been issued for many years, and in time, the remaining 12 rickshaws will become as extinct as the sedan chairs they supplanted.

Peak Tram

Hong Kong's famous funicular railway, the Peak Tram, is much more than just the quickest way to ride up the island's highest mountain—it is one of the most thrilling journeys you can make in the Territory.

The tram rises seemingly vertically (the incline is in fact 45 degrees) from the mass of Central's highrise blocks, reaching Victoria Peak 396 metres (1,302 feet) higher in around eight minutes. Views are magnificent—across Victoria Harbour to Kowloon and the distant hills of China, and down along the northern strip of Hong Kong Island to Wanchai and Causeway Bay.

Designed by a Scot with experience in Scottish Highland railways and opened in 1888, the Peak Tramway retains a solid late-Victorian aura, with green cars and smooth mahogany-slatted seats. Those apprehensive about the gradient (said to be the steepest in the world), the system's age or the slight bounce at mid-way stops should be comforted by the tram's perfect safety record.

Tickets cost HK$16 return and service is continuous from 6 am until midnight. It is worth making the trip by day and by night to enjoy the very different but equally breath-taking views. Try to schedule enough time to walk the almost level path around Mount Austin. If the thought of a return journey down the mountain is too daunting, you can always make your downward journey by road—double deckers, minibuses and taxis are all available at the upper terminus. A free bus runs every 20 minutes from the Star Ferry via Central MTR station to the tram's lower terminus in St John's Building, on the edge of Central, a little way up Garden Road opposite the US Consulate. The tram is far more than a tourist attraction, as the numbers of pinstriped commuters, schoolchildren and shoppers testify, but on Sundays and public holidays you can expect long queues of sightseers and locals.

Trams

Despite the seemingly perpetual redevelopment of the urban areas, Hong Kong's tram system, which was first set up in 1904, has not only miraculously survived, but is thriving; 130 million people ride the 30-kilometre (19-mile) system each year.

The distinctive double-decker trams adorned with sprawling, hand-painted advertisements rattle along the north side of Hong Kong Island from Kennedy Town through Central to Causeway Bay, North Point and Shaukeiwan, with a single branchline to Happy Valley. They are not for anyone in a hurry, but if you have a window seat on top and there is a breeze to relieve summer heat, this is a pleasant way to get a bird's eye view of some of the liveliest parts of town.

You enter at the back of the tram, making your way forward (no easy task if it is crowded) and pay as you exit at the front. The fare is a flat HK$1. The final destination of the tram is marked on the front (not all go as far as Shaukeiwan to the east or Kennedy Town to the west). If you are heading towards Causeway Bay or further east, make sure you do not get on a tram that will branch off at Happy Valley.

MASS TRANSIT RAILWAY (MTR)

The MTR has revolutionized transport between Hong Kong Island and Kowloon and along the northern face of Hong Kong Island. This is the world's first underground rail system to be totally air-conditioned; it also has the world's largest station (in Central). It copes with 1.8 million journeys a day. Each vast smooth-gliding carriage seats only 48 (on slippery stainless steel), but there is room for more than 300 to stand.

You need small change to buy your plastic, credit-card-sized, magnetically encoded tickets from machines. Fares range from HK$3 to HK$9, depending on the distance travelled. Look on the concourse wall for directions and a map of the most convenient exit; stations tend to have several, some of them considerable distances apart. If you plan to make more than a few journeys by MTR, consider investing in a stored-value card to avoid the recurring problem of insufficient change. These are sold in denominations from HK$50 to HK$200 at kiosks and banks inside the station concourses. There is a HK$25 card for tourists, but is worth only HK$20 in rides, as it is assumed that tourists will take the card away as a souvenir.

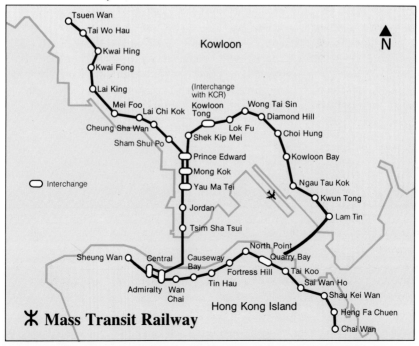

Dark Days

During the first weeks at Shamshuipo Camp, escapes, as has already been mentioned, were frequent, the escapees making their way into Chinese territory where they received assistance from the Chinese guerillas. Plans were pro-

posed for a general breakout from both Shamshuipo and Argyle Street Camps, but news of the plans reached the Japanese authorities. It is considered that the traitorous organisation, the Koa Kikan, recruited mainly from Chinese criminal societies, betrayed the Chinese patriots who would have helped with such a plan for mass escapes. The frequent escapes led to the Japanese re-organising the camps, and during the Spring of 1942, all officer POWs were moved from Shamshuipo to Argyle Street, with the exception of Major Boon who was left behind as Camp Officer together with some half-dozen Medical Officers.

'On Mondays and Fridays,' wrote Sergeant Salmon, 'friends and relations of the POWs were allowed to come within a hundred yards of the camp, and the men eagerly searched for acquaintances among the crowd on the opposite side of the wire. On these days, the cruelty of the Japanese was most evident. They would pick upon some small girl among the crowd and club her with their rifle-butts, strip her, and then throw her to the ground. We held great admiration for these Chinese women. We had seen them during the street fighting in Victoria when they fearlessly brought us out tea, even when the Japanese were machine-gunning us. The women picked up our wounded and took

Japanese air attack, 8 December 1941 (below);
receiving the Japanese surrender, September 1945 (right)

them into their houses. Now week after week they returned and would stand for hours, hoping to catch the eye of a friend.

When the guard's back was turned, they'd run to the wire and throw in a small parcel of food. I cannot speak too highly of the courage of these women.' Among those who braved the Japanese guards and came regularly to Shamshuipo Camp was Ah Suh, the Millingtons' amah. She brought food and clothing for the Millington men, grieving to hear that one of the sons, Sergeant Harry, had been killed. During February 1942, Sergeant Millington made this note:—'Ah Suh sent in a note (hidden in a pot of sugar) which said that our house has been taken over by the Japanese cavalry, the horses being kept on the vacant land in the front and back of the house. Ah Suh has moved next door and taken a few articles with her, because the Japanese ordered her out of our house, and told her to leave everything behind. She also said that most of our furniture including our piano has been chopped up for firewood.'

Ah Suh continued her weekly calls to the camp wire, but during March 1942, she was obliged to leave Kowloon. Sergeant Millington noted: — 'Ah Suh sent in another chit saying she was going back to her own country in a few days, so our parcels will cease in the near future. She has been a real brick. We have been able to send out money to her, and she sends us in all sorts of things. She has left a few articles next door with Mrs Castro's amah, and says that if we want her back after the war, we can get news of her through the Cast

John Luff, *The Hidden Years*, 1955

Hong Kong Island

The brief history of Hong Kong Island is a story of phenomenal growth. When Great Britain first occupied it in 1841, it was, according to Lord Palmerston's much-quoted description, 'a barren island with hardly a house upon it'. Today the island is the centre of one of the most buoyant economies in Asia, with some of the highest population densities in the world.

Hong Kong Island's rapid expansion has consistently astonished the world. The British had been in occupation less than three years when the first governor, Sir Henry Pottinger, reported to England that the settlement had made 'extraordinary and unparalleled progress'. By 1846, the population had doubled (to 24,000, of which 600 were Europeans) and a colonial lifestyle had evolved: horse racing had started in Happy Valley, amateur dramatics were underway and the Hong Kong Club was founded. Central was the first area to be developed, with unsanitary, overcrowded Chinese settlements to the east and west of it. Despite continuing bouts of plague and cholera, by the 1870s sinologist and clergyman James Legge spoke of the northern shore's imposing terraces and magnificent residences, and congratulated the colony on its triumph over the difficulties of its position. Travellers marvelled at the 'Englishness' of the houses and gardens, while a guidebook extolled the island's magnificent public buildings and hotels. By the turn of the century, the population of 300,000 had spread haphazardly from Western to Shaukeiwan and crept up to the Mid-levels and the Peak. Controlled urban planning and legislation, even in these early days, never quite kept up with the developers.

With the leasing of the New Territories in 1898, renewed confidence in the colony meant the injection of more public money into constructing reservoirs and reclaiming more land. The south side became more accessible when work on the first road to encircle the whole island began in 1915.

The rocky, scrub-covered, mountainous terrain, reminding many a British expatriate of Scotland's rugged west coast, looks wholly unsuited to accommodating persistent waves of immigrants. Yet today the 75-square-kilometre (29-square-mile) island has a population of 1.2 million. Most building has been constricted to the flat, narrow strip along the northern shore, and to small areas around Aberdeen, Repulse Bay and Stanley, spreading with extreme difficulty up steep slopes into chiselled-out terraces or onto land reclaimed from the sea. To the unaccustomed eye, it seems that every possible building site has been exploited to the last square foot. Yet engineers continue to do the impossible, driving four-lane highways through mountains and constructing immense concrete platforms up near-vertical slopes to create yet more building space.

While the urban concentrations of Hong Kong Island are now notorious, the beauties of the countryside are less well known. The visitor who ignores the south of the island misses some of the colony's most spectacular views, some stunning walks and country-side that combines subtropical vegetation and wildlife with open scrubland, some of it only minutes from Central.

Visitors to Hong Kong Island can experience with relative ease its extraordinary, intensely concentrated blend of oriental and occidental, of urban and rural, of unsightly poverty and ostentatious wealth, of a nostalgic past and an aggressively modern present.

Central

The Central District of Victoria, usually simply known as Central, is the traditional heart of Hong Kong. It was one of the first areas of the 'barren island' to be developed and today is the centre of Hong Kong's commercial life. Behind concrete and reflecting glass thrives the Territory's big business—finance, trade, banking. At lower levels, elegant stores in air-conditioned shopping arcades serve a cosmopolitan clientele. During office hours, the whole area hums with aggressive activity; at night it empties.

There is much of Manhattan in Central's concentrated jumble of highrise blocks, which grow almost visibly in a frenetic race to maximize land use. Down below, ambitious crowds surge through the streets, often spilling off pavements during the lunch hour. The jostling pedestrian flow pauses only at windows displaying the latest stock-market prices or at the lift lobbies when office staff all try to go back to work at the same time.

The first colonizers established in Central a pattern of rapid uncontrolled development that has barely been broken since. Within months of the British flag-raising in January 1841, a track along the coastline had become **Queen's Road**—still the district's main thoroughfare. European traders, including names familiar in China trading such as Jardine and Dent, grabbed lumps of shoreline for their godowns (warehouses) and almost at once began to expand their territory by filling up sections of Victoria Harbour.

The reclamation process has continually altered the shape of the area ever since. By 1860, enough land had been reclaimed to build another waterfront road—**Des Voeux Road**—running parallel to Queen's Road. **Connaught Road** became the third parallel waterfront road in 1887, a pet project of Sir Paul Chater, the grand old man of Hong Kong real estate and the co-founder of the giant property developers, Hongkong Land.

Few city centres can have experienced so many rapid changes in appearance as Central, where the tradition of tearing down buildings at short intervals to replace them with bigger ones is deeply entrenched. Early photos of Des Voeux Road show elegant, slightly Mediterranean three-storey buildings with verandas shaded by hanging bamboo blinds. Queen's Road had an exotic oriental look about it, packed with pigtailed men and rick-

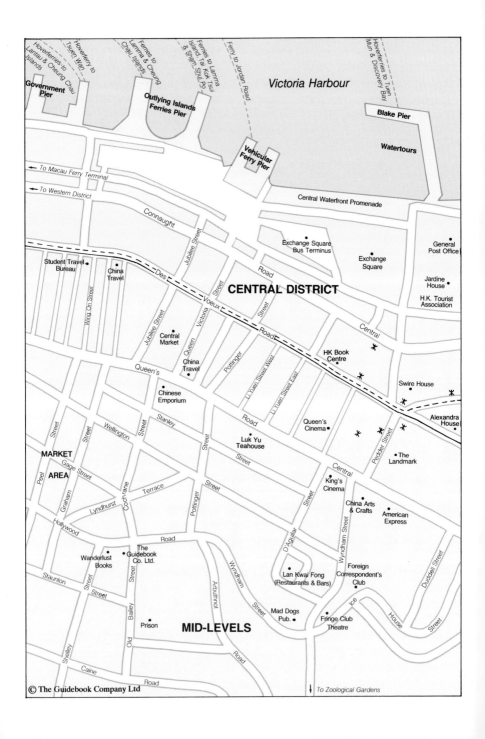

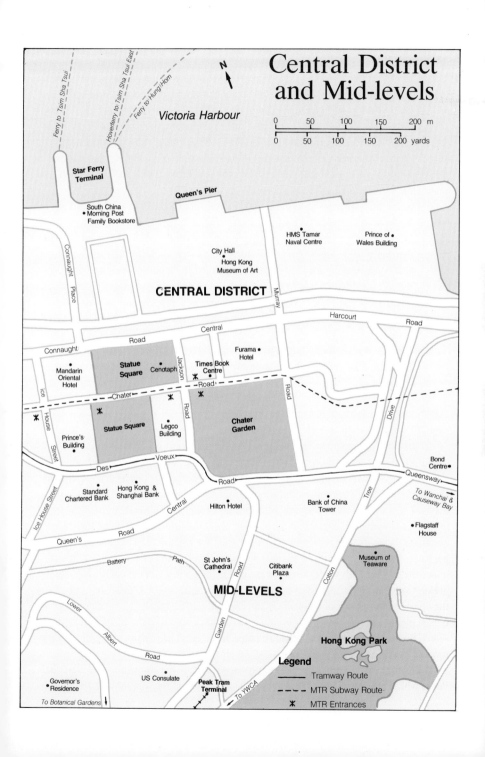

Central District
and Mid-levels

Victoria Harbour

| 0 | 50 | 100 | 150 | 200 | m |
| 0 | 50 | 100 | 150 | 200 | yards |

Ferry to Tsim Sha Tsui
Hoverferry to Tsim Sha Tsui East
Ferry to Hung Hom

Star Ferry Terminal

Queen's Pier

South China
Morning Post
Family Bookstore

HMS Tamar
Naval Centre

Prince of
Wales Building

City Hall
Hong Kong
Museum of Art

Connaught Place

CENTRAL DISTRICT

Murray

Harcourt   Road

Central   Road

Connaught   Road

Furama
Hotel

**Statue
Square**   Cenotaph

Times Book
Centre

Mandarin
Oriental
Hotel

Jackson

Ice

Chater

Road

Prince's
Building

Statue Square

Legco
Building

**Chater
Garden**

House Street

Des   Voeux

Road

Bond
Centre

Queensway

Standard
Chartered Bank

Hong Kong &
Shanghai Bank

Road

Hilton Hotel

Bank of China
Tower

Tree

To Wanchai &
Causeway Bay

Flagstaff
House

Ice House Street

Queen's   Road

Central

Battery   Path

St John's
Cathedral

Citibank
Plaza

Museum of
Teaware

Cotton

MID-LEVELS

Lower

Albert

Road

Garden

Hong Kong Park

Governor's
Residence

US Consulate

Peak Tram
Terminal

To YWCA

To Botanical Gardens

Legend

——— Tramway Route

- - - - MTR Subway Route

✳ MTR Entrances

shaws and flanked by colonnades of stores, the pillars strung with bold Chinese characters. (A few buildings in this style remain in Queen's Road West and Queen's Road East.)

Very few of the old buildings and little of the traditional Orient remain. Those buildings that have survived are in active use, as there has been no place for sentimentality for the past. As incomes and exports increase, so does the scale of the buildings. To office workers today it must seem that construction sites, pneumatic drills and pile-drivers are a permanent way of life.

Central's rich history exists in a less obvious way, not so much in the fabric of the buildings, but in the names of the streets, stores and buildings. **Pedder Street** was called after Lt W Pedder RN, a harbour master appointed by Captain Elliot. **D'Aguilar Street** is named after Major-General D'Aguilar, the first commander-in-chief of the army in Hong Kong. Duddell was a notorious businessman, Pottinger the colony's first governor, Captain William Caine the first magistrate, Bonham, Bowring and Des Voeux all governors. **Ice House Street** of course once served the ice house, which operated twice-daily delivery services of American-imported ice until the 1880s, when Hong Kong began to manufacture its own.

Some stores are also reminders of Central's early days. **Lane Crawford** was originally a ships' chandler, a far cry from its present-day status as Hong Kong's most prestigious department store.

Central is linked to Kowloon by the **Star Ferry** (a subway leads down from Chater Road beside the Mandarin Hotel to the pier) and by the MTR. A bus terminus to the west of the Star Ferry is a convenient place to pick up buses for all parts of the island.

At the heart of Central is **Statue Square**, an open area cut into two unequal parts by Chater Road. The square is virtually unrecognizable from the days when it was edged by ornate, whitewashed colonial-style buildings, each topped with cupolas and turrets and encircled by tiers of enclosed verandas behind Corinthian columns and bulbous balustrades. The design of today's square, with its angular layout of covered sitting areas, rectangles of water and organized tree clusters, was finished in 1966. Today there is only one statue here—that of Sir Thomas Jackson, chief manager of the Hongkong and Shanghai Bank, 1876–1902. On the north side of Chater Road, a simple cenotaph commemorates the dead of both world wars. On the east is the domed and colonnaded old **Supreme Court**, which in 1985 was converted into the home of the Legislative Council and the offices of the unofficial members of the Executive and Legislative councils. This typical piece of Edwardian public architecture (built between 1903 and 1911) was designed by Aston Webb, who was also responsible for London's Victoria and Albert Museum, the façade of Buckingham Palace and Admiralty Arch.

A brave expansion scheme was recently carried out by the **Hongkong and Shanghai Bank**, which has occupied the position on the south side of the square since 1865. Dem-

Pedder Street, 1870 (above); Victoria Waterfront, 1870s (below)

olition of the attractive 1930s block, pictured on millions of banknotes, took place in the summer of 1981. But the building replacing these famous head-quarters was designed to obliterate any momentary regrets with a dazzling dis-play of steel and glass. Architectural correspondents and others say that Brit-ish architects Foster Associates have given Hong Kong a much needed aes-thetic treat with one of the world's most-interesting and, at an estimated HK$1.4 billion, most expensive commercial developments.

With 47 levels above ground and four levels below, the bank's 183-metre (600-foot) tall headquarters dominates its banking neighbours. To the west is the **Standard Chartered Bank**, another established international bank. To the east is a chunky, grey building, the old **Bank of China**, its doorways guarded by solid square-faced Chinese lions.

Further to the east rises I M Pei's new **Bank of China** building. The 70-storey tower has distinct sections like the bam-boo, after which it is modelled. It is through this bank and a network of a dozen or so other China-controlled banks that Beijing holds sway over a sizeable proportion of Hong Kong's bank deposits.

A little way up Garden Road, past the Hilton on the right hand side, is the characteristically Victorian **St John's Cathedral**, built between 1847 and 1849 with a distinctive square, neo-Gothic tower. This is the oldest permanent centre of Christian worship in Hong

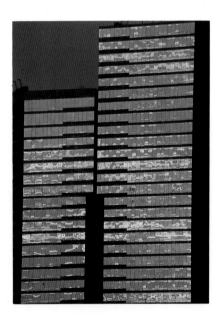

Kong and is still the focus of Hong Kong's Anglican community. The first bishop was a missionary named George Smith, who was given a diocese that, with the supreme self-confidence of 19th-century Britain, covered not only Hong Kong but also all of China and Japan. The ravages of white ants led to major restoration work in 1981.

A path from Garden Road leads past St John's Cathedral to a quieter green patch of mature trees and thick subtropical shrubbery. From here **Battery Path** slopes down to Queen's Road Central, past the recently restored red Amoy-brick former French mission. The building, which dates back to the 1880s, has a versatile past, at different times housing government departments, the Hongkong and Shanghai Bank junior mess, Butterfield and Swire, the Russian Consulate and, of course, the French mission.

The section of Queen's Road Central from Ice House Street to Pedder Street is dominated by towering buildings built by Hongkong Land, who are masters of the art of acquiring, pulling down and putting up property in Central. Covered walkways between the properties allow pedestrians to walk from Queen's Road to the MTR or Star Ferry without touching street level. The centre of this scheme is the **Landmark**, with its elegant window displays by chic, international stores. Eighty or so banks, airline offices, restaurants, jewellers and boutiques are housed here. Inside the Landmark, a vast air-conditioned hall incorporates the latest fashions in public indoor plazas.

The new face of Hong Kong

Escalators sail up past murals to suspended balconies; fountains disport in a circular pool; and overhead a kinetic glass fibre sculpture vibrates to light. At times the fountain in the high atrium is switched off and a platform erected over it to stage performances and displays of many kinds.

As you cross Connaught Road from Pedder Street, looking towards the harbour, the 52-storey **Exchange Square** comes into view. It houses the unified Stock Exchange, stockbrokers and other international firms, as well as a sandwich bar and a number of other eating establishments. Next to this is the massive, round-windowed, 52-storey **Jardine House**, built in 1974 and once the tallest building in Hong Kong. Both projects are owned by Hongkong Land. Behind Jardine House is the **General Post Office** and Government Publications Sales Office, and to the east is the Star Ferry pier. Beside the Star Ferry is an open promenade, Edinburgh Place, which overlooks the harbour, with City Hall's complex of buildings behind. Opened in 1962, these units were once the focus of Hong Kong's public artistic life and still house a couple of theatres (see Arts, page 128). The 12-storey High Block contains libraries, lecture halls and the Hong Kong Marriage Registry. The garden below is a favourite spot for photographing newlyweds.

East of the City Hall complex is **HMS Tamar**, the Royal Navy shore base in Hong Kong. The British armed forces have always been a dominant presence in Central, and their insistence on retaining large chunks of land and shoreline was a long standing frustration to planners and developers. Today's base—sometimes known as the Stone Frigate, since it is officially classed as a Royal Navy ship—is all that is left of the old naval dockyard, which before land reclamation stretched eastwards to Wanchai and right up to the old Victoria Barracks (now **Hong Kong Park**). The army was housed in Victoria Barracks, first established in 1843, until 1978, when the headquarters moved in with the navy to the 28-storey Prince of Wales Building, in the HMS Tamar compound. The tower's narrow base is a security feature, which allows the building to be sealed off in an emergency.

Occupying the eastern end of the old Victoria Barracks is the 22-storey **Supreme Court Building**, which was completed in 1984. Comprising a six-storey podium and a 16-storey tower block, it houses 36 court rooms and ancillary accommodation. In the newly opened Hong Kong Park, the old Flagstaff House, now the **Flagstaff House Museum of Tea Ware**, is one of the finest remaining colonial buildings in Hong Kong (see Museums, page 120).

Five minutes' walk up from Queen's Road Central is **Government House**, the residence of the governor. Entry is forbidden, but it is possible to look through the main gate in Upper Albert Road at the sweeping drive and façade. The building started life as a square neo-classical structure put up in 1855–56 under the watchful eye of Cleverly, a surveyor-general of Hong Kong. Considerable alterations and additions have since been made, the most incongruous of which is the prominent quasi-oriental tower constructed by the Japanese during the Second World War. The Japanese were also responsible for lengthening the roof corners, which are curved upwards and outwards, and for the portico. One Sunday a year, in spring, when the garden's magnificent azaleas are in bloom, the grounds are opened to the public. This is an immensely popular event and queues form several hours before the gates open.

Opposite Government House are the **Botanical and Zoological Gardens**, well worth a visit for anyone seeking a pleasant subtropical leafy retreat. The tiny gardens were created on the terraced hillside in 1860, and since then the varied lush vegetation has made them a favourite with residents. If you go early in the morning you can watch people going through their *tai chi ch'uan* exercises. On a fine Sunday it is a popular place for family outings.

The small zoo boasts an outstanding collection of birds, including many rarities like the Palawan peacock from the Philippines. The relatively small collection of mammals (orang-utans, monkeys, jaguars) still attracts more visitors than London Zoo—perhaps in part because entry here is free. You can enter from Garden Road, Albany Road, Glenealy or Robinson Road. The gardens are divided in two by Albany Road and are linked by an underground walkway.

The Peak

As orientation for the first-time visitor to Hong Kong, or for the sheer delight of the views, nothing can beat a trip up Hong Kong Island's highest mountain, Victoria Peak. Since the 1870s, when the governor, Sir Richard Macdonnell, took to spending the hot and humid months in his summer residence on the Peak, the area has become the enclave of Hong Kong's richest and most influential inhabitants. Many elegant houses are scattered over the slopes of Mount Kellet, Victoria Peak and Mount Gough, where the temperatures are lower but the social position is higher. Said a 19th-century traveller of the area: 'One can spend the summer in Hong Kong with a reasonable probability of being alive at the end of it.'

In the early days access to the Peak was only on foot or by sedan chair, but since 1888 the eight-minute ride on the Peak Tram has taken much of the effort out of the 396-metre (1,302-foot) climb. The No 15 bus from Central offers a longer (30–40 minute) but equally scenic route to the top.

Public transport terminates at the Peak Tower, which lies in the saddle between surrounding mountains. From the viewing platform or restaurants, there are splendid panoramic views of the northern shore of the island, across the harbour to Kowloon and Kai Tak Airport. In the opposite direction, the southern side of Hong Kong Island comes

Hong Kong's Buildings—Old and New

In the face of the myriad skyscrapers, it would be easy to think of Hong Kong as having no past. In fact, many reminders of the past await the patient explorer. The earliest prehistoric inhabitants left huge rock carvings, pottery and gigantic log slides. As the proposed new airport excavations get underway, archaeologists are racing to save as much as possible of the surrounding areas.

Central has its share of both historic and hi-tech buildings. Most visible is the former **Supreme Court Building**, which now houses the Legislative Council Chambers. Completed in 1912, it is particularly graceful when illuminated at night. Directly opposite sits the vast, grey, girder-like structure of **Hongkong Bank** headquarters, and next door is the small, squat ex-head office of the **Bank of China**—a building of pure communist style that now, ironically, houses the extremely élite and capitalist China Club.

Another former court building lies only 200 yards (180 metres) away, behind Beaconsfield House, on Battery Path. What was Victoria District Court has had a chequered history since it was first built in the mid-19th century as the French Mission. Restored in 1987 to an approximation of its 1915 lines, it now serves as an annex to the **Government Information Service**. The outside is charming in a dignified, restrained way, and the elegant proportions of the interior chapel create one of the most beautiful rooms in Hong Kong.

Go east, past St John's Cathedral to the former Victoria Barracks (now Hong Kong Park) with its 19th-century buildings for British army families, one of which houses the **Marriage Registry**. The treasure of the barracks is undoubtedly **Flagstaff House**. Completed in 1846, this is the oldest colonial-style building still standing in Hong Kong. Now a museum of Chinese tea ware, it was the official residence of the commander of the British forces in Hong Kong until 1979, when the entire barracks passed to the Hong Kong government. Between Garden Road and Cotton Tree Drive stands St John's Building, home of the **Peak Tram Terminus**, which looks down onto Admiralty and the bladelike structure of the new **Bank of China**, topped with what appears to be a rugby goalpost. This was Asia's tallest building, overtaken recently by **Central Plaza** in Wanchai.

For a feeling of what life must have been like a century ago, walk up into **Central Police Station** compound, which stands where Hollywood Road becomes Wyndham Street. The magistracy in the same complex dates from 1914, but most of the other buildings are known to be considerably older. Also interesting is the 1884 **Marine Police Headquarters** in Tsimshatsui. With its deep

verandas, watch towers and Round House—in use until the 1930s for the mid-day time signal—this enclave was originally on the waterfront.

Most of the more interesting old Chinese buildings are in the New Territories. It can be difficult to date rural temples, houses and ancestral halls with any certainty as rebuilding on the same site was commonplace.

If you discover a taste for Chinese traditional architecture, look at a large scale map and try exploring places where you see a temple indicated. Villages with the word *vai* or *tsuen* included in their names are worth exploring. The Hong Kong Museum of History sells a book entitled *History Around Us*, which considerably amplifies the admittedly arbitrary selection that follows.

Many villages have changed little in several centuries, and most have some unusual features worth seeking out, including roof ridges and the massive groups of interlocking beams that hold together many traditional buildings.

Railway buffs should not miss the chance to visit the **Tai Po Railway Museum**. When the railway line was fully electrified, the tiny station at Tai Po Market became obsolete. The Chinese decorations and roof trimmings have been repainted, shrubs have been planted, and a modest collection of memorabilia from the beginning of the Kowloon–Canton Railway has been installed. Go out on the tracks to get a good look at the painted bats under the eaves.

Only two minutes away stands the **Man Mo Temple**. In 1986, this was in a terrible state. HK$600,000 later with a new roof and substantial sections of new wall, the place provides a focus for the whole community.

New Territories clans are powerful and wealthy, both evident at the enormous **Man Lung Fung** ancestral hall at San Tin. This is virtually deserted except at festival time. A walk around the courtyards will reveal the subtle lines of beams which rise instead of lying truly horizontal. The Mans came to this area from Jiangxi Province in the 15th century. The hall is popularly believed to be 300 years old. To reach San Tin, turn off the Castle Peak Road where you see the signs for Wing Ping Tsuen and San Tin.

Not far away is one of the territory's most magnificent buildings, the **Tai Fu Tai**. Ask for directions to find it among the clusters of traditional village houses. It is currently undergoing substantial and sensitive restoration, thanks to a HK$2.6 million grant from the Royal Hong Kong Jockey Club. In the 1860s this was the home of an important government official. It is richly adorned with carvings, mouldings and other embellishments of uniformly fine quality. The pottery decorations on the roof ridge are from the Shiwan Wen Ru-bi kiln, one of the most famous in southern China.

into view across Aberdeen to Lamma, Lantau and the South China Sea. Many fine walks begin from the Peak Tower complex. One of the easiest and most satisfying is the 45-minute stroll round Victoria Peak along Harlech and Lugard roads, from where you can get striking views of the city, sea and outlying islands.

Western

For a taste of the traditional life in Hong Kong, there is no better place to go than Western District, to the outsider an exotic, crowded area extending westward from Central that combines the picturesque with the squalid. It is an old residential and commercial area of narrow streets with crumbling three-storey buildings, hawkers' stalls and small wholesale outlets.

It was in Western that the British flag was first hoisted in January 1841, at **Possession Point**. The event is commemorated in the name of a narrow, unprepossessing street, **Possession Street** (not worth a special visit) and, until recently, by a small square surrounded by tumbledown houses. New high-rise blocks and a covered hawkers' bazaar, painted in lurid turquoise, have now been put in the square.

But there are still several chunks of Western that are appealing for a glimpse of traditional urban Chinese life. Walk from Central or take a tram along Des Voeux Road to **Western Market**, a handsome old building in deep red Amoy brick recently renovated and converted into a shopping mall (see page 144). Turn up into **Morrison Street**, part of an asymmetrical jumble of streets lined with fruit and vegetable stalls. On the left, a herbalist sells two kinds of invigorating drinks—one dark and bitter and the other light and sweet. On the corner of **Bonham Strand**, several shops sell traditional everyday wood, rattan and bambooware—ginger graters, rattan pillows, wok brushes, fans and washboards. This is also the area for snake shops. At No 91 Bonham Strand the reptiles are kept in smart wooden boxes, fitted floor to ceiling, with red and gold plush. No 127 is more downmarket, with snakes quite visible in wire cages. In **Mercier Street**, amidst sellers of fishing tackle, string and tropical fish, is the Chinese Gold and Silver Exchange—a small, insignificant-looking building closed to spectators, although even a glimpse through the door gives a lasting impression of the frenetic activity inside.

Further west towards **Sai Ying Pun**, the banks and general stores of Des Voeux Road give way to ship's chandlers, and wholesalers and retailers sell a bewildering array of dried fish imported from China, Japan and Korea. There are shark's fins of all qualities, the best often kept behind glass and priced at over HK$500 a catty (about 0.6 kilogrammes or 1.25 pounds).

Some of the dried merchandise is recognizable—whole fish, shrimps, oysters, snakes and squid. Others are less so. The brown, two-centimetre (one-inch) discs in jars, for instance, are pieces cut from a scallop's root muscle, and the yellowish papery squares are jellyfish with tentacles removed. Other stores specialize in dried mushrooms, including an expensive, crinkly off-white fungus, which expands dramatically when soaked and is good for a clear complexion, and the popular 'cloud ear' which looks like scraps of charred paper until it is cooked and takes on the shape of an elephant's ear. Sacks of tangerine peel, red-brown melon seeds, dried lotus seeds, preserved bean curd and much else turn up in these shops.

Moving inland from here up **Centre Street** or **Eastern Street**, across Queen's Road West, the streets become very busy with markets selling Chinese vegetables, herbs, fruit, sweets, chickens and quails. At right angles, First, Second and Third streets are characteristic of old residential Western, the houses adorned with a tangle of curved wrought-iron balconies, pot plants, shrines, washing, wire-netting and bird cages.

Back eastwards a few blocks, the tiny streets around **Tai Ping Shan** (north of Hollywood Road) are interesting. This area was the site of a Chinese settlement before Hong Kong was ceded to the British (Tai Ping Shan, or Mountain of Peace, was the Chinese name for Victoria Peak). The early settlers were said to be followers of a notorious pirate who controlled the waters around Hong Kong at the end of the 18th century. Later, when the number of Chinese immigrants increased as the British settled in, the area became an important, densely populated, highly unhealthy commercial and residential centre. The original buildings were torn down and rebuilt at the end of the century after a particularly bad bubonic plague epidemic, but many of today's houses seem little altered from that period.

Three small temples stand in **Tai Ping Shan Street**. The surrounding steep lanes, narrow alleyways and steps paved with smooth stones are a mass of accompanying paraphernalia—joss sticks, paper offerings to be burnt and fortune tellers. On the corner with Pound Lane are the **temples of Kuan-yin** and **Sui-tsing Paak**, their origins going back to 1840. Women whose children are ill, or who have other domestic problems, flock to Kuan-yin. The General Sui-tsing Paak next door is believed to cure sickness. Several other gods are included in this temple, the sea goddess Tin Hau among them. An interesting hall has 60 images, each dedicated to one year of the Chinese 60-year cycle. Another has a replica of the mummified body of Hui Neng, founder of the Buddhist Vegetarian Sect. Outside is a much-used open shrine to earth gods, who protect the local community. The third temple is the **Paak Sing**, first established in 1851 (and rebuilt in 1985) to house tablets dedicated to the dead. The inner room contains photographs and over 3,000 tablets. Temple keepers burn incense and oil lamps in front of the tablets for a small fee.

Walking back towards Central you come across Hong Kong's famous ladder streets. The Cantonese equivalent of 'stair street' is in fact more appropriate for these narrow steep stone staircases. The most spectacular is **Ladder Street** itself, which climbs 65 metres (213 feet) up from its junction with Hollywood Road to Caine Road. A considerably shorter equivalent in Central, Pottinger Street, is lined with sellers of buttons and bows, sewing cottons, shoes, combs and other haberdashery.

Hollywood Road and **Cat Street** (Upper Lascar Road) have lost much of their character under an urban renewal scheme. The **Man Mo Temple**, 126 Hollywood Road—a fine example of a Taoist temple built on traditional lines—is well worth a visit if you are in the area. It is heavily used by worshippers who carry on apparently oblivious to the large number of tourists who go there. The temple is dedicated to two Taoist deities: Man Cheong, the god of literature, who also looks after civil servants; and Mo Kwan Kung, the martial god who, it is said, represents the qualities of the two influential Chinese community leaders who founded the temple in 1842. It was rebuilt in 1984.

Behind the fire screening door at the main entrance, the atmosphere is thick with smoke from the giant incense coils that hang in profusion from the ceiling of the section known as 'the smoke tower'. The coils, which burn for two weeks, are ideal for long-term offerings. The worshippers' prayers are written on the red tag that hangs from each. Below, paper offerings are burnt in the two stone incinerators and, on the other side, stand symbols of the Eight Immortals.

On the long marble-topped table at the top of the steps that lead to the main section (or palace) are two solid brass deer standing about a metre (three feet) high, symbolizing long life. And on the table in front of the main altar is a fine set of pewter Ng Kung, or five ritual vessels, as well as a central incense burner, a pair of vases and candlesticks on either side.

On the main shrine, Man Cheong (on the left) and Mo Kwan Kung (on the right) sit together. To the right is the shrine to city god Shing Wang, who looks after city dwellers, and to the left is Pao Kung, god of justice. The temple was in fact used early on as a Chinese court. Also in the temple are three finely carved teak sedan chairs, which until recently were used to carry the statues of Man and Mo through the street during festivals. The drum and bell (cast in Guangzhou in 1847) are on the right-hand wall. In the adjoining All Saints Temple a soothsayer waits to tell you what the gods have in store.

Wanchai

Wanchai is associated in most people's minds with Suzie Wong, sailors and lurid, neon-lit nightlife (see Nightlife page 133). But for anyone prepared to explore on foot, there is far more to this interesting old district, which was one of the five original *wan*, the areas set aside for the Chinese population who arrived on Hong Kong Island during the 1850s.

Wanchai was once a stretch of waterfront along Queen's Road East, but early this century reclamation provided new space for Wanchai's characteristic three- and four-storey tenements, ground floor stores with residential quarters above, which spread as far as Gloucester Road, the 1930s waterline. Today another broad strip of reclaimed land

Horse Racing

Beyond any doubt, the most popular sport of all in Hong Kong is horse racing. At least, it is the most popular spectator sport because it offers the Territory's only legal form of gambling. The Royal Hong Kong Jockey Club, which runs all the races at its Shatin and Happy Valley racecourses, was founded way back in 1884, but surprisingly professional racing was introduced only in the mid-1970s. The RHKJC operates betting shops throughout the Territory that are frequented by people from all walks of life. It also functions as an actual club, with paid-up members who pay exhorbitant fees to sit in boxes to watch the races. The amount of money wagered at major race meets is phenomenal and runs into billions of dollars. As a result, every year the Jockey Club donates a sizeable proportion of its huge surplus to charity and building sports-related facilities such as the Queen Elizabeth Stadium and the HK$50 million Jubilee Sports Centre in Shatin.

The Shatin racecourse was completed in 1978 and is equipped with every conceivable modern luxury, including piped music in the stables and heated swimming pools for the horses. The centre of the course is a beautifully land-scaped park, open to the public on non-race days. The stands are always packed, with attendance per meeting averaging 48,700 people. Racegoers sit pouring over their newspapers or listening to the latest totalizer odds on their transistors. Shatin has the world's biggest trackside video matrix, on which punters in the stands can read the rapidly changing odds or watch a close-up of the action. Since the races are held alternately at Shatin (Saturdays) and Happy Valley (Wednesdays), the big screen is used in each case to display the race to usually packed stands at the other stadium. It also provides slow motion film and instant replay of a race and displays information in English and Chinese (the messages being illustrated by animated cartoons). The atmosphere is electric, and a massive swell of noise from the crowd can be heard as each set of horses thunders down the home straight. It is a strange sight to see the crowd go crazy under the blazing floodlights at Happy Valley when there isn't a horse in sight; the audience are simply watching the action in Shatin on the vast video screen.

The racing season runs from September to May, and admission to the General Grandstand is HK$10. If you are at least 18 and a bona fide visitor in Hong Kong for less than 21 days, you can go to the races in style in the HKTA's Come Horse Racing tour, which includes access to the members' enclosure of the Jockey Club.

on the north side of Gloucester Road has filled up with highrise office blocks, a sports-ground, the Arts Centre and the APA (see Arts, page 128) and a ferry pier.

The face of pre-war Wanchai is rapidly disappearing as developers take over in this frenzy of office-block construction. The tallest of these is the **Hopewell Centre**, which rises an improbable 66 storeys out of Queen's Road East. Apart from restaurants on floors six to eight, the revolving restaurant on top and two shopping floors, the whole cylindrical building is taken up by office space—a daring and highly successful venture by a local developer born and bred in Wanchai.

The Hopewell Centre is incongruously surrounded by several historical sites. Almost next door is the tiny Wanchai Post Office, one of the area's few protected remnants from the last century. A little closer to Central is the single-storey **Hung Shing Temple**, dedicated to a god of seafarers. Although the building was constructed in 1860, a shrine inside is dated 1847–8. The splendid line of Shekwan pottery decorating the roof was added at the turn of the century. On the other side of the Hopewell Centre, a picturesque alley with its name, Tik Loong Lane, written over the entrance, leads up steps to a crumbling terrace of 19th century houses. Several of these incorporate the **Sui Pak Temple**, which was probably founded in the 1870s and is especially popular with people seeking medical help. The interior contains many mirrors inscribed by grateful worshippers who have recovered from illnesses. Upstairs is an interesting collection of antiques.

In the narrow side streets that lead into Queen's Road East, you may stumble over traditional shops selling birds, crickets, snakes or fragile, brightly coloured paper offerings. Fortune tellers, traditional hairdressers and professional letter-writers have set up their tables on the pavements hereabouts. **Wanchai Market**, which runs from Queen's Road East down to Wanchai Road, is one of the most interesting to wander through (go round 9–11 am, or in the late afternoon).

Happy Valley

Racing began in Happy Valley in 1845 and has been one of the major preoccupations for Chinese and expatriates ever since (see opposite page). The height of enthusiasm was perhaps reached when Governor Sir Henry May, a keen horse-owner, took to the tracks as a jockey with some success.

Aside from the racecourse, Happy Valley, once swampy and malaria-ridden, is now a pleasant residential area, which first became fashionable in the 1870s when the wealthy began to move away from Central. On the south side of the racetrack is an entrance to Happy Valley's Colonial **Cemetery**, established in 1845. It can also be approached via another entrance much higher on Stubbs Road. Amidst flowering trees and well-kept hillside gardens (the setting for a key scene in John Le Carré's *The Honourable School-*

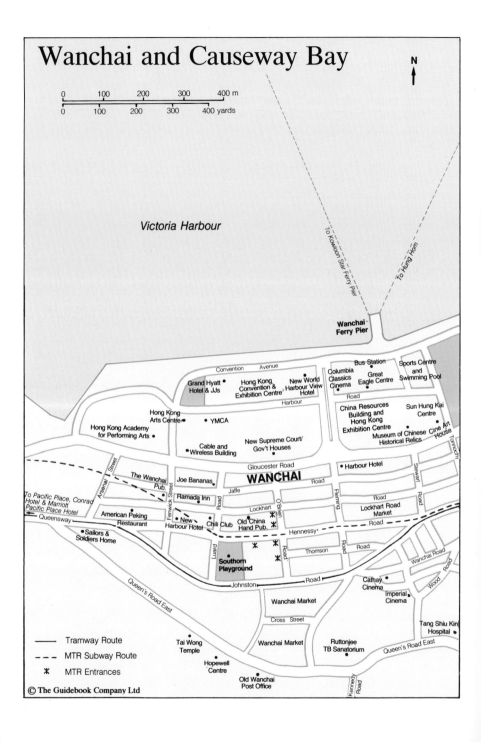

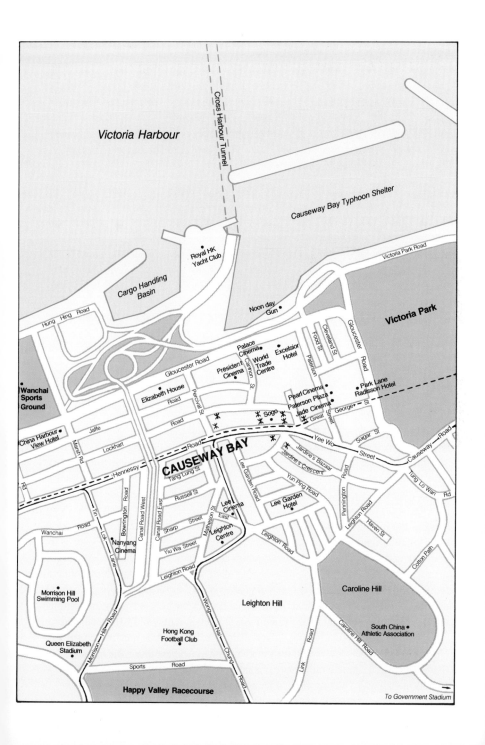

boy), the gravestones vividly bring to life much of Hong Kong's early history. There are graves bearing British, Russian, German and Chinese names. The many monuments include one to the American naval officers and crew who died in an attack on a fleet of piratical junks in 1855, one in memory of a French crew that disappeared in a typhoon in 1906 and, of course, many to the British soldiers and their families who died of fever. The Aberdeen Tunnel emerges nearby.

Causeway Bay

Wanchai merges imperceptibly into Causeway Bay, the busy area most favoured by locals for shopping and eating. Innumerable restaurants, jewellers, camera shops, boutiques and electrical stores mingle with the largest China Products store in Hong Kong, three big Japanese department stores, a branch of Lane Crawford, several shopping malls and a few garment factory outlets in back streets behind the Excelsior Hotel. Prices throughout are better than in Central, and the area is often thronged with shoppers taking advantage of the range of goods and the late closing hours (9 or 10 pm).

Trading is not new to Causeway Bay. The most famous hong (trading house), Jardine, Matheson & Company Limited, set up shop here in 1841. Jardine's most famous relic is the Noon-Day Gun, made known to the world by Noel Coward's *Mad Dogs and Englishmen*: 'In Hong Kong they strike a gong/And fire off a noonday gun.'

Causeway Bay long ago lost its bay to extensive reclamation, but it still has a **typhoon shelter**, where between April and November you can enjoy a floating dinner. Hire a sampan on the waterfront (most easily reached via the pedestrian bridge from Victoria Park) to take you out into the shelter. The food (not cheap) is chosen from the boats that cluster round the sampan, and for extra dollars a music boat will serenade you.

One bonus of the reclamation completed some 30 years ago is **Victoria Park**. Opened in 1957, the 7.7-hectare (19-acre) park is not especially beautiful, but it is an accessible place for an insight into Hong Kong's early morning life. (Between 6 and 7.30 am is the best time to go). Under clumps of trees groups of people of all ages go slowly through their *tai chi ch'uan* exercises. Impressively fit individuals practise various forms of kung fu, while others jog round the flat central grass area. Bird cages are hung in the trees to give the birds an airing while their owners chat below. The park is heavily used throughout the day. It has swimming pools, mini-soccer pitches, tennis and basketball courts.

A bizarre park of another kind is **Tiger Balm Gardens**, a place much maligned but offering a fascinating view of Buddhist mythology and Chinese taste. The founder, Aw Boon Haw, was a Chinese millionaire philanthropist who made his money with the most famous of cure-alls, Tiger Balm, used for asthma, lumbago, scorpion bites and more.

The garden was built in 1935 on eight acres of very steep hillside behind Causeway Bay. Grotesque and amusing plaster figures depicting Chinese folktales or Buddhist stories ornament every ledge and corner. Most lurid (and furthest to climb to) are those representing the Ten Courts of Hell. There is also a monument to Aw's parents and a decorative Tiger Pagoda, with 149 steps up its six storeys. Open daily 9 am to 4 pm.

North Point and Shaukeiwan

East from Causeway Bay to North Point, Quarry Bay and Shaukeiwan, population density and industry intensify. These areas are for anyone who wants to see something of Hong Kong's industrial life or low-cost housing estates. **North Point**, sometimes called 'little Shanghai' because of all the Shanghainese who have settled there, is an oppressive mass of 1960s residential blocks, vast restaurants, street markets and heavy traffic.

Quarry Bay is the oldest industrial area in Hong Kong; shipbuilding began here with the establishment of Whampoa Dock in 1863. The Taikoo Dockyard, founded by Butterfield and Swire, was in full operation in 1908. Today, much of it has been redeveloped as a large private housing estate—Taikoo Shing—while the remaining yards are operated by a joint concern, the Hong Kong United Dockyard Company.

Shaukeiwan was for a long time a small fishing village, persistently bothered by pirates, the most notorious of whom was based on the mainland opposite at Lei Yu Mun. This is the shortest stretch of water to the mainland—the one the Japanese used when invading Hong Kong Island. Today the crossing can be made by public ferry to eat at one of Lei Yu Mun's seafood restaurants (see New Territories, page 90).

Shaukeiwan today is the base of Hong Kong's second-largest fishing fleet (Aberdeen's is bigger) and a densely populated residential area. The traditional craft of junk building carries on in **Aldrich Bay**, but there is much new industry as well. If you have time, visit the **Tin Hau Temple** opposite the fish market or the **Tam Kung Temple**. Tam Kung, with his ability to heal the sick and control the weather, became the boat community's second-ranking patron deity after Tin Hau. His festival, on the eighth day of the fourth moon, is one of the island's most spectacular celebrations. Boats carrying shrines come from all over Hong Kong, offerings are made, and dragon and lion dances are performed.

Repulse Bay and Stanley

No perspective of Hong Kong Island would be complete without making the easy trip to the south side of the island. Until 1920, when a road to Repulse Bay was completed, the

fishing settlements at Repulse Bay and Stanley were small and isolated, accessible only by a narrow track or by boat. Today there is a constant stream of traffic to these now popular residential areas, served by regular buses and plenty of taxis. The route along Stubbs Road and Wong Nai Chung Gap Road winds above Happy Valley racecourse and crosses to the greener side of the island. The road curls past smart houses and residential blocks in leafy settings—with superb views across to **Deep Water Bay**, where there is a pleasant though crowded beach—to Repulse Bay and, another ten minutes on, to Stanley.

Sandy, shallow **Repulse Bay** got its name from a 19th-century pirate-chaser, the HMS Repulse. For some the name has strong colonial associations, largely because of the old **Repulse Bay Hotel**, which was built in 1918. It was demolished to make way for a high-rise development, but a replica of the original restaurant has been built. It is the site of the island's most accessible beach, which unsurprisingly is also its most heavily used.

The road through Repulse Bay towards **Stanley** passes glorious views and elegant residences. Stanley had the largest population (some 2,000 people) of any settlement on the island when the British arrived in 1841, but did not develop until the 1920s, when the island road reached it. The village has strong military associations. Part of the headland, first set aside for army use in the 1930s, is still a restricted army base. Stanley was the scene of the most heroic, and inevitably hopeless, resistance to the Japanese invasion in December 1941, and it was here that many of Hong Kong's civilians were herded together in a camp (now Stanley Prison) until the Japanese surrender in August 1945.

Most visitors to Stanley these days are in search of bargains in the small market. Bundles of jeans, T-shirts, sweaters and jackets, as well as silk dresses and suits, are stacked unceremoniously on stalls and sold at low prices, taking all the glamour out of the (not always genuine) designer labels. Small rattan and porcelain shops cater increasingly to tourists, whose recent influx has led to a rise in prices and a general smartening up of the narrow pedestrian market streets.

Yet, despite the influx, Stanley village is still a pleasant place to spend a couple of hours. If you go by bus, get off at the small, grassy triangle and walk down Stanley Market Street, which slopes towards the fruit and vegetable market. On the right is a small fish market (best in the morning) and food stalls that cook the fish you buy for yourself in the market. To find the market (situated next to the China Products shop) turn left off Market Street. If you feel like a swim, Stanley's **main beach**, facing Tai Tam Bay, is five minutes away past the bus stop. At the other end of the village is a **Tin Hau Temple** thought to be around 200 years old and so the oldest on the island. Turn right at the bottom of Stanley Market Road into Stanley Main Street and walk along the promenade past the squatter huts to the temple where a statue of Tin Hau, the Queen of Heaven and guardian of all connected with the sea, stands looking out across the ocean.

The unpretentious temple has much in common with Hong Kong's other Tin Hau temples. One unusual feature is the metre-high (four-foot) stone ledge that runs round

Causeway Bay typhoon shelter at dusk

three walls of the main hall and carries an awesome array of black and gold gods thought to date back some 200 years. On the wall to the left of the altar, look for the dirty skin of a tiger said to have been shot only a hundred yards from the temple by Japanese soldiers during the occupation of Hong Kong.

Shek O

Although today largely occupied by commuters, Shek O still has the air of an unkempt Cantonese village. The countrified surroundings include a large golf course and even a few vegetable farms. It is not easily accessible from Central: take a No 9 bus from Shaukeiwan (about 30 minutes) or a taxi from Central (off-peak 50 minutes). At weekends the village attracts large crowds, but on weekdays the wide sandy beach is emptier, and a walk through the warren of narrow pedestrian streets around a tiny Tin Hau Temple gives a glimpse of a lifestyle far removed from the dense urban living on the island's north shore. Good, plain Cantonese food is served in several simple restaurants. Walk through the village along the main street to reach Shek O headland, bordered by luxury houses, and go down a footbridge across to the tiny rocky island of Tin Tau Chau.

In 10 minutes you can climb up the path to a lookout position with splendid views north to Joss House Bay and the mainland, and south to Stanley Peninsula, with a satellite communications station at its tip and the Po Toi Island group in the distance.

Ocean Park

Around two million visitors a year flock to Ocean Park, which opened in January 1977. The 65-hectare (160-acre) park is set in rocky terrain just east of Aberdeen; the lowland and headland areas are linked by cable car and escalator. The lowland area is the home of Water World, which has giant slides, a wave pool, a rapids ride and a toddlers' pool. There is also an Omnimax cinema, zoo, children's playground, goldfish exhibition, dolphin feeding pools, garden theatre, where regular entertainment is given by sea lions and others animals, and plaza area, where trained cockatoos and macaws entertain, and the Middle Kingdom theme park.

It is the spectacular seven-minute ride to the headland in six-seater gondola cars high above the rocky slopes that makes the visit worthwhile. On the headland itself is the world's largest marine mammal tank and aquarium. The Ocean Theatre, with its panoramic backdrop, holds 4,000 people and stages performances by dolphins, sealions and

TREAT THE KIDS

Highly urbanized Hong Kong is not an obvious destination for holidays with children, but it's surprising how many things there are for kids to do—and lots of activities are free. Here are a few suggestions; ask the HKTA for more details.

* See how many different kinds of birds the kids can spot at the Hong Kong Park aviary, a vast netted area off Cotton Tree Drive in Central high enough for the birds to fly around in. Entrance is free.

* Spend a morning at Kowloon Park's Creative Playground and be amazed at how much Chinese the kids pick up. There's also a museum, an aviary, water gardens and a Sculpture Walk. Entrance is free.

* Splash out on a day at Water World in Aberdeen, where you can ride a giant water-shoot, zoom down a gigantic slide and battle the elements in the wave pool. Open 9 am–9 pm. Entrance is HK$60 for adults, HK$30 for children.

* Watch the killer whales jump at Ocean Park's Ocean Theatre (shows from midday onward). If you have the nerve, take the ride of your life on the spectacular one-kilometre (half-mile) roller coaster, which perches on the cliff edge of the peninsula above Aberdeen, before the trip home by cable car. Open 9 am–9 pm. Entrance is HK$140 for adults, HK$70 for children.

* Ride the world's longest escalator back in time to Middle Kingdom, a HK$70-million theme park, and experience for yourself the 5,000 years and 13 dynasties of Chinese history. Watch traditional painters and potters at work, have your fortune told, and marvel at the acrobatics show. Part of Ocean Park—details above.

* Ride the ferry from Central to the fishermen's island of Cheung Chau and choose your own live fish and shellfish to eat at an open air restaurant. This is your chance to learn how to peel prawns with chopsticks.

* Get up early and watch Hong Kong's elderly people practise the graceful martial art *tai chi ch'uan* (a kind of slow-motion shadow-boxing) at the leafy Zoological and Botanical Gardens (Upper Albert Road, Central). If you can't

make it quite that early, at least try to get there before 8 am for feeding time. There are several endangered species, including the beautiful lion tamarind monkey. Entrance is free.

* Climb in and out of the coaches and operate the signals at the Tai Po Railway Museum, at Tai Po Market in the New Territories right opposite the KCR station. Entrance is free.

* Ride the terrifyingly steep Peak Tram to the top of the Peak and see how many of Hong Kong's landmarks you can identify with the telescope on the terminus roof.

* Trundle by tram along the length of Hong Kong Island's northern shore all the way from Kennedy Town to Shaukeiwan and see life at street level. At just a dollar a time, you can simply get off anywhere you want, have a look around and get on the next tram.

* If you are stuck in Central, visit the high-tech Hongkong and Shanghai Bank headquarters, at No 1 Queen's Road, and ride the chain of escalators high up into the tower.

* Find the Asian food halls in the basement of the Sogo department store in Causeway Bay or Seibu in Pacific Place, Admiralty, and taste a huge range of foods—baby octopus, crab sticks and eel for the adventurous; fried rice, noodles or even a burger for the more cautious.

* Have a real *dim sum* experience. Try the eatery in City Hall, Central, or even the floating Jumbo Restaurant at Aberdeen. Get there before midday, or all the tastiest snacks will have gone.

* Have your photo taken standing on a giant turtle at the ghoulish Tiger Balm Gardens (Aw Boon Haw Gardens) above Causeway Bay. And, if you think this is bad, the gaudy and gory frescoes will show you just how many kinds of hell exist. Entrance is free.

* Strap on your skates and hit the ice or roller rinks at Cityplaza, Taikoo Shing. Go in the morning when it is less crowded. Charges are HK$20 for the morning session and HK$30 for the evening. Open late on Fridays and weekends.

* Hear thousands of songbirds chirp away at the Bird Market in Hong Lok Street, Mongkok, and watch them eat live locusts and grasshoppers for breakfast.

* Get your legs in gear and climb up to the world's tallest outdoor bronze Buddha at the Po Lin Monastery (Temple of Precious Lotus) on Lantau Island. Luckily, there is an excellent vegetarian restaurant to satisfy your appetite once you reach the top. And if you still do not have the energy, you can always take the bus.

* Hire a sampan from the pier at Aberdeen Harbour and watch the fishermen hang fish out to dry from their brightly painted green-

and-red boats. This should not cost you more than HK$50 per hour per person, but don't forget to haggle.

* Go computer crazy at the incredible Golden Arcade in Shamshuipo, Kowloon, where you will find the latest in every kind of computer hardware and software crammed into the smallest space imaginable. You will have to drag computer whizz-kids away from this place—or at least buy them the latest Gameboy!

* Experience kite-flying Chinese style. First visit Chinese Arts & Crafts in Tsimshatsui to choose your kite. Then find a large open space such as the one on the Peak to fly it.

* Enjoy a day at the beach in Repulse Bay plus the spectacular bus trip there and back. Take bus No 6 or 61 from Central Bus Station and don't get off until you see a coloured block of flats with a hole in the middle of it to your left and the beach to your right!

killer whales, all compered by a remarkable, bilingual master of ceremonies.

The vast Atoll Reef, a seawater aquarium, holds 200 different species of fish, which swim around in an enormous tank that has been designed to give the impression of a coral reef. Viewing galleries take the visitor down from the shallow upper reef levels to depths normally reserved for deep sea divers. A Wave Cove with 100 metres (328 feet) of coastline and a wave-making machine is a splendid home for sealions, seals and penguins and can also be viewed from an underwater gallery.

The entrance to Ocean Park is opposite the southern end of the Aberdeen Tunnel.

Aberdeen

The old fishing town of Aberdeen has traditionally been included on the Hong Kong Island tourist route, but recent changes have been so sweeping that many visitors feel it is hardly worth a special visit. The area is fast developing into an urban-industrial district to equal North Point, Quarry Bay and Shaukeiwan. Reclamation of the harbour has all but destroyed the old character of the waterfront. Apparently undeterred, the boat people still sell their fresh catch to passers-by, and noisy sampan ladies tout for customers. The famous floating restaurants were moved away from the waterfront in 1978 to less spectacular moorings in a secluded part of the typhoon anchorage. On shore, the town centre is a Western-style shopping complex surrounded by high-rise resettlement blocks.

For a fine overview of the harbour you can climb up some steps onto the Ap Lei Chau Bridge pedestrian walkway. The bridge, opened in 1979, enabled the 20th century to spill onto this tiny island, which earlier had existed entirely on its flourishing shipbuilding industry.

For boat enthusiasts, the shipyards around Ap Lei Chau are a paradise. Many kinds of small craft are built here—including, of course, junks, which are still made by skilled carpenters who have added electric drills to their traditional tools. Diesel engines, which have replaced the picturesque sails, are repaired here. Scrap iron and steel from ships broken up here are converted into metal products used in the construction industry.

Due to the large boat population, Aberdeen's Tin Hau Temple is heavily used. It was built in 1851 on what was the shoreline, but today it is in the centre of town set in a small garden. The bell, on the left as you enter the temple, was made in 1726 and reputedly dredged up from the sea by local fishermen. The one on the right dates from 1851. A statue of Tin Hau sits in the central shrine with a smaller image in front (this is carried out of the temple at festivals). Two almost life-size generals stand in front of her—Thousand-Li Eye on the left, who could see a thousand li (500 kilometres or 300 miles), and Favourable Wind Ear on the right, who could hear distinctly over the same distance. To the left and right are shrines to Pi Tai, who fought the demon king barefoot.

Kowloon

Little is known of Kowloon's early history, though the Lei Cheng Uk tomb (see Museums page 119) in Lai Chi Kok just north of Kowloon is evidence of Eastern Han Dynasty (25–220) settlers. In 1277 the Song Dynasty's last emperor, Ti Ping, and his brother, Ti Ching, under the guardianship of their uncle, Yang Liang-chieh, found refuge in Kowloon. The Mongol army, from which they were fleeing, had captured and disposed of their eldest brother, the former emperor, and taken the Southern Dynasty's capital of Hangzhou. On arrival in Kowloon, a temporary court was set up near the present airport. Here the eight-year-old emperor and his brother are said to have spent many hours playing in the shadow of a great rock overlooking the sea. Some years later the rock was engraved with the message 'Song Wong Toi' (Terrace of the Song Emperor). Sadly, during the Japanese occupation in the Second World War it was broken up to make way for the Kai Tak runway, though a fragment bearing the inscription was saved and can be seen today in the **Song Wong Toi Garden**.

On his arrival, the young emperor asked the name of his new home and was told that it was Kowloon, meaning 'nine dragons' after the peaks in the ridge of hills which lie behind it. Dragons are a traditional symbol of imperial majesty and are believed to inhabit mountain ridges. When the boy remarked that he could only see eight—today there are fewer as some have fallen foul of the developer's dynamite—he was told that he, the emperor was the ninth.

The next major event in Kowloon's recorded history was in 1860, when it was ceded to Britain following the Second Opium War. In 1895, Kowloon was described by the traveller Henry Norman as the 'ground floor' of the colony, the Mid-levels being the 'second storey' and the Peak the 'top storey'. In other words, Kowloon was one of the mercantile centres, Mid-levels was for executive living, with the Peak for the taipans (bosses). This is very much the feeling of Kowloon today—a bustling market-place.

The Kowloon Peninsula is surrounded by one of the most breathtaking and vibrant scenes in the world—**Victoria Harbour**, with the startling backdrop of mountainous Hong Kong (Victoria) Island and its multitude of buildings, some climbing precariously up to the Peak. This perfect natural harbour of 60 square kilometres (23 square miles) is a constant hive of activity. It plays host to all manner of craft—aged junks from mainland China propelled majestically by great patched sails; jetfoils and hydrofoils plying between Hong Kong and Macau; the more sedate lozenge-shaped Star Ferries; the numerous Hong Kong and Yaumatei Ferries serving the outlying islands; sleek warships; container vessels and bulk cargo carriers; tugs and lighters; police launches and every imaginable type of pleasure vessel. Once a year the liner Queen Elizabeth II docks at Ocean Terminal. Harbour-watching, a constant pleasure whether from land or sea, was enhanced in 1981 by the completion of a walkway along the waterfront from Kowloon

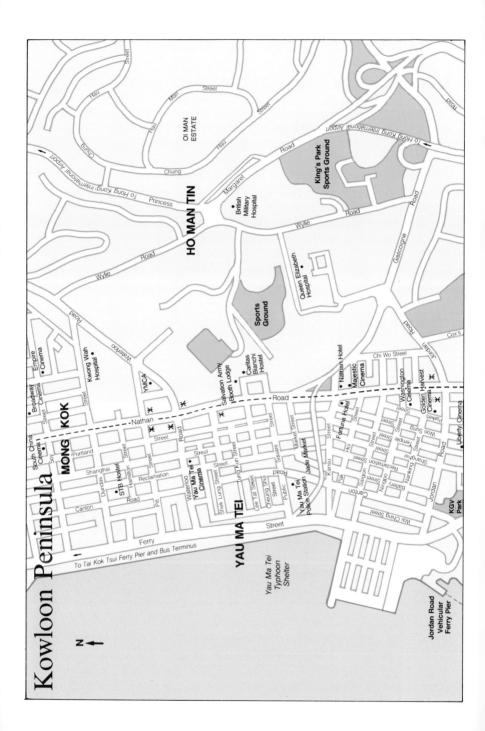

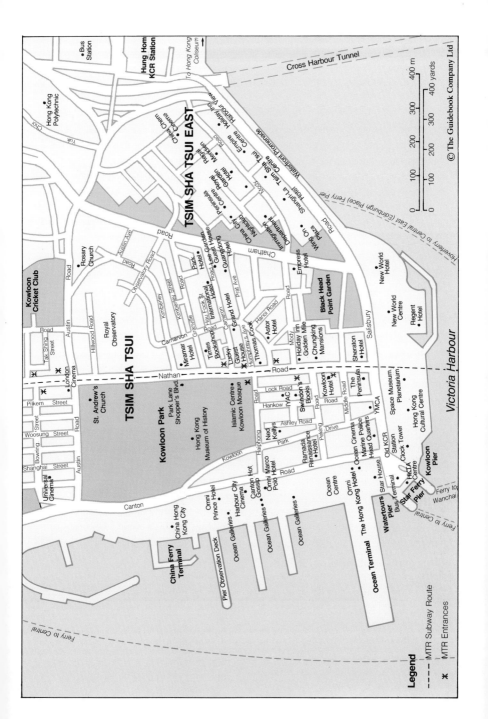

Pier to Hunghom. A night-time crossing on the Star Ferry is particularly spectacular.

The area of the Kowloon Peninsula is 11 square kilometres (4.3 square miles) stretching north from the waterfront to Boundary Street, which marks the extent of the land ceded in 1860. Tsimshatsui—a tongue-twister pronounced 'Chim Sa Choy', which means 'sharp sand point'—is the peninsula's old town. Surprisingly, many of the neighbouring districts such as Lai Chi Kok and the **Walled City of Kowloon** are, strictly speaking, not in Kowloon. The so-called Walled City was built in the 1840s by a group of Chinese who wished to protect themselves from the British barbarians. The walls, like the Song Wong Toi Rock, disappeared during the Second World War when the Japanese needed stones to build the Kai Tak runway, so today little remains of the old city, an unsanitary slum that is now being demolished and turned into a park.

The best way to see the southern part of Tsimshatsui is on foot. If you arrive on the Star Ferry, just prior to docking you will see on the right a fine orange and white Clock Tower built in 1910 to commemorate the Victoria Jubilee. This is all that remains of the old railway station, which was demolished in 1978 to make way for the Cultural Centre. The clock, protected from the wreckers' hammer, has caused certain amusement in the past by occasionally running backwards. Just to the left of the Star Ferry exit is Harbour City, the vast shopping complex formed by **Ocean Terminal**, **Ocean Centre** and other buildings running up Canton Road (see Shopping, page 144). In addition to the cornucopia of shops and restaurants, there are occasionally Chinese cultural shows in the main concourse of Ocean Terminal.

Walking along Salisbury Road, in the first block on the left (opposite the bus station) is Star House. On the ground and first floors is the large and well-stocked **Chinese Arts and Crafts Store**. On the second floor is the **Chinese Export Commodities Exhibition Hall**, which is mainland China's showcase for displays of archaeological treasures or products ranging from tractors to exquisite silk embroidery. Often there are visiting craftsmen demonstrating how handicrafts are made in different provinces.

Leaving Star House, continue walking east past the imposing portico of the **YMCA**. On the opposite side of the street is the **Space Museum** and the virtually windowless **Cultural Centre**. Walking further along Salisbury Road you pass the venerable Peninsula Hotel (see Hotels, page 205). Turn left up Nathan Road, the main artery of Kowloon. This five-kilometre (three-mile), tree-lined boulevard was laid down at the turn of the century during the governorship of Sir Matthew Nathan. At the time sceptics dubbed it Nathan's Folly: what possible use, they asked, could this boulevard serve in a sparsely populated, unfashionable area?

However, times have changed and the southernmost mile is a densely populated, highly commercial area considered the prime beat of shoppers. The streets to the right and left offer a host of diversions, nearly anything anyone could desire.

The Kowloon–Canton Railway clock tower

A Law Unto Itself

As I write (for it will not be there for long), if you walk up Tung Tau Tsuen Road north of the airport, just over the line between Kowloon and the New Territories, you will discover on your right-hand side a row of establishments curious even by the standards of this recondite place. One after the other, glass-fronted to the street, they are the surgeries of unqualified dentists. Their windows are full of pickled abscesses, illustrations of impacted wisdom teeth, grinning rows of dentures, and in the background of each shop a dentist's chair stands waiting, sometimes with the dentist himself reclining in it between customers while his ornamental goldfish (good for patients' nerves) circumnavigate their illuminated tank in the background.

Unqualified doctors and dentists practise all over Hong Kong, but these particular practitioners are there for a historical reason. They believe themselves to be beyond the reach of Government regulations and inspectorates, because that side of that stretch of Tung Tau Tsuen Road once formed the rampart of the old Kowloon City. This was the place, you may remember, which the Manchus maintained as a fortified headquarters before the British ever came to Hong Kong, and in which they reserved their authority when the New Territories were ceded in 1898.

In their time it was a walled city, rebuilt in 1847 specifically as a defence against the British across the water. It had six watch towers, walls fifteen feet thick, a garrison of 500 soldiers and a yamen, the administrative office, securely in the middle of it. Its guns were black with red muzzles, and its demeanour could be fierce: there are pictures of convicted criminals crouched outside its gates with placards round their necks, and of pirates, apprehended by the Royal Navy, decapitated on the nearby beach courtesy of the yamen.

When the British took over the New Territories they very soon got rid of the Chinese officials at Kowloon, relying upon loose wordings in the Convention of Peking, and subsequent legal quibbles never quite settled the status of the place. It became a sort of no man's land, known simply as *The Walled City. The Chinese objected whenever the British proposed to pull the place down; the British never applied to it all their usual municipal regulations, and as late as the 1970s it was said that its only real administration was provided by the Triads.*

For as the city grew around it, the Walled City became a famous resort of villains. Never being absolutely sure what their rights were, the British generally let it be, hoping that it would wither away of its own accord. It very nearly did; in 1933 there were only some 400 inhabitants, and by 1940 almost all its houses had been demolished. However, it revived remarkably after the Second World War, when squatters by the thousand moved in, and by the late 1980s it was thought to house some 30,000 people.

By now the quarter bears no resemblance to the fortified town of the Manchus. Its walls were all torn down by the Japanese, to be used as rubble for extensions at the airport, and very few of its structures are more than thirty years old. Nevertheless it still feels like an enclave within the city, extra-territorial and even slightly unreal. It is a frightful slum. No vehicle can enter it—there are no streets wide enough—and its buildings, rising sometimes to ten or twelve storeys, are so inextricably packed together that they seem to form one congealed mass of masonry, sealed together by overlapping structures, ladders, walkways, pipes and cables and ventilated only by foetid air-shafts. . .

Well before 1997 the Walled City of Kowloon is going to be demolished at last, the British and the Chinese no longer being at odds about it. With it will disappear from Hong Kong an ancient thrill. Though in my own experience everyone within the Walled City has been kindness itself, and though in recent years Hong Kong policemen have been patrolling it, still even now tourists are warned against entering the place, for safety's sake, and are sometimes to be seen enjoying an anachronistic frisson, a last shiver of the Mysterious Orient or the Inscrutable Chinese, as they peer past the preserved abscesses into its unenticing purlieus.

Jan Morris, *Hong Kong*, 1988

The next stop on this expedition is the **Yaumatei Typhoon Shelter**. Take the MTR to Yaumatei Station, emerge at the Portland Street exit and then walk east three blocks. As you approach the last block on the left, you will hear a strange clack-clack noise coming from an old building where there is a wholesale fruit market. Salesmen tout for business by clacking their mini abacuses like castanets.

Across the road is the Yaumatei Typhoon Shelter. It was built in 1915 after a disastrous typhoon and today is home to hundreds of families. These boat people are made up of two groups, the Tanka and Hoklo. The Tanka (immortalized by Chinnery in many works) are said to be the indigenous fisherfolk of the South China Sea, while the Hoklo came later, possibly from Fujian Province. They speak different dialects and can also be told apart by their junks and distinctive horizonal brim, the Tanka's resembling a solar topee. The Tanka fish the deep waters and have larger vessels, whereas the Hoklo stick nearer to shore with their low-gunwaled, high-sterned craft.

Historically, the boat people have suffered badly from discrimination. The Guangzhou authorities used to refuse them the right to settle onshore, marry non-boat people or sit for civil service examinations, thereby excluding them from official positions. In Hong Kong, they were barred from living onshore until 1911, but today these communities are shrinking as many of their young people, no longer victims of discrimination, prefer to live on land. It is still fascinating to walk along the shelter: the community is almost self-sufficient with its shop sampans, barbers, schools, doctors and so on. Some of the older junks are magnificent and serve not only as the homes of several generations but also of their dogs, chickens and invariably a Tin Hau shrine (see Festivals, page 111) wherein a light burns continuously.

One block beyond the south end of the shelter is Man Cheong Street, where a delicious smell of baking will make even the most disciplined nose twitch. Halfway along this street of bakeries is Heyton, which makes mouthwatering Chinese custard tarts and other delights for the peckish adventurer. After indulging in these refreshments, cross Ferry Street, go along Kansu Street, and there, between 10 am and 4 pm at the intersection with Battery Street, you will find the **Jade Market**.

The pavement is covered with travelling salesmen's suitcases displaying all sorts of jade objects—predominantly bangles and pendants. Some lay their wares on gleaming white satin while others make do with crumpled newspaper. The more serious salesmen produce theirs in blue cloth boxes with white toggles. People are everywhere, browsing and haggling. Every now and then a small group gathers to examine a special piece. Serious sales are conducted silently with the aid of sign language, tick-tack style. In Qing times (1644–1911) interested parties would slip their hands inside each other's ample silk sleeves indicating their price by finger pressure.

The Chinese regard for jade is perhaps best expressed by Confucius: 'It is soft, smooth and shining like kindness; it is hard, fine and strong, like intelligence; its edges seem sharp, but do not cut, like justice; it hangs down to the ground, like humility; when struck, it gives a clear, ringing sound, like music; the stains in it which are not hidden and add to its beauty are like truthfulness; its brightness is like heaven, while its firm substance, born of mountains and the water, is like the earth.' In religious and domestic life jade has played an important role, as the early Chinese believed it held the elixir of life. During the Han Dynasty (206 BC–AD 220), the wealthy were buried in suits of jade. Some of the greatest treasures of the Ming and Qing dynasties (1368–1911) are of finely worked jade. Today, many people, even small children, wear a piece of jade as a talisman. It is said to be difficult to pick up a true bargain at the jade market, but you never know your luck.

At the intersection of Canton Road and Jordan Road is **King George V Memorial Park**. Early in the morning this is crowded with people practising *tai chi ch'uan*. When performed by an expert, these balletic movements are a pleasure to watch, the idea being not only to exercise the body but also to achieve harmony of body and mind. It is worth looking in the park even later in the day as you may still find a late riser exercising.

Walk along Jordan Road eastwards and turn right up Shanghai Street into a bustling market area: slippery mounds of sea cucumber (thought by some to be a delicacy) in pink buckets, neat squares of beancurd on thick wooden slabs, herbalist stalls and medicine shops emitting a strange yet nostril-cleaning smell are all interesting to see. Turn left into Bowring Street and find shop No 36. This is filled from floor to ceiling with little bamboo cages holding birds of all sizes and colours, and even some crickets and squirrels. Outside the shop you may see a huge pile of small brown paper parcels. When unpacked, more bamboo cages are revealed, complete with charming blue and white porcelain food and water bowls.

If you are able to resist the temptation of stopping for a delicious *dim sum* lunch at Evergreen Restaurant, 136 Woosung Street, or one of the many other restaurants in this small area, continue on eastwards along Bowring Street into Nathan Road and the Jordan MTR Station for your return to the modern world. At a gentle pace, this meander around Kowloon will take you about four hours.

There are a few other sites in this part of Kowloon that ought not to be missed and are worth making another expedition. For Public Square Street, take the southernmost exit from the Yaumatei MTR Station and walk two blocks south. Here you will find a temple complex, fortune-tellers and public letter writers—surprisingly, a number of middle-aged Chinese are illiterate, though this situation is improving. Nearby in Temple Street, Kun Wo Tung sells his famed turtle meat soup—a medicinal cure-all. At dusk this street, which in the old days was a favourite haunt of prostitutes, turns into a colourful night market. For the **Bird Market** take the MTR to Mongkok Station, go two blocks

Good or Bad Chih?

The man I had arranged to meet was standing by one of the two bronze lions that snarl in the forecourt of the new Hong Kong and Shanghai Bank. He wore a blue silk Nina Ricci tie; a gold wristwatch with a crocodile strap, and an immaculate worsted suit the same Wehrmacht grey as the building.

He handed me his card on which was written, in embossed letters:

LUNG KING CHUEN
Geomancer

Searching and fixing of good location for the burial of passed away ancestors; surveying and arranging of good position for settling down business and lodging places, in which would gain prosperity and luck in the very near future.

The building—to which workmen were adding the final touches— has forty-seven storeys (including the heli-pad on the roof) and stands on the site of the Bank's former Head Office, overlooking the Cenotaph, on the south side of Victoria Square. It is the work of the English architect, Norman Foster, and is, by any standards, an astonishing performance.

I heard it called, variously, 'the shape of things to come;' 'an act of faith in Hong Kong's future;' 'something out of Star Wars;' 'a cathedral to money;' 'a maintenance nightmare,' and 'suicides' leap.'

Having overrun its budget three times over, to the tune of $600 million U.S., it had also earned the distinction of being the most expensive office block ever built.

Architecturally, I felt it was less a 'vision of the future' than a backward, not to say nostalgic look at certain experiments of the Twenties (when buildings were modelled on battleships, and Man himself was thought to be a perfectable machine): buildings such as Charreau's Maison de Verne or, more specifically, the unrealised dreams of the Early Soviet Constructivists—the PROUNS of El Lissitzky; Vesnin's project for the offices of Pravda.

Mr. Lung, on the other hand, is a modest practicioner of the venerable Chinese art of geomancy or feng-shui. At the start of the project, the Bank called him in to survey the site for malign or demonic presences, and to ensure that the design itself was propitious. Whichever architect was chosen, there was bound to be some anxiety; for the Hong Kong and Shanghai Bank is the pivot on which Hong Kong itself stands or falls. With 1997 in sight, prosperity and luck must either come 'in the very near future'—or not at all.

The afternoon was overcast and a sharp wind was blowing off the harbour. We rode the escalator to the first floor, and took shelter in the Cash Department. It was, it must be said, like entering a war-machine: the uniform grey, the absence of 'art': the low hum of computerised activity. It was also cold. Had the building been put up in Soviet Russia there would at least have been a touch of red.

Behind a gleaming black counter sat the tellers—unscreened and unprotected—since, in event of a bank-raid, a kind of portcullis slices sideways into action, and traps the raiders inside. A few potted palms were positioned here and there, apparently at random.

I sat down on a slab of black marble which, in less austere surroundings, might have been a banquette. Mr. Lung was not a tall man. He stood.

Obviously, the surroundings were too austere for many of the Bank's personnel: and already, in the executive suites on high, they had unrolled the Persian carpets, and secretaries sat perched on reproduction Chippendale chairs.

'This,' Mr. Lung began, in a proprietorial tone, 'is one of the Top Ten Buildings of the World. Its construction is particularly ingenious.'

'It is,' I nodded, glancing up at the cylindrical pylons and the colossal X-shaped cross-braces that keep the structure rigid.

'So first,' he continued, 'I would like to emphasise its good points. As far as feng-shui is concerned, the situation is perfect. It is, in fact, the best situation in the whole of Hong Kong.'

Feng-shui means 'wind-and-water.' From the most ancient times the Chinese have believed that the Earth is the mirror of the Heavens; and *that both are living, sentient beings shot through and through with currents of energy—some positive, some negative— like the messages that course through our own central nervous systems.*

The positive currents—those carrying good 'chih', or 'life force'— are known as 'dragon-lines' and are thought to follow the flow of underground water, and, conceivably, the direction of magnetic fields beneath the Earth's surface.

The business of a geomancer is to make certain, with the help of a magnetic compass, that a building, a room, a grave or a marriage-bed is aligned to one or other of the 'dragon-lines', and shielded from dangerous cross-currents. Without clearance from a feng-shui expert, even the most 'westernized' Chinese businessman is apt to get the jitters: to say nothing of his junior staff.

At a lunch I happened to tell an 'old China hand,' an Englishman, that the Bank had taken advice from a geomancer.

'Yes,' he replied. 'It's the kind of thing they would believe in.'

Yet we all believe that some houses are 'happy' and others have a 'nasty atmosphere'. Only the Chinese, however, have come up with cogent reasons why this should be so. Whoever presumes to mock feng-shui as a superstitious anachronism should recall its vital contribution to the making of the Chinese landscape in which houses, temples and cities were always sited in harmony with trees and hills and water.

Perhaps one could even go a step further? Perhaps the rootedness of Chinese civilization; the Chinese sense of belonging to the Earth; their capacity to live without friction in colossal numbers—have all, in the long run, resulted from their adherence to the principles of feng-shui?

'Now it so happens,' Mr. Lung said, 'that no less than five 'dragon-lines' run down from The Peak and converge on the Central Business District of Hong Kong.'

We looked across the atrium of glass, towards the skyscrapers of what is—and may yet still be—the most expensive patch of real-estate in the world.

Some of the lines, he went on—not by any means all—were punctuated here and there with 'dragon-points', (or 'energy-centres') like the meridien-points known to acupuncturists: points at which a particularly potent source of chih was known to gush to the surface.

'And the site on which the Bank stands,' he added, 'is one of them.

It is, in fact, the only 'dragon-point' on the entire length of the line.'

Other lines, too, were known to have branches, like tap-roots, which tended to siphon off the flow of chih, and diminish its force.

'But this line," he said, 'has no branches.'

Yet another favourable point, he went on, was the Bank's uninterrupted view of mountain and sea. Had there been naked rocks or screes on the mountain, these might have reflected bad chih into the building.'

Similarly, because the new building was set well back from the waterfront— and because the sun's course passed to landward— no malign glitter could rise up from the sea.

Mr. Lung liked the grey colour which, he felt, was soothing to the nerves. He also liked the fact that the building absorbed light, and did not reflect glare onto its neighbours.

I questioned him carefully on the subject of reflected glare, and discovered that glass-curtain-wall buildings which mirror one another— as they do in every American city, and now in Hong Kong—are, from a feng-shui point of view, disastrous.

'If you reflect bad chih onto your neighbours,' Mr. Lung said, 'you cannot prosper either.'

He approved, too, of the two bronze lions that used to guard the entrance of the earlier building. During the War, he said, the Japanese had tried to melt themdown:

'But they were not successful.'

I said there were similar lions in London, outside the Bank of England.

'They cannot be as good as these two,' he answered sharply: so sharply, in fact, that I forgot to ask whether the lions had been put away in storage three years ago, when Mrs. Thatcher made her first, ill-informed foray into Chinese politics—and so gave the Hong Kong Stock Exchange its major nervous breakdown.

There are rumours—in this city of innuendo and rumour—that it was the Bank's directors, backed up by other Hong Kong nabobs, who, with fifteen years of the lease to run, were so alarmed for the future of their investments that they pressured the Foreign Office in London to clarify the position: hoping, no doubt, for the continuation of British rule.

The result, of course, was the historic slap from Deng Xiaoping himself.

Other experts will tell you that Communist China never recognized the validity of the lease (the original document is in Taiwan) and that without Mrs. Thatcher's 'Falkland-ish' rhetoric, thereby forcing the Chinese hand, the situation could have drifted on indefinitely.

Others, again, think it ironic (and perfidious) that Britain, so concerned for the fate of 1800 Falklanders, should have signed away the rights of more than 5 million Hong Kong citizens without so much as a nod: leaving them with vaguely formulated promises that the ex-colony will be allowed to keep its 'life-style' and commercial system for a further fifty years.

The fact is, however, that the agreements have been signed. The Mainlanders are coming in 1997. And as a herald of their coming, the Bank of China (Mainland China) has commissioned from I.M. Pei a soaring pinnacle that will soon rise up on a nearby site, dwarfing the Hong Kong and Shanghai Bank by more than twenty storeys.

'So what about the bad points?' I asked Mr. Lung.

'I'm coming to them now,' he said.

The Hong Kong waterfront, he continued, was built on reclaimed land and there were stories....No. He could not confirm them but there were, nevertheless, stories.... of sea-monsters and other local ghouls, who resented being dumped upon and might want to steal into the building.

This was why he had recommended that the escalator to the first floor— which was, after all, the main public entrance—should be so angled, obliquely, so that it ran along a 'dragon-line.' The flow of positive chih would thus drive the demons back where they belonged.

Furthermore, since all good chih came from the landward, he had advised that the Board Room and Chief Executive offices should turn away from the sea: away, that is, from the view of Kowloon and the mountains of China; away from the cargo-ships, tugboats, ferries, drifters, coaling-barges, junks; away from the White Ensign, Red Ensign and that 'other' red flag—and turn instead to face the 'Earth Spirit' descending from The Peak.

The same, equally, would apply to the underground Safe Deposit— which has the largest, circular, stainless-steel door ever made.

Finally, Mr. Lung said, he had to admit there were a number of

A Taoist priest officiates at a ceremony

danger zones in the structure—'killing-points' is what he called them
- where, in order to counteract negative chih, it had been necessary to
station living plants: a potted palm at the head of the escalator 'in case
of a fall': more potted palms by the lift-shafts; yet more palms close to
the pylons to nullify the colossal downward thrust of the buildings.

'Right,' I said. 'I'd like to ask you one thing. I believe that 'dragon-
lines' should never run straight, but be curved.'

'True,' he said.

'And isn't it also true that traditional Chinese buildings are almost
always curved? The roofs are curved? The walls are curved?'

'Yes.'

Chinese architecture in fact—like Chinese art, Chinese language
and the Chinese character—abhors the rigid and rectilinear.

'Now, as a feng-shui man,' I persisted, 'how would you interpret
this rigid, straight-up-and-down Western architecture? Would you
say it had good or bad chih?'

He blanched a little, and said nothing.

'These cross-braces, for example? Good or bad? Would you consider putting plants underneath them?'

'No,' he said, blandly. 'Nobody sits there.'

My question, I have to confess, was most unfair: for I had heard on
the grapevine—true or false I cannot say—that the cross-braces were
terribly bad feng-shui.

It was soon obvious that I had overstepped the mark, since, at the
mere mention of cross-braces, Mr. Lung moved onto the defensive. He
backpedalled. He smiled. He re-emphasised the good points, and
glossed over the bad ones. He even left the impression that there were
no bad ones.

His reaction, I felt, was comparable to that of most Hong Kong
Chinese when forced to contemplate the unpalatable fact of 1997:
'Smile.' 'Hedge your bets.' 'Hope for the best.' 'Take a gamble.' Indeed,
what else to do but gamble in this volatile city whose people bet $6
million U.S. on every horse-race at Happy Valley?

At the foot of the escalator Mr. Lung shook my hand and said:
'I have done feng-shui for Rothschilds.'

Bruce Chatwin, 1987

west and then left into Hong Lok Street. The birds in this truly fascinating spot are probably more pampered than any other pets.

Further afield and not technically in Kowloon (but easily accessible by MTR), Lai
Chi Kok and Wong Tai Sin both offer sights of interest.

For the **Song Dynasty Village**, take the Tsuen Wan Line to Mei Foo Station and walk
or catch a taxi north. This is a sensitive and faithful re-creation of one of the richest
cultural periods of China's history (AD 960–1279). Chinese garden architects have always dealt with small spaces very effectively, allowing the visitor to see only limited
sections of an area at any one time, thereby creating the illusion of greater size. To some
extent, this 5,570-square metre (60,000-square-foot) village follows this concept. The
overall plan is a rectangle, edged with buildings and a picturesque stream bordered by
open-fronted shops and mature trees. Once inside the great entrance gate the tour begins
in earnest. First comes a monkey show, then a contemporary weapons display in the
village tower, followed by calls at quaint stream-side shops where, with the help of the
Song paper money coupons handed out on arrival, one can buy sesame seed cookies and
a longed-for cup of jasmine tea while listening to musicians accompanying a young
singer. All the villagers are dressed in Song costume, in which they seem quite at home,
and they use the available props well. Against a beauty's recline—the slanted bench of a
pavilion—lounges a comely maiden while others sing prettily from a canopied boat. In
the village square itself, a bride arrives in a red sedan chair; the bridegroom's first
glimpse of his bride was when her veil was lifted as she alighted from her sedan chair. In
summer it is a relief to reach the rich man's house, which is powerfully (albeit anachro-
nistically) air-conditioned and contains a number of interesting antiques. There is an
excellent variety show—acrobats, dancers and a performance of martial arts. You can
visit a fortune-teller before repairing to the Restaurant of Plentiful Joy for a snack and
some more music. The final exhibit is a large wax museum that includes a tableau of the
Song boy Emperor Ti Qing being carried on his uncle's back into the sea to drown, thus
escaping capture by the invading Mongols.

The Song Village is one of Hong Kong's most popular attractions. It has been well
constructed with much attention to architectural details—the project took five years and
cost HK$15 million. The shop houses are more successful than the larger buildings,
which look too new and glossy. Admission is HK$110 (children HK$60) weekdays and
HK$75 (children HK$30) on Saturdays, Sundays and public holidays. Visitors are admitted weekdays 10 am–8.30 pm, and 12.30–5 pm weekends and public holidays. Ask your
hotel for details about coach tours. Children love this tour.

When taking the dinner tour, it is possible to combine a visit to the adjacent **Lai Chi
Kok Amusement Park**, but you will have to take a taxi or bus back to your hotel. Although the park is a conventional fun fair with ferris wheels, candyfloss and so on,

Chinese opera is performed here every evening from 7 pm to 7.30 pm. Another site well worth visiting in this area is the **Lei Cheung Uk Tomb and Museum** (see Museums, page 119).

Another option is to take the Kwun Tong Line to Wong Tai Sin Station, and follow the signs to the **Wong Tai Sin Temple** right beside it. This large, new temple in traditional design, which opened in 1973, is a *miu*, in other words a temple dedicated to several creeds—Taoist, Buddhist and Confucian in this case. It is one of Hong Kong's most popular temples, and the crowds thronging it generate a sense of excitement. The site is in the midst of a concrete jungle of flats and is overlooked by the majestic Lion Rock, which gives it excellent *fung shui*. (*Fung shui*—literally meaning 'wind and water'—is said to influence the pattern of people's lives both for good and evil. To achieve the best *fung shui*, whether for a religious or secular building, the site is chosen by a professional geomancer and must combine harmony of the elements and the celestial world). Enter the temple through its main gate, paying the nominal entrance fee (which goes to charity), pass Lord Buddha's delightful small pagoda, and continue up to the terraces. Here the air buzzes with the shaking of *chim*, bamboo cylinders containing thin bamboo sticks, which are shaken until a stick drops out. The number on the stick corresponds to a message, which is then bought from and interpreted by a soothsayer.

Unlike those of most temples, the inner sanctum is cordoned off, and entry is left to the discretion of the gatekeeper. The inside is very ornate, and in the centre of a huge gilt altar stands a portrait of the Taoist god Wong Tai Sin, who is thought to possess the power to heal. Many believers say that the water at his temple—although it comes straight from the public mains supply—has medicinal qualities. Down one side of the temple runs an alley full of soothsayers' stalls, decorated with all manner of charts and gaudy red Chinese calligraphy advising would-be customers of their talents.

New Territories

Technically the area known as the New Territories includes all of Hong Kong except Kowloon, Stonecutter's Island and Hong Kong Island, but this section will deal only with the 728-square-kilometre (281-square-mile) land mass that sprawls between the Chinese border and the Kowloon Peninsula.

The New Territories acquired their name on 11 June 1898, when Britain signed a 99-year lease with the Chinese on the pretext of providing a line of defence for Hong Kong Island and Kowloon. As part of the same concession, Britain secured sole trading rights up the Yangzi River, thus protecting vital commercial interests from ambitious French and Russians. Soon after this acquisition 'tales of its beauty and enchantment,' wrote a British historian, 'were passed back across the Kowloon hills—tales of paved mountain paths, walled villages of the plain . . . silent bays and silver sand'. Much of this unspoilt magic can still be found, but today it co-exists with dense urbanization. Indeed the New Territories are undergoing one of the world's biggest urban development programmes. Nearly half of Hong Kong's population is being rehoused in a series of vast new towns— some with populations of more than 500,000.

The duality of New Territories towns is exemplified by **Shatin**, once a small seaside town of 40,000 inhabitants. It is said that the rice once grown here was so succulent that it was sent north to the emperor's table. Today its harbour has been filled in by bulldozing a hilltop into the water, and along with the surrounding fertile valley it has been transformed into a jungle of skyscrapers. But don't let this put you off; side by side with its concrete and steel Shatin offers plenty of cultural interest. Spectacularly sited in a bowl of jagged hills, it is an exciting first stop for a tour around the New Territories.

Shatin lies beyond the mountain range that protects Kowloon from the north. To get there by road drive through the Lion Rock Tunnel. You emerge below the **Amah Rock** (or Waiting-for-Husband Rock), shaped like a mother carrying her child. One legend is that the woman's husband, a bodyguard at the Song court in Kowloon (See Kowloon, page 61), was killed after a battle against the Mongols. Every evening she would climb this hill and vainly await his return, until eventually the gods took pity, released her soul and turned her body into stone. The rock can best be seen further down the Shatin Valley against the southern skyline, where it is prominent.

Just before you reach Shatin is a living memento of the past, the well-preserved walled village named **Tsang Tai Uk**. High up on the tree-clad hill, **Tao Fong Shan**, overlooking Shatin from the northwest, is the **Chinese Mission to Buddhists** (strange as it may seem, it is a Lutheran organization). In 1929, Karl Ludwig Reichelt, who had spent many years in China teaching Christianity to Buddhists, arrived in Hong Kong in search of a perfect site for a centre to study Buddhist literature. An expert in Chinese Buddhist architecture was employed, and in 1931 the foundations were laid for a delightful complex of buildings. An archway leads to the collection of blue-roofed whitewashed houses. The central building is a striking hexagonal chapel. A new guesthouse to accommodate 44 people was more recently built. There is a pottery decoration shop where the work is carried out by former Buddhist monks; the motifs are mostly floral or religious, but special orders are accepted. Throughout the compound are lovely plants and flowers, and the view of Shatin Valley is spectacular. There is no better place to spend a couple of calm days if you can spare the time.

On the next hill stands the **Ten Thousand Buddha Monastery**, with its hexagonal pink pagoda. It is reached by a stiff, 500-step climb through a pine and bamboo wood—pretty except for the empty cans thrown everywhere. Round the walls of the main temple (built in 1950) are some 12,800 Buddhas of varying size. In front of the temple is the pink pagoda and to the right—a bizarre touch—a collection of children's fairground cars. If your tastes tend towards the macabre, climb a little further up to the three temples above. Here you can see the embalmed body of the monastery's founder, the Reverend Yuet Kai. He died in 1965 aged 87, and according to his wishes was buried in a sitting position. Eight months later the body was exhumed and was said to be in perfect condition. It was then covered in gold leaf, and now sits in a glass case on the altar. The wisps of hair protruding through the gold on the chin are said to be growing still.

While in Shatin it is impossible to miss the imposing **Shatin Racecourse**. Opened in 1978, the 250 acres of reclaimed land accommodated three tracks, stands for 37,000 racegoers, a central public park and a multitude of other buildings. Next door is the site of the impressive **Jubilee Sports Centre**.

Shatin boasts several delicious restaurants: **Luk Yuen** and **Lung Wah Hotel**, which specialize in pigeon, and the **New Shatin**, famous for stuffed nightshade flowers. But for a real surprise, go down a small steep track to the left of the main road descending from the Lion Rock Tunnel to the **Shatin Seafood Restaurant**. In addition to a menu of marine delicacies this obscure restaurant has one of the most distinguished wine lists (notably the first growth clarets) in Asia.

Continuing north from Shatin on the old Tai Po Road you see the **Chinese University**—an imposing 1960s acropolis commanding views both over the Shatin Valley and the serene lengths of the Tolo Harbour to the east. The university has some 4,500 students. Unlike in the older Hong Kong University, the language of tuition is Chinese. Its museum is well worth a visit.

A little further on towards Tai Po, built at the end of an isthmus, is **Island House**. During the occupation it was used as the headquarters of the Japanese commander of the New Territories. Stop on the road and contemplate a breathtaking view down Tolo Harbour—sparkling water, the occasional junk and mountains receding in layers, as is characteristic of Chinese landscape.

At Ma Liu Shui, a ten-minute walk from the Taipo KCR Station, ferries leave twice a day for **Tap Mun Island** at the mouth of Tolo Harbour. The four-hour round trip, with stops at several islands and villages, affords an excellent glimpse of rural life. There are many permutations of this journey: the HKTA will give you all the timetables and advice needed. One can also get a ferry here for Ping Chau in Mirs Bay—not to be confused with Peng Chau, near Lantau—which is practically in Chinese territorial waters.

As early as the eighth century Tolo Harbour was known to have been a centre of the pearl fishing industry—in those days an extremely dangerous affair. The divers (who were Tanka people) were conscripted by the imperial household. They frequently had to be supervised by military guards to ensure that they worked and to prevent smuggling. The fishing system is described in a Yuan-dynasty petition that brought about its abolition on humanitarian grounds: 'The method of gathering them is to tie stones onto a man and lower him into the sea so he will sink quickly. Sometimes he gets pearls and sometimes not. When he suffocates he pulls the rope and a man in the boat hauls it up. If this is done a fraction too late the man dies.'

Tai Po itself, once a sleepy market town, is like Shatin undergoing a metamorphosis. Fifty hectares (120 acres) have been reclaimed from its seashore to build an industrial estate alongside the remains of the old market town (the market itself still operates nine times each lunar month). In June, Tai Po is a favourite venue for the popular Dragon Boat Festival. On the road to Plover Cove Reservoir is a 280-year-old temple dedicated to Tin Hau, goddess of the sea.

Along the street is the marble-faced factory of the **Tai Ping Carpet Company**. Established in 1956, it is particularly proud of its list of prestigious installations, such as those in Buckingham Palace and the home of Bob Hope. The workshop has now moved to China, but interested buyers may view the company's products at the showroom in Wing On Plaza, G/F, 62 Mody Road, Tsimshatsui East. Several types of pile and non-pile carpets are produced in both traditional and modern designs.

Continue along the north side of Tolo Harbour to the **Plover Cove Reservoir**; the next few miles over the watershed and down into Starling Inlet feature some of the most beautiful scenery accessible by road in the New Territories. **Brides Pool**, a little way off the road and along a stream, is a perfect picnic spot. In summer, these hills are covered with flowers, wild gardenias, honeysuckle, rose myrtle; they are a flower- and butterfly-lover's dream.

Where the road joins Starling Inlet is the **Luk Keng Egretry**. From April to September this tree-clad hill is crowded with noisy egrets (small crane-like birds). Three species are indigenous to Hong Kong, and all of their members, numbering about 800, nest here. These elegant birds can often be seen standing in a paddy, or sometimes on the back of water buffalo.

Farming is intensive between Luk Keng and Fanling, mainly in the form of small,

The March of Progress

How would you like a road from Wireless Bay to Sheung Tsuen?' asked the Magistrate suddenly.

Old Liu exposed his five teeth in a stupid grin.

'There already is a road, Magistrate,' he said.

Everyone roared with laughter, one brown old face nodding to another, while, behind the men, the women cackled at the Magistrate's not knowing that there was a road already.

With them, however, the wicked interpreter was also laughing, louder and longer than all the others.

'You old dunderhead!' he said to Old Liu at last, when he could make himself heard. 'The Magistrate isn't talking about the old stone footpath. He means a big motor road, wide like this, like in the big city—you know, poop-poop!'

The laughter and chatter dwindled away into silence. Nobody could understand what the interpreter meant.

The Magistrate continued: 'All those old deserted fields on the hillside could be used again. If you had a motor road you could grow vegetables and get them through to Wireless Bay in time to catch the early ferry into the big city. Your vegetables would reach there in time for the morning market.'

Old Liu wiped the beer off his lips and laughed stupidly again.

'But we don't grow vegetables, Magistrate,' he said.

'I know,' replied the Magistrate, 'But you could, in the future, if you had a motor road.'

Old Liu looked embarrassed, turning to the other old men in the hope of finding another laughing expression that would give him the courage to tell the Magistrate how funny his idea was. But all the other old men's faces were blank with liquor and incomprehension. Timorously, he turned back to the table.

'No one in the village knows how to grow vegetables,' he said.

The wicked interpreter chuckled. The Magistrate said: 'We can teach you.'

Old Liu shook his head, then looked down and scratched it. Fai could understand how it was that the old fellow could not explain to the Magistrate, for he himself also could not have explained it. People from the city could not easily understand the village and the valley. How could anyone teach them to plant vegetables? And why should vegetables be connected with a motor road to Wireless Bay? A larger boat might be useful for transporting their fish catches. Yet, even with that, would the dealers on Little Island, where they traditionally sold their fish, be any more lenient with credit? In any case, most of the fish caught was eaten in the valley. Only a small portion was sent to Little Island.

'There's so much land wasted and unused,' said the Magistrate.

People wagged their heads, smiled at the Magistrate and looked emptily at one another.

'If I can tell the Government that each village on the new road will contribute free labour, there's a chance the Government will agree to giving the money for it,' the Magistrate went on. 'Otherwise, I'm afraid they'll say it's too expensive.'

Like everyone else, Fai was completely confused by this talk about vegetables. The city people always talked in a mad way, all upside down and back to front. The meeting began to vibrate with loose chatter.

The interpreter grinned round at everyone.

'Do you want a road?' he asked, holding his glass in his hand and drinking from it rapidly. 'A good road, maybe with a bus, so you can get quickly into Wireless Bay—in twenty minutes, maybe—then into the city by ferry.'

People tittered, because no one knew quite what twenty minutes was. It was possibly something good, by the way the wicked interpreter spoke, but it was meaningless.

'Do you want a road?' he asked again, banging the table with his now empty glass.

The old men in the front row of the school benches began nudging each other and giggling.

'Yes, Magistrate!' one piped up. 'We'd like a road!'

Everyone laughed with relief, because it was better to be with the Magistrate than against him, and the meeting had been so hard to follow that unfortunately they had all put themselves in the wrong position of being against the Magistrate, which was improper—at least, at a public meeting it was.

Austin Coates, The Road, 1959

neat squares of vegetable gardens. The farming methods are still old-fashioned, with night soil often the only fertilizer used. The farmers are predominantly elderly, the young preferring easier factory work, and many of them are Hakka people. The Hakka women bending in the fields wear crownless straw hats with black cloth hanging from the brim—like a horse's tail, it keeps the flies away when swished. The Hakka have their own dialect and are one of the four groups of people in the New Territories, the others being the Punti, who speak Cantonese, and the two boat peoples (see Kowloon, page 70). For those interested in architecture, this area is rich in fine buildings, including five walled villages (see the government's excellent publication *Rural Architecture in Hong Kong*).

For a clear view of China go to **Lok Ma Chau** (Dismount Hill) border post. Legend has it that the last Song emperor rested here, when fleeing from the Mongols, so those on the hill at the time had to dismount and kowtow in respect. The energetic can get an even clearer view by climbing up **Robin's Nest**.

Crossing over to the western side of the New Territories, you reach **Kam Tin**, where there are three walled villages, all dating back some four or five centuries. Among the settlers who arrived during the late Song Dynasty were the five Great Clans. The Tangs, who were the earliest to arrive, chose the most fertile land and became the most powerful. To protect themselves against bandits, they surrounded their villages with sturdy walls that are still standing. **Kat Hing Wai** is the best known and is geared up for tourists with trinket-covered souvenir stalls. More interesting are **Wing Lung Wai** and **Shui Tau Tsuen**, particularly the latter's ancestral hall and Hung Shing Temple.

In the aftermath of the 1949 Chinese Revolution, many thousands of refugees poured into the New Territories with little or no money to restart their farming activities. The philanthropic Kadoorie brothers realized the need for agricultural education and set up the Kadoorie Agricultural Aid Association. In the subsequent years the project has snowballed: 1,218 villages have received help; 199 miles of road and 254 bridges have been constructed making formerly inaccessible areas available for cultivation; and through research and husbandry courses at the **Kadoorie Experimental Farm** (near Taipo), new farming methods have been accepted. It is possible to visit this 360-acre farm and garden by appointment with at least two days' notice (tel 488 1317). It has been beautifully landscaped, with exotic and native trees and plants blooming profusely.

Vast piles of empty oyster shells herald the fishing village of **Lau Fau Shan**. These oysters are either dried or made into oyster sauce rather than eaten raw. Situated on Deep Bay, the village is within a stone's throw of the mainland. Indeed it is across this stretch of water that many refugees have attempted to swim. Seafood auctions are held every day in the main street, and the **Sun Tao Yuen Restaurant** provides all manner of seafood including, of course, oysters, which should be eaten only well-cooked. You can buy your own seafood and vegetables in the market and ask one of the restaurants to cook them up for you.

In the southwest of the New Territories are three monasteries. **Castle Peak Monastery** is steeped in history. It stands high on Ching Shang (Green Mountain) overlooking Tuen Mun New Town and the long-since silted up Castle Peak Bay. This bay was the staging post for ships trading in and out of China (the pearls from Tolo Harbour were probably brought overland and shipped from here). Tuen Mun means 'garrisoned entrance', and the foundations of a fort believed to date from AD 750 have been found near the monastery. The monastery was founded, tradition says, by an eccentric Buddhist monk named Pei Tu (literally 'cup ferry', referring to the wooden bowl he carried around and, aboard which, he apparently used to cross water). A stone image of Pei Tu stands in a dark cove above the monastery, where he used to meditate. A military commander is said to have put it here in his honour in AD 964. During the following centuries the monastery prospered, was rebuilt several times, and at one time was taken over for a short spell by the Taoists. Today it is inhabited by two Buddhist monks and three followers. The delightful complex of buildings includes a large, slightly tilted restaurant that serves vegetarian meals. This leads onto a spacious terrace backed with evening fragrance bushes, whose exquisite smell is not just confined to the evening. The stunning view was beautifully described in AD 820 by the Confucian scholar Han Yue, who 'looked over the vast unfathomable ocean and the forests and water and felt that it was indeed a sacred spot'. Another of the monastery's treasures is the 10,000-year-old bone of a dragon, which is housed in a cage under an ancient, gnarled tree literally balancing on its roots. If possible, visit this outstanding monastery with a Mandarin speaker. The abbot has a wealth of historic anecdotes.

Some early foundations from the Han Dynasty have also been found at **Lingtou Monastery**, though the present building, with its seven altars, is only 200 years old. It is inhabited by one monk who has to cope with severe security problems arising from the monastery's isolated position. Indeed, although it is only 15 minutes from Castle Peak Monastery, many local people do not know of its existence, so go armed with precise instructions from the HKTA.

The Taoist monastery **Ching Chung Koon** (close to Castle Peak Hospital), although of traditional design, was founded in 1949. It includes an old peoples' home, which is funded with the help of the monastery's popular vegetarian restaurant. It has an extensive library and some priceless works of art. For those interested in bonsai, there are marvellous examples everywhere.

Far away at the eastern entrance to Hong Kong is the fishing village of **Lei Yue Mun**, traditionally the haunt of pirates and until recently only accessible by boat (still the most exciting way of getting there; a pre-dinner trip through the harbour is particularly rec-

Farmers still practice centuries-old watering techniques

ommended). Today, it is the haunt of seafood lovers. The system of dining here requires a curious division of labour. Wander down the narrow streets edged with bubbling fish tanks and gaudy signs, bargain for the fish of your choice (a Cantonese-speaking friend will be invaluable here), then, armed with flapping plastic bags, choose a restaurant in which to have your purchases cooked and served. **Wai Lung Seafood Restaurant** is popular, always jostling with people both eating and playing mahjong. Finish off a delicious meal by stopping at a stall making fresh, paper-thin egg rolls. A blob of batter is dropped onto a sizzling pan and then deftly rolled up. The stall next to No 41B on the playground corner is recommended.

A separate limb of the New Territories land mass is the extravagantly beautiful and mountainous **Sai Kung Peninsula**, which contains lovely parkland for hiking and swimming. Sai Kung town, half new, half old, has a typically cluttered Chinese market. Along the waterfront are several restaurants, their outside tables decked with bright tablecloths. The brave can take their fish to the Sam Hoi (Three River) Restaurant, which is built on stilts over the sea and serves delicious noodles. Before leaving visit the attractive Tin Hau Temple.

Many traditional beliefs are still adhered to in these rural areas. In Long Keng, near Sai Kung, an ancient banyan tree is worshipped. Trees reputedly house the soul of a god who can prevent sickness and aid fertility. A shrine is often placed on or at the foot of the tree and, to ward off evil spirits, strips of red paper decorate it. Another important village deity is the Well God, who keeps the village water supply both topped up and pure. His shrine will often be found beside wells.

One of the most picturesque features of the Sai Kung Peninsula is **Rocky Harbour**, an enormous island-strewn stretch of water jutting out from its southeast flank. A trip undertaken by few visitors but well worthwhile is an exploration of Rocky Harbour by boat, hiring a small craft from Hebe Haven pier (the HKTA will suggest whom to contact). This opens up endless possibilities to visit sandy coves, small islands and remote villages.

Outlying Islands

Lantau

The Hong Kong archipelago, covering 1,068 square kilometres (411 square miles), consists of 235 islands, many of them just a few rocks. Lantau, the largest, is twice the size of Hong Kong Island. This is a staggeringly beautiful world of mountains, mists and monasteries —it is sometimes called the Island of Prayer. Lantau supports a population of only some 20,000. Try and visit during the week, as it becomes crowded with day trippers and campers at weekends.

Although knowledge of Lantau's early history is sparse, it is believed to have been settled since prehistoric times. In 1277, the doomed last emperor of the Song Dynasty fled to Lantau from the New Territories. Some say a temporary court was set up in Tung Chung Valley—indeed several families claim to be direct descendants of Song courtiers.

Discovery Bay, in the northeast, is a commercial/residential resort, with a commuter as well as a weekend population. Discovery Bay Golf Club and Village Resort are open to the public, offering a wide range of recreational facilities. Discovery Bay has its own high-speed ferry service, which runs from Blake Pier in Central.

Ferries to **Silvermine Bay** (about one hour) on the east coast run from the Outlying Districts Pier in Central. From Silvermine Bay you can hire a car or take a bus across the island to Tai O. Some of the Silvermine Bay ferries stop at Peng Chau. (Do not disembark unless you wish to visit Lantau's **Trappist Monastery** dedicated to Our Lady of Joy. The monk's boat meets every Peng Chau ferry and will take you across the small channel to the foot of a flight of steps leading to the monastery. You can walk from here to Silvermine Bay in about two hours.)

At Silvermine Bay the bus terminal and taxi stand are just opposite the ferry exit. To hire a minibus or car with driver, telephone Lantau Tours at 984 8256 before leaving Hong Kong Island. There is little to see in Silvermine Bay itself (silver was mined there only briefly during the last century). Along the beach are a group of good seafood restaurants; the Sampan and Seaview also serve Western food. **Pui O**, nestling under the majestic Sunset Peak, is the next village along. It has a selection of guesthouses and restaurants, and across some meadows is a long, slightly grey beach. Lantau's most beautiful beach accessible by road is at **Cheung Sha**, between Pui O and Shek Pik Reservoir.

For the walker, Lantau is paradise, but it is easy to get lost (or worse) on its precipitous terrain. Wear snake-proof shoes and take a strong stick, a good map and sensible precautions. *Selected Walks in Hong Kong* and the HKTA's leaflet *Lantau Walks* are useful companions. For a beautiful walk that is neither particularly hazardous nor too taxing,

Po Lin Monastery, Lantau Island

turn left down Wang Pui Road just after the Shek Pik Reservoir (if you are in a car you will have to leave it by the waterworks barrier) and take the path along the headland to Fan Lau (about three hours) where there is a ruined fort and two small isolated beaches. From Fan Lau it is possible to hire a junk or if you feel energetic to walk the five miles round to Tai O to catch the homeward bus or taxi.

Continuing on from Shek Pik Reservoir, the road winds up between dense vegetation, opening out into a valley with the Pearl Estuary beyond. The hillside on the right is dominated by two monastery buildings, Po Lin and Yin Hing, their yellow roofs shining against the dark green vegetation. No fewer than 135 monasteries dot Lantau, the most famous and largest is **Po Lin Monastery** (Temple of Precious Lotus), now home to the world's tallest outdoor bronze Buddha, the 34-metre-high Temple of Heaven Buddha. Despite the hype about size, the Buddha is impressively serene and well sculpted. The monastery is situated 2,500 feet above sea level and was first used by monks in 1905 but not inaugurated as a monastery until 1972. Its present buildings date from 1970. There are 100 resident monks and nuns who, with the help of about a hundred retired people, look after the monastery and manage a commercial tourist enterprise. Two thousand tourists visit the community most weekends, many stopping for lunch in its vegetarian restaurant. The ornate main temple is dedicated to the Three Precious Buddhas, and the

THE GREENING OF HONG KONG

Today's concrete jungle sprouting from the rocky hillsides of Hong Kong is hardly a cause of delight for nature lovers, but the apparent lack of greenery is no new phenomenon. Scientists believe that some 300–400 years ago, Hong Kong was covered with rainforests and populated by elephants and tigers, but by the time the British arrived in 1841, large sections of the colony's hillsides had already been denuded and the early houses stood on bleak, stoney slopes.

In an attempt to improve the situation, the colonists quickly began to plant trees—many of which were foreign species imported from Australasia —and today's green-covered hills are witness to their efforts. Some 40 per cent of modern Hong Kong is designated as country park, land that can be used by the general public for recreation, and also as vital water catchments.

As vast numbers of people fled to Hong Kong after the communist take-over of China in 1949, and the colony's economy began to take off, the scorching pace of development soon took its toll on the local environment. By the early 1980s, Hong Kong was a mess: its waters—only decades earlier fit to drink—were fetid with sewage, crowded with floating refuse and poisoned with chemical overflows; the air was choked with sulphur from the thousands of small factories churning out dirty emissions and the ever-increasing numbers of vehicles; and traffic clogged the roads, buildings mushroomed in a haphazard, short-term fashion without any proper planning, and daily noise levels rose to unbearable heights. Life was becoming distinctly unpleasant and it was clear that something had to be done.

There is much of worth in Hong Kong that deserves to be saved and treasured. Its waters are home to the few remaining examples of temperate water corals in southern China, as recorded by many of the local diving clubs. Fish, crab and shellfish are all plentiful in areas where the water is still relatively clean, such as Mirs Bay in the Sai Kung area.

There are also some interesting marshlands left near the Chinese border, the best known of which is Mai Po, where migratory birds rest on their journey between Siberia and Australia. There is also a sizeable local bird population that draws ornotholigists from around the world, while the mudflats attract their own collection of admiring scientists.

There are also a surprising number of trees still to be found on less developed streets—some even growing straight out of walls! Hong Kong's greenery is definitely hanging on and fighting back; it needs only a helping hand from the hoards of humans with which it is forced to share a very small piece of land.

In June 1989, the government published a major policy paper on the environment entitled *Pollution in Hong Kong: A Time to Act*, which outlined a structured process for cleaning up the Territory over a ten-year period. Included was a sewerage-improvement plan, a waste-collection network, a centralized chemical-waste centre and revisions to laws on water, air and waste. The introduction of a compulsory low-sulphur fuel had an instant and dramatic effect, as the clouds of smog that lingered over Hong Kong's industrial areas cleared overnight, but many other parts of the plan have since been delayed.

Victoria Harbour, into which most of Hong Kong's small factories pour their effluent, will not become a water control zone as early as hoped, and although the harbour's strong tidal currents have a flushing effect the body of water is still filthy. Two million cubic metres (70 million cubic feet) of sewage flows into Hong Kong waters every day, 90 per cent of which goes virtually untreated, and yet construction for the new sewerage system is still not underway. Although the government expects pollution from vehicles to increase by up to 65 per cent by the year 2000, regulations on car emissions remain non-existent. And municipal waste continues to grow, while landfill space is running out fast.

Nevertheless, all is not doom and gloom. There is little doubt that Hong Kong's population is as feverishly occupied as ever with earning money, but there is a growing number of people who are starting to demand more from their local environment. People are fed up with the dirt, noise and pollution—and are becoming more outspoken in voicing their opinions on the issue. This is reflected not only in the growth of local membership of such green organizations as Friends of the Earth, Green Power and the Worldwide Fund for Nature, but also in the increase in coverage of environmental issues in the local press and in corporate sponsorship of green community projects. The authorities are also reacting to public demands, as illustrated by the fact that several of the Legislative Council members who came to power in the recent elections rode at least partly on an environmental ticket.

stone floor is inlaid with the lotus pattern. To Buddhists the lotus is the symbol of the attainability of nirvana, whatever one's past: 'It grows out of mud but it is not defiled.' You can reach the monastery by bus or on foot, spend the night there, then climb neighbouring **Lantau Peak** (934 metres or 3,065 feet above sea level) and watch the sunrise.

A ten-minute walk from the monastery, on Ngong Ping Plateau, is a **tea plantation**. In 1959 a British barrister with experience in Ceylon noticed some disused tea terraces in the area. Today, there is a 70-acre farm producing 36,000 pounds of tea (both Indian and Chinese) each year.

The road to the small town of **Tai O** is bordered by the dry fields of old salt pans. Two hundred years ago, Tai O salt factories flourished, and today Tai O remains a large producer of salt fish. The village is built half on Lantau, half on another island, and is connected by a flat-bottomed ferry pulled and poled by two old ladies (fare 50 cents). At the far end of the village on the island side is **Hou Wang Temple**, built in 1699 (reigned over by the Qing Emperor Kang Xi) and dedicated to Marquis Yang Liang Xia, uncle and guardian of the last Song Emperor. Each year a festival is held in his memory: an enormous theatre is constructed in the temple's forecourt and opera performed. The houses along the shore, made of upturned boats incarcerated in metal sheeting, are curious looking, to say the least. Even two-storey affairs are contrived, complete with verandas and roof gardens. Often the house fronts are supported on stilts. Every second shop sells the famed salt fish, which hang like Italian salamis, their heads neatly packaged in paper. Tai O has some other old shops, including an 80-year-old traditional medicine shop (on the Lantau side of Wing On Street), where sandalwood and herbs perfume the air.

The only road to **Tung Chung** on the northern shore climbs over the central spine of Lantau, overlooked from their hillside vantage points by several monasteries, and with Sunset Peak towering to the right. The remains of a 17th-century fort stand guard over Tung Chung; its six cannons have been recently restored.

Cheung Chau

Lantau's small neighbour Cheung Chau has a thriving fishing community. For hundreds of years this island was the haunt of pirates, traders and smugglers; today, with an area of 2.5 square kilometres (one square mile), it has almost double the population of Lantau. Its main street buzzes with the activity of a typical market, with plenty of food and drinks stalls for the hot and footsore visitor. Try the seafood at the floating restaurant, **Cheung Chau Marriage Boat**.

After wandering in the market and its side streets—there are several good jade shops where occasionally bargains can be found—visit the **Pak Tai Temple** (to the left when where occasionally bargains can be found—visit the **Pak Tai Temple** (to the left when you get off the ferry). This is the setting for the famed **Cheung Chau Bun Festival** (see Festivals page 112). The temple, built in 1783, houses an early statue of Pak Tai, the god of the north, and a Song Dynasty sword salvaged from the sea during the last century.

By crossing the thin central strip of land, it is possible to make a circular walk around the southern part of the island. The **beaches** along Peak Road (named somewhat obscurely Tun Wan, Afternoon, Morning and Italian) are all good for a cooling swim. Just beyond the Italian beach is the Cheung Po Tsai hideout cave. From Sai Wan village, either walk or take a sampan back to the ferry pier.

Peng Chau

Peng Chau is a much quieter place. Although its 8,000 inhabitants are predominantly fisherfolk, there is some cottage industry, including several porcelain factories; Yuet Tong has a factory employing 100 people. Like Cheung Chau, the island has no motor cars and you can wander peacefully through the narrow streets. There are noodle stalls and restaurants aplenty. You can buy your fish on the pier and take it to **Sun Kwong Restaurant** (tel 983 0239) to be cooked. On the way to the porcelain factories, depending on the weather, you may see tray upon tray of tiny fish drying in the sun.

Lamma

Just south of Aberdeen lies Lamma, Hong Kong's third largest island at 13 square kilometres (five square miles). Fragments unearthed in Shan Wan Bay and stone rings attributed to the Shan Yao aboriginal people provide evidence of Lamma's prehistoric past. This rugged, mountainous island of sparse vegetation has a mixed population of vegetable and fish farmers and commuters, a large number of them Europeans.

There are two main villages on Lamma, both served by ferries leaving from Hong Kong's Outlying Districts Pier. Alternatively you can take your life in your hands, hire a sampan from Aberdeen as you make a dash across the paths of giant container ships into **Sok Kwu Wan**. There is little to see in the village but plenty to eat, as a whole series of outdoor restaurants lines the shore. The beaches are good, but sadly often polluted.

From Sok Kwu Wan it is a hilly 90-minute walk, mostly along the coast, passing desirable (depending on the tides) **Hung Shing Ye Beach** to **Yung Shue Wan**, where you can catch a ferry back to Central. This small town also has a number of seafood restaurants where you can enjoy a good meal before the ferry ride.

The Cheung Chau Bun Festival celebrations

Country Parks and Open Spaces

Walking boots may not be the first item you would pack for a trip to Hong Kong, but if you enjoy wide open spaces, the solitude of mountain tops and the call of woodland birds, you may well find yourself making a quick visit to one of Hong Kong's many shoe shops to buy some sneakers before setting off to explore the less well-known side of the Territory.

Hong Kong's buildings are packed so densely together that it can come as a surprise to realize about three-quarters of the total land area is without buildings of any sort. No matter where you stand in the city, it is almost always possible to see hills, luring you to explore.

Despite Hong Kong's perennial land-development hunger, where it seems every square centimetre must yield a quick profit, around 40 per cent of the total area of 1,070 square kilometres (413 square miles) is officially designated as country park, which means there can never be any building. The 21 parks plus two 'Special Areas', as they are described, cover many types of landscape—including some of Hong Kong's most beautiful beaches and rocky shores, as well as soaring mountain chains rising to almost 1,000 metres (3,300 feet).

The parks range from the 4,477 hectares (11,062 acres) of Sai Kung East, to the 270-hectare (667-acre) reservoir catchment area that is diminutive Pokfulam Park. The terrain varies from the bleak grandeur of the Pat Sin Range and much of Lantau, to fine, golden sand off Sai Kung Peninsula and thickly forested Tai Lam and Tai Po Kau.

Hong Kong's actual open land area may be limited compared to that of other places, but it encompasses an impressive diversity of features. Despite many common boundaries, each country park is unique in some respect. Whether you fancy a gentle stroll along shaded paths or a strenuous climb rewarded by a 360-degree panoramic view, the parks offer you an experience of Hong Kong far removed from the glitzy shopper's paradise that is the everyday tourist beat.

You may see traditional Chinese omega-shaped graves on slopes overlooking the sea. These are always sited with great attention paid to the principles of *fung shui*. The science (literally 'wind and water') is often translated as 'geomancy', and experts dictate everything from where you place your goldfish tank and office desk, to which building you should live in and when you should marry. In most parts of Hong Kong you can see eight-sided mirrors, which are believed to deflect bad fortune. As you pass traditional settlements, look out for *fung shui* woods, planted near newly-established villages three or more centuries ago. Different varieties of bamboo plus many trees with medicinal powers have been allowed to flourish in magnificent profusion. Once your eyes tune in, you can soon pick out other features which are clearly part of the *fung shui* system.

The **MacLehose Trail**, in the New Territories, is named after one of Hong Kong's former governors who was very active in promoting the Country Parks concept in Hong Kong. Linking eight parks, it stretches for 100 kilometres (62 miles) through some of Hong Kong's most beautiful and remote areas, including the territory's highest mountain—Tai Mo Shan.

Detailed leaflets highlighting the features of individual parks and the MacLehose Trail are available from the Agriculture and Fisheries Department headquarters, 393 Canton Road, Kowloon. As you go into each park you will find an information centre and detailed map of its special attractions.

Thanks to its geographical position—just within the tropics—Hong Kong's plant and bird life is unusually rich. Virtually all the 2,500 species of flowering and green plants, trees and ferns can be found within the country parks. Azaleas light up low ground and hillsides in late spring, and tiny blue gentians carpet mountain tops in early summer. Orchids and ferns lurk in unexpected places at all seasons, a surprise to the innocent eye. Hong Kong's native plants are protected by law, which should encourage them to flourish more abundantly with every passing season.

Such rich plant life in turn encourages abundant butterflies, some of which are relatively rare in world terms. Local moths include the giant silk worm moths, among which the atlas has an average wing span of 23 centimetres (9 inches) and the moon, 18 centimetres (7 inches). More than 200 recorded species and forms of butterflies have been found here. Between April–May and September–November, almost overwhelming numbers of these gaudy, fragile creatures may be encountered at any turn of the path as you explore.

Hong Kong's indigenous animal life has been much reduced by urbanization, and most of the remaining species (barking deer, pangolin, porcupine and wild pig among them) are nocturnal anyway, so your chances of seeing them are slim. Birds, however, are more resilient in the face of progress, and you do not need to be a keen ornithologist to enjoy their presence.

Serious birdwatchers have a number of favourite spots. Several informative books are available on Hong Kong birds, the best of which is undoubtedly the recently revised *New Colour Guide to Hong Kong Birds*, by Clive Viney and Karen Phillipps, published by the Government Printer, Hong Kong. The Hong Kong Bird Watching Society arranges regular field trips for its members. If you would like to participate during your stay, contact the HKTA, which will put you in touch with the appropriate person.

The **Mai Po Nature Reserve** is a collection of mudflats, fishponds and mangrove swamps in the extreme northwest of the New Territories, partly inside the closed border area with China. It constitutes a unique environment for migrant and resident birds. More than 250 species have been recorded in this area, at least 110 of them rarely encountered elsewhere in the Territory. On account of its international significance, the reserve is administered by the World Wide Fund for Nature (WWF). Access is freely available to the WWF information centre at Mai Po, but the bird-watching hides lie within the closed border area, which can be entered only with a permit. WWF organizes guided tours daily; the price is HK$30 per head. Tickets should be collected in advance from WWF's head office in Central. Telephone 526 4473 for further information.

During the breeding season from April to July at the **Yim Tso Ha Egretry** near Shataukok, you can see as many as 1,000 egrets, including a few pairs of the very rare Swinhoe's egret, plus as many as six species of herons. You cannot enter the egretry, but with the help of binoculars you can have a good view from the perimeter.

Public transport takes you to your starting point when exploring Hong Kong's open spaces. Most weekdays you can be sure to have the destination of your choice more or less to yourself—unless you have chosen the same day and the same place as a swarm of schoolchildren out for a picnic or field trip. Keep walking, as few of them will venture far from their jumping off point. The same applies to weekend and holiday excursions: use your initiative and it is easy to move beyond the hordes.

Remember also that Hong Kong's open spaces are by no means confined to country parks. A number of the Outlying Islands have not been included in the scheme, but they, too, make fascinating destinations (see page 91).

Mai Po

—Clive Viney, co-author of *Birds of Hong Kong*

Many international flights approach Hong Kong by following the Pearl River to its mouth on the South China Sea. From the air this is an endless waterscape of small ponds along the banks of the mighty river until, as the plane begins its descent, the industrial development around the Shenzhen Special Economic Zone is clearly visible. Then, amidst the greys, blues and browns, a patch of vivid green stands out like an emerald—Mai Po.

The green is the great, thick belt of mangroves on the eastern shore of Deep Bay. They survive only because Mai Po is a nature reserve. Elsewhere around the bay, the mangroves originally were cropped for fuel but in recent years have been cleared for reclamation, river training, rubbish and ash lagoons and even industrial feasibility studies. This is a sad loss, for precious little mangrove remains anywhere on the China coast. It is not just the unique community of salt tolerant plants and animals that is lost but also an essential nursery for prawn and fish stocks.

Mai Po sits almost in a no-man's land between Hong Kong and China, but administratively it is part of the New Territories. Behind the mangrove belt, the reserve comprises a collection of large and very long ponds. Most of these ponds are tidal with water levels artificially controlled for prawn and, to a lesser degree, fish farming. However, the Hong Kong chapter of the World Wide Fund for Nature (WWF) has secured the control of several of these ponds and manages them especially to attract wildlife. For instance, when the tide is high in Deep Bay, covering the vast mudflats, mud is available, in the safety of the reserve, for the hundreds, and sometimes thousands, of feeding and roosting birds. For the visitor, viewing hides or blinds have been strategically placed to permit close observation, and an education centre provides much background information and a useful bookshop.

Internationally, Deep Bay is vitally important as a stopping-off and feeding point for migratory birds. These are the birds that breed in the far north during the brief summer but spend the remainder of the year in warmer climes away to the south, even as far as Australia and New Zealand. Obviously, such long journeys, which are undertaken twice a year, cannot be

Deep Bay, Mai Po Marshes

made without safe resting places. And with the rapid development of China such staging posts have all but vanished. If the vast nutrient-rich mudflats of Deep Bay (a misnomer for its average depth is just three metres) were to disappear, either through reclamation or more insidiously through pollution, then these migratory birds would die. Entire species might vanish. Already a number of species that visit annually are close to extinction; these range from huge Dalmation Pelicans to the extraordinary Spoon-billed Sandpiper, but others include a gull so rare that its breeding grounds have only just been discovered and an egret that has all but disappeared.

Because the mud is treacherously soft, the bay is difficult to approach. Local fisherman use mud scooters, propelled by one foot, to tend their oysterbeds. A viewing hide which rises and falls with the tide can be approached by a floating broadwalk through the mangroves. Perhaps Hong Kong's greatest wilderness experience is to sit in this outer hide and watch the rising tide creep over the mud, moving the great mass of feeding birds closer and closer until they are forced to rise up, as the last vestige of mud is covered and seek sanctuary in the reserve.

In the context of Hong Kong, Mai Po is vital. No other place in this over-populated Territory can boast such a wealth of wildlife. Well over 270 species of birds have been recorded and mammals include leopard cats, civet cats, Javan mongoose and even the occasional otter. It is quite unbelievable that only 45 minutes from Central or Tsimshatsui, by car, there is true wilderness. From the minute of arrival birds are evident everywhere. Overhead are herons, egrets, ibises and brilliant blue kingfishers; the bushes and reeds are full of warblers and white-eyes, and on the path ahead are invariably wagtails and buntings. It is not just the birds that make a trip to Mai Po worthwhile; venture forth into the mangroves and watch the antics of the calling fiddler crabs or the comical mudskippers, fish that live both in and out of water.

The Chinese government has also recognized the importance of the area and declared 11 kilometres of the Deep Bay shoreline, contiguous with Mai Po, a strict nature reserve. On the face of it, the future looks rosy. However, the hinterland is developing at an alarming rate and the fragile ecosystem of the mud itself is under constant threat from pollution.

Despite these worries, everybody involved with the Mai Po project is highly optimistic. It has become an oasis for wildlife amidst an urban desert. Every season more and more birds, in an ever-increasing variety, visit the reserve. Even at the height of summer, usually the quietest time, Mai Po is well worth a visit as, apart from sheltering the many breeding birds, the mangrove and shore communities are at their most active.

The WWF organizes daily guided tours (contact 526 4473 for information). Individual visits are possible for bona fide naturalists but a permit must first be obtained from the Agriculture and Fisheries Department of the Hong Kong Government. The Hong Kong Bird Watching Society holds regular weekend field meetings and is always ready to welcome visiting birdwatchers. A captive wildfowl collection housing up to 40 species of Asian birds was set up in 1989 and forms part of the guided tour.

Mai Po is a little known face of Hong Kong that should not be missed.

Beaches

Hong Kong's rocky coastline is dotted with beaches. Some 38 of these on the mainland and some islands are maintained for public use—they are manned during the summer season by lifeguards and beach cleaners and offer changing rooms, umbrellas, barbecue pits, refreshments stalls and bathing rafts. The HKTA has a useful leaflet that shows all maintained beaches, lists the facilities and describes how to get there.

However enthusiastic the HKTA may be, no realist would deny that the Territory's crowded beaches come a poor second to the glorious stretches of sand in nearby Malaysia, Thailand and the Philippines. Yet, there may be days when beach conditions in Hong Kong are nearly perfect. The sand at times may be clean, the water may be as clear as the South China Sea ever is and, midweek, the beach may be almost deserted—but the chances of this magic combination are small. Winds and tides carry piles of debris (driftwood, plastic bags and worse) onto all beaches at some time or other. Heavy rain leaves both sand and sea muddy and grey. On Saturday afternoons, Sundays and public holidays, huge crowds of garrulous swimmers with barbecues and radios descend on beaches almost everywhere in the Territory.

The best beaches are inevitably the most inaccessible. If you have the time (and good weather) to devote a whole day to the beach, then it is possible to treat yourself to an interesting expedition that will give a glimpse of some of the most beautiful parts of Hong Kong. On Lantau, the 914-metre (almost 3,000-foot)-high Lantau and Sunset peaks form a stunning backdrop to a string of long, sandy beaches along the island's southern shores. On the mainland, the beaches of Clearwater Bay on the Sai Kung Peninsula are mostly unspoilt and sometimes breathtakingly beautiful. The inaccessibility rule even applies to Hong Kong Island, where the least crowded beach is at Big Wave Bay.

(following pages) The Dragon Boat Festival

Festivals

All the world loves a festival, an excuse for colour, feasting and a change from routine, and Hong Kong's calendar is punctuated by special occasions for celebration of many types. Some are major events, marked by processions, operatic productions, firework displays and similar public happenings on a large scale. Others are equally significant, but take the form of intensely personal devotions, inaccessible to outsiders. Unless you are fortunate enough to have Chinese friends, you will have to be content with the public faces of local festivals.

Most Hong Kong people are only one or two generations removed from the soil. Their peasant ancestors followed the rhythms of the seasons, the phases of the moon and the all-important signs that this might be the right time to plough, to plant or to harvest. They needed the security of a vast almanac telling them what was appropriate on every day of the year. Life in today's highrises has changed beyond recognition in most respects, but the lunar calendar still dictates many of Hong Kong's public holidays in celebration of major Chinese festivals, as well as such traditional Western holidays as Christmas and Easter.

Festivals are family-centred occasions. For centuries the two major events of the year—Chinese New Year (nowadays renamed the People's Spring Festival in the People's Republic of China) and the Mid-Autumn festival—were the only times of reunion for far-flung relatives. Today most small to medium-sized factories and workshops in Hong Kong still close down completely for as long as two weeks at this time of the year. The owners say they find it easier to give all employees their statutory 14 days of annual holiday at the same time, rather than stagger leave dates throughout the year. And certainly the employees seem to favour this approach, many seizing the chance to travel, visiting relatives in China or venturing further afield.

The major festivals are all marked by a public holiday, although in recent years the tendency has been to observe it the day after to allow everyone to recover from late-night celebrations. Minor festivals take place virtually every day, but only a few members of the older generation follow them all faithfully, with the help of the almanac, which is still issued annually.

Some of the most interesting festivals are little known outside a particular section of the community—the boat people, or the residents of a single island or walled village in the New Territories, for instance. The HKTA can supply a list of events, which will include some of these, such as the Cheung Chau Bun Festival. Others like the Ten-Year—or even more important 100-Year—clan celebrations may be encountered only by chance.

The easiest signs to spot as you tour the rural areas of Hong Kong are the temporary theatre and other structures put up for these celebrations, usually on open ground out-side a village. Made of bamboo with tin sheets for roofing, these are minor marvels of traditional engineering in themselves. The design has probably varied little in the past millennium, but these days they are for the most part held together with plastic stays rather than the traditional rattan bindings. The biggest of these matsheds, as they are known, is the theatre for performances of Chinese opera to entertain the gods, whose colossal paper effigies are housed in their own matshed. A smaller structure houses a communal kitchen.

Outsiders will attract plenty of stares but are always tolerated at such events. Even in the daytime there is a bustling, festive atmosphere. Visitors light joss sticks, chat and bargain for windmills, gilt bells and other souvenirs. If the community is rich, opera may continue round the clock, by relays of performers, the best being reserved for the late show in the evening. Do not be surprised to find yourself virtually the only person in the audience in the daytime.

With the exception of a few fanatics, the Chinese attitude to religion has never been dogmatic. The sixth-century scholar, Fu Hsi, was the epitome of Chinese eclecticism; he dressed in a Taoist cap, a Buddhist scarf and Confucian shoes. In more recent centuries, Western missionaries were appalled when converts simply absorbed the Trinity into their existing collection of deities. The popular belief has always been that it is impossible to have too many gods: each represents additional insurance—for this world or the next.

Official figures list a total of 600 temples in the whole of Hong Kong, of which 100 represent a mixture of religions, while 300 are Buddhist and 200 are Taoist. Temples go in and out of fashion. If a devotee obtains valuable advice when consulting the wooden fortune sticks or other sources of guidance, word spreads quickly and the temple is soon buzzing with worshippers in search of similar good luck. This may continue for months or years, the profits from sales of *heung yau* (incense and lamp oil) plus donations from the faithful going into extensive and frequent renovations or innovations. Such popular-ity is as fickle as fate, waning as readily as it waxes, leaving some of Hong Kong's most interesting temples virtually deserted year round.

LUNAR NEW YEAR

Otherwise known as Chinese New Year, this festival falls in late January or early Febru-ary and is the most widely observed. Each year is assigned to one of 12 animals (which follow each other in rotation), each possessing different characteristics. The legend con-cerning this 12-year cycle tells how the Lord Buddha summoned to him all Earth's ani-mals but only 12 obeyed and, as a reward for their loyalty, he named a year after each one. Your fate in any one year may be determined by the relationship between the ani-mal of the year in question and that of the year of your birth. The coming of a New Year means a period of goodwill, the settling of debts and quarrels and a visit to the fortune-

teller. Ancestors are worshipped—the spirit of an uncared-for ancestor can turn very nasty—and special attention is paid to the Kitchen God, for it is thought that at the end of each year he returns to the Jade Emperor to report on the family's conduct during the past year. Special food (often vegetarian) is prepared and presents of New Year biscuits (*chau mai beng*, stamped with messages such as 'Harmony and Prosperity', 'May sons and wealth be yours') are exchanged. To the delight of children, they are given little red *lai si* packets containing money—the colour red being lucky. Everywhere you will hear or see the words *Kung Hei Fat Choi* (Best wishes and prosperity), though to young couples the greeting is *Kung Hei Tim Ding* (Best wishes and have more sons).

For the visitor, though, this thoroughly family festival can be a bleak time. The statutory holiday spans three days, but many shops and restaurants close for two weeks. Hundreds of thousands of people return to China to visit relatives, so it is definitely not the best time for a quick trip across the border. Central District, though dressed in decorative lights with the animal of the year shining down from prominent buildings, tends to be deserted. To get an authentic feeling of this festival, visit one of the special new year fairs in the final week of the old year. Fragrant Chinese narcissi, huge blossom-covered peach branches and mini orange trees are given as symbols of long life and prosperity. The oranges are later dried and stewed to make medicine. The largest market is in Victoria Park, Causeway Bay, where, especially at night, there are row upon row of exquisite blooms, food stalls, side shows and thousands of jostling men, women and children in holiday mood. The end of Chinese New Year, on the 15th day, is marked by the lighting of traditional lanterns.

Springtime Birthday of Tin Hau

The Taoist Empress of Heaven has a lavishly celebrated day in her honour. Tin Hau is the patron saint of fishermen and they depend on her to keep them safe throughout the year. Many temples to her can be found in the Territory, although, thanks to reclamation, many are now well back from their original waterfront vantage point. The most popular temple is in Joss House Bay and dates from 1266. The harbour becomes a sea of rippling silken banners as convoys of boats sail to this remote rendezvous.

Roast suckling pigs, joss sticks and other offerings are made ashore, where the insistent drumming of lion dance teams heightens the festive atmosphere. Individual boat shrines are taken into the temple to be blessed for another year by the Taoist priest. (It is estimated that 20,000 people visit this tiny temple during the birthday celebrations. So be prepared for dense crowds if you decide to go along.) Special commercial tours are organized for the festival, and there are usually excursion ferries too.

Many legends surround Tin Hau's earthly existence. The daughter of a 10th-century Fujian fisherman, she is reputed to have sailed on a straw mat into the eye of a typhoon

Dragon Boat races

and guided an entire fishing fleet to safety. Faith in her supernatural powers continued to grow after her death until, in the Qing Dynasty (1644–1911), she was given the title Empress of Heaven.

CHEUNG CHAU BUN FESTIVAL

This three-day festival is celebrated in May with a unique procession. Three vast wooden towers, each covered with some 5,000 white buns stamped with a goodwill message, are erected near Pak Tai Temple. The purpose of these bun towers is to appease the hungry spirits of pirate victims, whose mutilated bodies were found in the 1880s on this small, dumbbell-shaped island on the west side of Hong Kong's archipelago. This Taoist festival also gives thanks to Pak Tai, Emperor of the North and God of the Sea, for protecting the islanders since the 1770s from various plagues. The festivities include Chinese opera, lion dances, stilt dances and a fabulous procession, featuring many legendary figures as well as more contemporary celebrities. Small children in elaborate costumes are strapped to the top of tall poles, which are then carried through the streets to give the appearance of floating in mid-air.

Get to the island early in the day and wander through the back streets to discover the secret of this particular brand of magic. At midnight on the third day, a gong sounds, and the destruction of the 60-foot bun towers begins. In the past young men scaled them with the object of collecting as many buns as possible—the higher the bun, the greater the luck it was supposed to bring them. Since a tower accidentally collapsed one year, the scramble has been discontinued and the buns are distributed by the priests. Special tours go to the island for the festivities and there are supplementary ferry sailings throughout this period.

DRAGON BOAT FESTIVAL

Known in Chinese as *Tuen Ng*, this event is a noisy affair held in June. Teams from across the Territory and even from overseas compete in boat races to the beat of a huge drum. The races commemorate Chu Yuan, a fourth-century scholar, who was so distressed by the corruption of local government officials that he threw himself into the Mei Lo River in Hunan. To keep the fish from eating his corpse, the local people scattered rice dumplings over the water and beat drums—perhaps as one sees Chinese fishermen today, rowing from one end of their net to another, beating a drum or thrashing the water with a long stick, to scare the fish into their nets.

Today, the craft used for the races that celebrate this distant event are long, slim and gaily painted, with the ornately carved head and tail of the fearsome dragon. Depending on their size, they carry 10 or 20 oarsmen with an additional person acting as coxswain, beating on a large drum to keep time for the rowers. An international dragon boat competition is staged in the weeks following the festival, drawing teams from many parts of the world. The accompanying razzmatazz makes this a colourful and enjoyable event.

Mid-Autumn Festival

Altogether more tranquil, this was traditionally a harvest festival, but it also had a political significance. During an uprising against the Mongol Yuan Dynasty in the 14th century, messages were passed to conspirators in moon cakes. Today these cakes no longer contain messages, but they do have an exotic range of sweet and savoury fillings. The mixture includes pork fat, duck egg, lotus seeds, sugar and red bean—an acquired taste for most people. In the weeks before the festival sales are brisk, and streets and markets are festooned with colourful lanterns. Some are in traditional shapes, like rabbits, starfruit and goldfish, while others are modern novelties like rockets and aeroplanes. On the night of the festival, many families take their moon cakes and lanterns to one of the Territory's peaks, where they can enjoy the rising of the moon—always unusually large and brilliant at this season. In recent years a lantern carnival has been organized in Victoria Park, Causeway Bay, and another in the Ko Shan Theatre in Kowloon. These feature displays of magnificent lanterns as well as opera and other entertainment. The sight of the lanterns flickering among the trees is one of the prettiest experiences Hong Kong has to offer. Make the effort to visit the Peak or one of the parks.

Ching Ming and Chung Yeung

These are the times when families visit the graves of their dead to clean and sweep them, make offerings and pay their repects. Ching Ming is in the spring, and Chung Yeung in the autumn. There's nothing morbid about the rituals, which are usually rather colourful, informal family picnics.

Yue Lan

This is otherwise known as the Festival of Hungry Ghosts, who are released from the underworld for one lunar month. At this time food and paper offerings are prepared to appease the spirits of the dead. At the side of the road, particularly in residential areas, you may see some elaborate paper models of houses, motor cars, horses and furniture waiting to be burned to help the spirits on their way.

Winter Solstice

This festival, important in the Chinese calendar, comes in the third week of December. However, it catches most non-Chinese completely by surprise, since there is no public holiday, and the celebration is very much a family affair. Most smaller shops and offices close early or take the whole day off, and many taxi drivers take at least half a day off.

Ritual Obeisance

Fong was discharged in time to sweep the ancestral graves at the Ching Ming festival, that annual obeisance the quick paid to the dead in the season of renewal. The Ching Ming rites were hard work at the best of times; in the unprecedentedly hot spring weather they would be a physical ordeal. Wallace doubted the wisdom of having Fong accompany the family to the graves while she was still recovering but kept his misgivings to himself.

The cemetery was on the other side of the small mountain ridge that formed the spine of the island, on the Pacific Coast, near the fishing village where the first British naval landings had taken place. The graves were cut into the hillside in steeply ascending terraces, platforms so narrow that unsubstantiated rumour had it that coffins had to be slotted into the cheaper plots in an upright position.

The morning buses were crowded, and Mr Poon let several pass before supervising a mass embarkation. Soft drinks stalls and flower stands were already doing a roaring trade at the cemetery's imposing porcelain gates when the Poons arrived. The family waited while Mr Poon bargained unsuccessfully for a small wreath; the boys stared at a row of frosted bottles, licking beads of perspiration from the soft black down on their upper lips.

At length Mr Poon retired, empty-handed, from his negotiations. He waved the family on. Following him down a steep flight of steps, they had to run the gauntlet of yapping dogs that, day or night, were to be found by the gates. Wallace found their well-fed appearance sinister.

The full extent of the day's demands broke in on him as he came out of the shade of an avenue of trees and saw the graveyard in the midday sun. The architecture of the cemetery was itself a cogent reminder of the continuing power of the dead over the living. Mr Poon's ancestors were dotted in random, disobliging clumps over the entire hillside, thus attesting to Wallace that key characteristics of that irksome family were transmitted beyond death itself. Or, at the least, the Poons died in character.

For the next four hours the family descended, back-tracked, and circled in the hottest part of the day. Trips to the different burials could

Ching Ming Festival, watercolour, Tingqua (Kwan Luen Cheung), Hong Kong Museum of Art

not be scheduled according to any logical plan, so far as considerations of time and effort were concerned, but had to be made in strict order of familial precedence. The men's shirts stuck to their backs in transparent patches. Mr Poon set a gruelling pace, never turning to look behind himself. His black trousers, stretched taut across the rump, were speckled with silver friction marks. They glinted like a mirage before the family, always at the same distance. Even had he wished to do so, Wallace would have been unable to overtake the old gentleman. Mr Poon still prided himself on his agility but, more than this, he drew strength from the discomfiture of the others.

May Ling and Fong brought up the rear a little distance behind the sisters, as Mr Poon arrived at the first tombs. He had economised on tips to the groundsmen the year before with the consequence that the Poon plots were now heavily overgrown with weeds. Ah Lung's sons, in their school uniforms of blue canvas trousers and white shirts, produced trowels from their satchels. There were not enough of these tools for the entire party but numbers were made up with the distribution of European-style cutlery. Wallace found a fork more efficient than a spoon or knife.

At a major grave such as this, the tomb of Mr Poon's grandfather, thick stacks of counterfeit money would be sacrificed, while the family bowed their heads in contemplation. The money burnt fiercely but inconspicuously in the bright sunshine, crumbling into flakes which were carried upwards on shimmering waves of heat. It was almost as if the stack was being destroyed by the concentrated energy of prayer. Then a single pale finger of flame would point skywards and the pile collapsed upon itself.

Before departing, Mr Poon appropriated a wreath from a nearby plot, which looked recently swept, and placed it on the grave of his ancestor.

Timothy Mo, *The Monkey King*, 1978

Museums

Hong Kong is uniquely placed to record and study Chinese history and culture. The past 20 years have seen the opening of a number of small museums. Because their size is limited, these are highly selective and are all very good.

SPACE MUSEUM

Of the four centrally located museums, the Space Museum, on the Kowloon waterfront opposite the Peninsula Hotel, offers a spectacular experience. Opened in October 1980, this HK$60-million project consists of a 300-seat Space Theatre, a Hall of Solar Sciences, an Exhibition Hall, a lecture hall, an astronomy bookshop and a snack bar.

The **Space Theatre's** programme (changed roughly every six months) is consistently captivating. Films are projected onto the domed roof 23 metres (75 feet) in diameter. In the centre of the auditorium, a weird-looking space monster—in fact the Zeiss Planetarium projector—moves up and down on its axis throughout the hour-long show. In addition there is an Omnimax projector with over 100 precision lenses capable of slotting onto a gigantic 'fish eye', many special-effects projectors and a multi-channel sound system—all automatically controlled by a computer in the centre of the theatre. The result is both absorbing and spectacular. The entire screen is used throughout the show, with a commentary in Cantonese, but headphones at every seat provide English, Japanese or Mandarin versions.

In the **Hall of Solar Sciences**, a solar telescope gives the visitor a close look at the anatomy of the star on which we all depend. Other exhibits delve into subjects such as solar phenomena and solar energy with copious use of audiovisual devices and microcomputers. Before you leave, a quizzing computer can test the knowledge acquired during your visit. The **Exhibition Hall** explores man's advancement in the fields of astronomy and space exploration. An interesting exhibit is the Aurora 7 space capsule, in which Scott Carpenter made three orbits of the Earth in 1962. Telephone 721 2361 for current programme times and other details. The exhibition halls are open 2–10 pm Monday–Saturday and 10.30 am–10 pm Sundays and public holidays (closed on Tuesdays). Tickets are available for an all-in price of HK$25 (seniors and children HK$15).

MUSEUM OF ART

The most recent addition to the group of cultural facilities along the Tsimshatsui waterfront is the Hong Kong Museum of Art. The museum's collection—including oil paintings, drawings, etchings and lithographs of old Hong Kong—is displayed in six galleries: Historical Pictures; Contemporary Hong Kong Art; Chinese Fine Art; Chinese Antiques; the Xubaizhai Gallery; and the Special Exhibitions Gallery.

The museum is open 10 am–6 pm weekdays and Saturdays, 1 pm–6 pm Sundays and public holidays (closed Thursdays). Admission HK$10 (seniors and children HK$5).

MUSEUM OF HISTORY

This is now in two pre-war buildings in Kowloon Park, a little way up Nathan Road, past the Hyatt Hotel. Exhibits chart Hong Kong's archaeological and ethnological background and development. A highlight of the permanent exhibition is a series of detailed models of fishing junks and their tackle, illustrating traditional fishing methods. Special exhibitions, such as 'Hong Kong Before 1841', are invariably clearly captioned and well laid out. Those especially interested in 19th and 20th century Hong Kong should ask to see the albums of old photographs, which provide a revealing insight into the Territory's development and social life. From time to time major exhibitions are brought in from outside Hong Kong; watch for announcements of these as they are always superb.

A newly opened branch that is worth a detour is the **Law Uk Folk Museum**, which houses artifacts of Hakka village life in a 200-year-old Hakka house at 14 Kut Shing Street, a short walk from the Chai Wan MTR Station.

TSUI MUSEUM OF ART

Situated on the 11/F of the old Bank of China building on Des Voeux Road Central, is Hong Kong's first private museum. It displays over 2,000 pieces of Chinese antiquities: the most important is a collection of ceramics spanning a period of about 5,000 years. Museum hours are 10.00 am–6.00 pm weekdays and 10.00 am–2.00 pm Saturdays. The entrance fee is HK$20 (students and children HK$10).

FUNG PING SHAN MUSEUM

Further afield, at the University of Hong Kong in Pokfulam, is the Fung Ping Shan Museum. This imposing building, with its circular main exhibition hall, was originally opened in 1953 primarily as a teaching museum for the university's art students. The bronze and early pottery collections are particularly fine. The earliest pieces are ritual vessels from the Shang (1600–1027 BC) to Zhou (1027–256 BC) dynasties. There are bronze mirrors from the Han (206 BC–AD 220) to Tang (618–907) dynasties. Also notable is the collection of 967 Nestorian crosses, dating back to the Yuan Dynasty (1279–1368). The museum also houses a fine ceramic collection of late Ming and Qing paintings. Opening times are 9.30 am–6 pm daily (closed on Sundays and public holidays).

LEI CHENG UK

The Lei Cheng Uk Branch Museum (part of the Museum of History) houses a well-preserved tomb of the Eastern Han Dynasty (25–220). Following the devastating squatter hut fires of 1954, the tomb was discovered during the foundation work for Hong

Incense burners

Kong's first public housing estate at Shek Kip Mei. Subsequent excavation was carried out by the University of Hong Kong and the find was opened to the public in 1957. Driving through this densely populated concrete jungle one suddenly comes upon an incongruous grassy knoll beside a park. In front of the tomb stands a small museum building, which exhibits drawings and stone rubbings depicting life in Han times, as well as recording the excavation of the site. Replicas of worldly possessions to help in the afterlife have always played a part in Chinese burial custom, and on display are numerous bronze and pottery items found in the tomb: model houses complete with animal yards, and pottery storage jars, much like those found today in many a rustic kitchen. Open 10 am–1 pm and 2 pm–6 pm daily (closed Thursdays) and Saturdays 1 pm–6 pm.

MUSEUM OF CHINESE HISTORICAL RELICS

Opened in 1984, this 1,200-square-metre (13,000-square-foot) museum is a permanent exhibition of cultural treasures from China. The display changes twice a year and features some of China's most recent archaeological discoveries. Prerecorded tapes in English or Cantonese are available, as is an expert to answer questions. Located in the Causeway Centre, near the Wanchai Ferry Pier, the museum is open 10 am–6 pm virtually every day of the year. Admission is HK$20 (students and children HK$10), HK$5 for groups of 10 persons or more.

FLAGSTAFF HOUSE MUSEUM OF TEA WARE

The Flagstaff House Museum of Tea Ware is housed in the oldest Western-style building still standing in Hong Kong. Located in Hong Kong Park, just off Cotton Tree Drive, its elegant verandas, tiled roof and tree-shaded setting recall the ambience of the mid-19th century. Other Victorian restorations in the vicinity include the Marriage Registry.

The collection includes about 500 pieces of tea ware, mainly of Chinese origin, dating from the Warring States Period up to the present day, among which the Yixing teapots are the most notable. There is also a special display on the history of tea. Opening hours are 10 am–5 pm except Wednesdays.

SAM TUNG UK MUSEUM

As the satellite industrial town of Tsuen Wan grew up in the New Territories over the past decade, three lines of 200-year-old houses survived intact. These formed the clan home of the Chan family, immigrants from Fujian province. At the end of 1987, Sam Tung Uk became Hong Kong's newest museum, containing period house displays and giving a lively insight into the lifestyle of the Qing Dynasty (1644–1911) scholar class. Ironically, as part of the process of metamorphosis, the original buildings were demolished and what you see today are reinforced-cement replicas. The place is worth visiting and is readily accessible as it is only minutes away from the Tsuen Wan MTR station.

Food

— Harry Rolnick

With more than 95 per cent of Hong Kong's people originally from the bordering province of Guangdong, it is hardly surprising that the overwhelming majority of the Territory's restaurants should be devoted to Cantonese cuisine. Fortunately, just as France could be called the apex of European cuisine, so Cantonese has long been regarded as the most subtle, multifarious, ingenious and interesting of all the Chinese cuisines.

Equally fortunately, the Cantonese are not quite so prejudiced against other cuisines as, say, the metropolitan Parisian might be against 'inferior' foreign dishes. The Cantonese diner may habituate himself to his native fare, but he has nothing against a spicy night out with some Sichuan food; he loves his oily, warming Shanghai dishes during the wintertime; and for those very special occasions, he'll impress everybody by taking them to a Peking banquet, the centre of which is Peking duck or Hangzhou beggar's chicken.

The third part of Hong Kong's culinary good fortune is that the expatriates, predominantly from the US, Scotland and England, have eschewed their own provinciality and are willing to indulge in foods from all over Asia—if only as a reminder that many of these exotic foods came from one-time colonies. In addition the burgeoning tourist trade over the past decade has meant that many European restaurants of high quality have made their mark here, to the benefit of all.

THE CHINA SYNDROME

For a casual visitor, the words 'Chinese restaurant' might suffice, but to those who truly enjoy their eating, the words mean practically nothing. Outside of the major differences in the regions, there are so many different types of restaurants, so many seasonal imperatives and so many different ways of eating, that the syndrome of Chinese food is virtually infinite.

The most informal and least expensive eateries are the *dai pai dongs* —street restaurants or noodle stalls—which are set up in market and shopping areas. The variety of foods can extend from ox, pig and cow offal to the freshest seafood. There are a dozen different kinds of noodles, and noodle soup with *wonton* or meats and vegetables. And of course nearly everything is accompanied by rice.

Up a few grades are the morning *dim sum* restaurants. In fact almost every Cantonese-style restaurant serves *dim sum* from 6 am through to lunch time. The food is not so much a meal as a very happy ritual—*yum cha* to the Cantonese— of drinking tea and eating a variety of dishes at a leisurely pace. *Dim sum* has two distinct advantages. First, the food is usually on display, passed around in little bamboo baskets, so you do not need to understand a word of Cantonese to order. Simply point a finger and the basket is placed on the table. You do not need to worry about a written bill. At the end of the meal, the baskets are added up and the price is paid; invariably it is very reasonable too. The other advantage is that these little Chinese *hors d'oeuvres*—literally 'little hearts'—are delicious.

Third up the scale are the ordinary meals in Chinese restaurants. Except for very small restaurants (equivalent to indoor noodle stalls) and the monstrous ones in far-out sections of Hong Kong where foreigners rarely wander, nearly all restaurants have English-language menus. Unfortunately, even with lists of up to 500 different dishes, some of the best are not even mentioned. Your best bets in this case are: a) to enlist the assistance of a friendly waiter; b) go with some Chinese friends; c) if you spot something good on another table, do not hesitate to ask what it is.

A point to remember is that Chinese dishes here are very different from those in your own country. The great pride of Cantonese food is that it is always fresh. And as the greens in London or seafood in San Francisco are different from the *choi* or shrimp of Hong Kong, the ingredients and tastes will be unlike those you know back home.

The most important thing in Chinese dining is ordering. Remember that democracy at a large Chinese party is unheard of. The host will take the menu and decide what the others will have. After checking food prejudices (that is, whether eel or pork or fish lips is acceptable to all), the leader will begin ordering. A basic plan is to start with a cold dish, then order one beef, one pork, one vegetable, one seafood or fish, one soup, some noodles or fried rice. Traditionally, a single plate should be ordered for each member of the party, plus one more. The waiter will determine what size platter to bring: for up to four, a small serving will do, up to nine or ten a medium-sized dish, and after that, a large portion.

As Chinese food has been an 'in' thing in most occidental capitals, most visitors have some idea of the differences between the regions, but here is a rundown:

Cantonese The best Cantonese food in the world is in Hong Kong. The preparations are traditional (as they are in Guangzhou itself), but the ingredients come not only from China but Hong Kong (the New Territories was once called 'The Emperor's Rice Bowl' for the richness of its produce) and the rest of the world. The emphasis is on fast cooking to bring out the best of each dish's natural taste and colour. No greasy dishes are ever served. If they are not fast-fried in a minimum of oil, they are steamed or broiled. Few spices are used but there are many sauces. The Guangdong coast supplies remarkable seafood, as well as an abundance of fowl, meat and vegetables, including an endless variety of mushroom. Truly this is the world's greatest cuisine—as even the Parisian practitioners of *nouvelle cuisine* are happy to point out.

Pekingese The arid desert of northern China has little in the way of natural ingredients, unlike tropical and sub-tropical Guangdong. But as Beijing has been the capital of China since early times, the best produce was sent up to the Emperor's palaces, and

The floating Jumbo Restaurant, Aberdeen

some fine recipes were devised. The best known dish is Peking duck, but the Mongolian hotpot is popular, as are lamb and mutton dishes, especially during winter. You rarely eat rice with this food. Instead, ask for some dumplings (perhaps half steamed, half fried). You should wind up the meal with noodles and vegetables.

Sichuanese This is the spiciest of all Chinese food. Garlic, pepper, fennel and star anise all grow in Sichuan province and are added liberally to the steamed, simmered, smoked dishes. These include excellent seafood, superb fowl and eggplant, as well as an intriguing sour-and-hot soup to finish off the meal. Be prepared for a *lot* of garlic.

Shanghainese This is a bit greasier than some, a little sweeter, and the dishes are fried for a long time in sesame or soy sauce. The seafood—especially eel and winter crab—is good, and the portions are enormous. The dumplings are tasty, and the little shrimp with pieces of garlic and pepper are excellent. Many of the dishes come from other provinces, befitting Shanghai's status as the largest port in China and its most cosmopolitan city.

Hakka and **Chiu Chow** Both of these cuisines come from the south of China, and neither is very popular outside the Far East. But Chiu Chow food is gutsy, with thick shark's fin soup, goose doused in soy sauce, excellent seafood and all kinds of bird's nest dishes. Usually these restaurants do not close until 3 am. Hakka food comes from a nomadic people who of necessity preserve their food. Consequently, many of the best dishes are salted down (like salt chicken or salted cabbage) and are not terribly appealing, save the mixed vegetable dish *lo han* which is probably the best of all vegetable dishes.

In the top grade of all Chinese food is the Man Han Banquet—and should you be so lucky as to be invited to one of these rare occasions, do go. A traditional banquet is not simply one dinner—it consists of at least three days of dining. And of the 100-odd dishes, not a single one is duplicated.

To quote an old Chinese saying: 'Let there be plenty of food and plenty of clothing, and propriety and righteousness will flourish.'

THE TABLES OF ASIA

With immigrants from all parts of Asia, and with a European population always on the look-out for different foods, it is little wonder that Hong Kong can serve dishes from all over the Orient. Granted, some of the restaurants aren't always the cleanest (one thinks immediately of the Indian restaurants in Chungking Mansions, on Kowloon side), but for the most part health laws are so stringent that you can eat safely.

For the record, countries represented include India (mainly North India, but with a few Madras dishes served in Chungking Mansions), Pakistan, Indonesia (spicy, with coconut milk and *sambal* hot sauces), Malaysia (virtually the same as Indonesia, but with less variety, as the restaurants are run by Chinese), Japan, Korea (very spicy, marvellous barbecued beef), Thailand (spicy tangy lemon grass and good curries) and Vietnam (where the food is mild except for the vinegar and includes dewy-fresh greens, mint and lettuce).

FOOD FROM THE LONG-NOSED BARBARIANS

Traditionally, European food was as much an anathema to the Chinese as were the Europeans themselves. In multi-national Hong Kong, this has obviously changed—and rare is the young Chinese who does not indulge at fast food joints like McDonald's.

Every hotel has its restaurants and first-class hotels nearly always have European managers. Prices are fairly reasonable for cuisine, fairly unreasonable for wines. (Hong Kong is duty free in everything except cigarettes and liquor.) The best bargains are the buffets, listed daily in the *South China Morning Post*. The Hilton, Furama, Peninsula and The Hongkong Hotel all have superb buffets.

At private restaurants, the *prix fixe* lunches are about one-third the price of *à la carte* meals. Gaddi's, Chesa and Au Trou Normand are usually expensive, so these set lunches fall into the bargain class.

Outside the hotels, a number of ethnic restaurants are around: little Mexican cafés, pizzerias, a few delicatessens, some Hungarian food and, around Wanchai, very inexpensive European dishes can be found. Sandwich bars are mushrooming with an imaginative choice of fillings and breads.

When dining out in Hong Kong the main rule is to be adventurous about trying new dishes and restaurants off the beaten path. If Hong Kong people are handsome, healthy, hard-working and hearty, they are the prime heirs of the dictum offered by Confucius, back in the fifth century BC. 'Great food,' he said, 'is the first happiness.'

Afternoon Tea

—Jeffrey Hantover

"When we consider how small after all the cup of human enjoyment is, how soon overflowed with tears, how easily drained to the dregs in our quenchless thirst for infinity, we shall not blame ourselves for making so much of the tea-cup. Mankind has done worse." Kakuzo

When one first thinks of teatime in Hong Kong, one likely has visions of the Peninsula, doyenne of hotels. You imagine English ladies and gentlemen fresh from the Kowloon–Canton Railway Terminus sitting where you now sit in the ornate lobby with its bas-reliefs and gold trim. Unfortunately, you hear more than echoes from the gracious past; you hear the clatter of dishes and the babble of voices. You are smack in the middle of a busy lobby that is itself a tourist attraction and sits above and below an arcade of fine shops, a magnet to throngs of Japanese tourists.

If the Peninsula evokes memories of luxury train travel, the Mandarin Oriental's Clipper Lounge with its low ceiling and masthead at the top of the stairs (from the film *Billy Budd*) has the Art Deco feel of a 1920s luxury ocean liner. At afternoon tea (HK$60 for one, HK$113 for two), locals outnumber tourists. Elegant, well dressed Chinese women parade by—an informal fashion show, and the air is filled with lively chatter of what's on sale, or on life in Vancouver, Bangkok and Singapore. A Filipino combo play light popular music as you nibble blueberry tarts, *petit fours*, madeleines, Windsor cake, scones with jam and clotted cream, tea sandwiches and savoury puffs. You can choose from a range of teas, leaf infusions and coffees, all brought by smiling and courteous staff.

The new rich kid on the block, the Tiffin Lounge at the Grand Hyatt, may throw his money around, but he has learned his manners. Tea here (HK$68) is as gracious or more so than at the Mandarin, and the offerings more extensive. Those who find the Clipper Lounge claustrophobic will find the Tiffin Lounge airy to the point of being as cavernous as an airplane hangar. Despite its newness, it has the grandeur of an old style hotel with its comfortable chairs, tasteful decor and delicate bone china service. A string quartet provide the musical background, and though they can churn out 'Memories' with the best of them, they also play a frothy Strauss waltz. From the glass walls is a magnificent view of the harbour and a sweep of the city all the way to the Macau Ferry Terminal that captures the modern architectural gems as well as the landscaped garden and waterfall across from the hotel where brides and grooms often pose for pictures.

The food matches the surroundings: smoked salmon, egg salad and crunchy cucumber tea sandwiches, scones served warm with kiwi and blackberry preserves along with the *de rigueur* clotted cream. Though there is no chocolate mousse or savouries as at the Mandarin, there is a wonderful miniature cheesecake topped with orange segments and candied orange peel and mixed fruit tarts. Off the set tea menu there is a wide selection of pastries including apple crumble, chocolate cake and a light airy éclair.

For tea with an equal, if not more magnificent, view there is the Convention Centre's Gallery Café, serving an English, Chinese and Deluxe tea at reasonable prices (HK$40–50). For a moving experience of another sort the Star Ferry Afternoon Tea Cruise (HK$110 for adults, HK$70 for children) takes you on an hour and a quarter tour of the harbour, offering in addition to Chinese teas, cakes and sandwiches a Chinese calligraphy demonstration.

Finally, at the austere end of the spectrum and not truly afternoon tea in the English fashion is tea at the Lian Tan Buddha Statue Square at the Po Lin Monastery on Lantau island. For HK$5, you can sip a cup of Chinese tea outside under the shade of an umbrella and look in one direction at mist covered mountains and in the other at the 34-metre-high bronze Buddha. Here you can, in Kakuzo's words, 'dream of evanescence, and linger in the beautiful foolishness of things'.

Packing tea for export, *watercolour, by unknown artist, Hong Kong Museum of Art*

Arts and Entertainment

Hong Kong's cultural fare has improved greatly in the last few years, and visitors will find plenty of artistic sustenance to complement their diet of sight-seeing, shopping and eating. If you happen to visit during the Hong Kong International Arts Festival in January/February, there will be a broad selection of world-class theatre, dance and music to choose from, but even at quieter times of year, you will find Asian and Western dance, drama, music, mime and art happening somewhere in town.

This change in climate has been helped along by the opening in November 1989 of the Hong Kong Cultural Centre's auditoria complex, after over ten years of planning and construction. Behind the Clock Tower, where once stood the Kowloon–Canton Railway Terminus, the HK$600 million complex overlooks the harbour, a two-minute walk from the Star Ferry pier. 'Ski slope' and 'public toilet' are some of the milder epithets showered on this salmon-tiled structure that has only a thin sliver of window onto the magnificence of the harbour and the Hong Kong skyline.

But what the Cultural Centre lacks in taste, it makes up for in size. The 2,100 seat Concert Hall contains Southeast Asia's largest organ, an 8,000-pipe, 93-stop Reiger, on which are performed monthly midday free concerts. The Grand Theatre, with 1,750 seats, was designed for dance and Western and Chinese opera and theatre. Despite its size, it has a small, intimate feeling. The Studio Theatre is a flexible space for contemporary dance and theatre that seats 300 to 500 people.

The Cultural Centre has already been host to an array of international stars, including jazz musicians Wynton Marsalis and Sadeo Watanabe, the Bolshoi and New York ballet companies, opera singers Placido Domingo and Jesseye Norman and great orchestras such as the Philharmonia and the Boston Symphony. On Wednesday and Saturday afternoons and early Friday evenings, a variety of free entertainment is offered at the centre, from Chinese folk dancing and mime to belly dancing and Western string quartets. The HKTA Cultural Diversion tour on Monday and Thursday evenings (HK$290 for adults and HK$240 for children aged 6–12) includes a guided tour of the Centre, performances of traditional Chinese dance, folk songs, acrobatics or classical drama and an eight-course Chinese banquet at the centre's Serenade Restaurant.

Other venues for the performing arts are the City Hall Theatre and Concert Hall (near the Star Ferry in Central), the Academy for the Performing Arts (a short walk from the Convention Centre in Wanchai), the Coliseum (in Kowloon, alongside the Hunghom Railway Station), the Queen Elizabeth Stadium (in Wanchai), the Sir Run Run Shaw Hall (on the campus of Hong Kong University) and the Koh Shan Theatre in Hunghom. More alternative, experimental or simply aspiring performers of all kinds can

Lam Kam Tong, a Cantonese opera leading actor

be found in the appropriately named Fringe Club (2 Lower Albert Road, South Block) next to the Foreign Correspondents' Club. The Fringe Festival in January/February presents both local and international visual and performing artists.

The 'What's On' column in the HKTA's *Hong Kong This Week* lists highlights of the city's cultural events, and the free *HK* magazine, *TV & Entertainment Times*, *The Hongkong Standard's* Talk of the Town column and the Information page of the *South China Morning Post* provide a comprehensive list of cultural happenings in the Territory. On the newsstand and often found free in your hotel room are *HongKong Tatler* and *Artention* magazines, which list cultural events.

A quick and convenient way to learn what's on is to drop by the lobby of the City Hall Theatre on your way to or from the Star Ferry. Posters adorn the walls, and descriptive brochures for all Urban Council-managed venue events can be found there. URBTIX, which sells tickets for these events as well as those at the Academy for the Performing Arts and the Arts Centre, has an outlet here. There is another URBTIX outlet at the Arts Centre.

The HKTA or your hotel concierge can help you track down Chinese performing arts. If the Hong Kong Chinese Orchestra is performing during your stay, give them a try. A large orchestra composed solely of traditional instruments, they play both traditional and modern Western and Chinese works. The music can be hauntingly beautiful—Vaughan Williams' 'Lark Ascending' is written for the plaintive voice of the *erhu*.

The Festival of Asian Arts, held every other year in October, brings together dance, music and the visual arts of varying quality from most countries in the region, which can provide unique opportunities to enjoy some fascinating performances.

Visual Arts

The newly opened Hong Kong Museum of Art next to the Space Museum in Kowloon is a spacious, modern museum with special exhibitions as well as its permanent collection of Chinese art and antiquities. The museum section (see page 117) will give you an idea of where to see antique Chinese ceramics and paintings. Those interested in more contemporary art will find it displayed in private galleries, exhibition spaces in commercial buildings and even the restaurants of Lan Kwai Fong. Again, check the newpapers, *Tatler* and the listings in *Artention* for current exhibition information. The first place to check after the Hong Kong Museum of Art is the Pao Galleries at the Hong Kong Arts Centre. This venue has been the most consistent exhibitor of both Chinese and Western art, and recent shows have ranged from Western calligraphy to contemporary acrylic works by young Hong Kong artists.

The Art Gallery at the Chinese University of Hong Kong at Ma Liu Shui, just north of Shatin in the New Territories, is mainly for teaching purposes. Located in the middle of the university's impressive, modern campus, the entrance is via a contemporary interpretation of a traditional Chinese courtyard garden. Decorative carp flourish in the miniature canals around the perimeter. The interior exhibition space is on four split levels. The museum houses several important collections, of which the most notable are the Jen Yu-wen collection, consisting of 1,300 items from the Ming Dynasty to recent times, and the Min Chui Society of Hong Kong's bequest of 463 exquisite Ming jade flowers. Opening times 9.30 am–4.30 pm daily, Sundays 12.30 pm–4.30 pm.

Other spaces that exhibit on a regular basis are: the Rotunda in Exchange Square, Plum Blossoms, Altfield Galleries and Altfield Fine Arts, Hanart TZ Gallery, Devon Art Gallery, Le Cadre at the Fringe, Lok Ku Gallery, Alisan Gallery, Wattis Fine Art and the Seasons restaurant in On Lan Street.

Cinema

We find it hard to imagine someone who travels several thousand miles to spend two hours in the dark watching a film that could easily be seen back home. But if that's your idea of a vacation, there are enough luxury commercial cinemas to keep you satisfied, like the Palace in the World Trade Centre and the UA Queensway quadriplex at Pacific Place.

For newly released films in Hong Kong you can buy your tickets in advance at the box office. Though prices are relatively inexpensive at HK$30–40, you may not get all you paid for as the result of the censor's scissors or an avaricious theatre owner trying to fit the film into a neat two-hour programme slot. Check the film listings in the paper regularly, since good films without Hollywood hype can come and go overnight.

Easier to recommend is the special film series shown at the Arts Centre or at City Hall, often featuring top-quality films from the past or contemporary ones without wide commercial distribution. The Arts Centre (open daily 10 am–8.15 pm) puts out a monthly programme of its film offerings, and tickets can be bought in advance at URBTIX outlets. The Goethe Institute, Alliance Française and the British Council also run film series. Check the Talk of the Town and Information pages of the *Hongkong Standard* and *South China Morning Post* for information about time and place.

The Hong Kong International Film Festival is held in the spring. Tickets sell out well in advance. Apart from the Asian Cinema section, it is likely to seem familiar to visitors accustomed to the rich fare of cinema in the West.

Chinese Opera

Whether it is broadcast, televised or live in a theatre, performed by people or by puppets, Chinese opera has a devoted following in Hong Kong. The Territory has a number of professional troupes, which include some excellent young performers trained in China. Visiting troupes from different regions of China always are extremely popular.

Like Western opera, Chinese opera depends heavily on colour and theatrical effects for its impact. Traditionally, scenery was not used beyond a plain wooden chair or table and, as in the Elizabethan theatre, everything else is supplied by the imagination. These days realistic sets are more common, but the performer still dominates the stage. Actors specialize in a certain category, which they continue to play throughout their careers. All singing is in a characteristic falsetto voice that takes many years to perfect. Although it may sound harsh, it can still be highly expressive. In the past only men could become actors, but today all roles are unisex, depending on the talent of the individual.

Platform shoes, lofty headdresses, and brilliantly coloured, padded costumes laden with sequins make the actor appear larger than life. Extra-long 'water sleeves' of white silk are attached to basic brocade, to be used to emphasize gestures. The orchestral accompaniment uses gongs and drums to heighten the drama as a significant character moves on or off stage.

The cast of a Chinese opera

Stylized movements make it instantly clear that the hero is in a boat, riding a horse or in a carriage, in the dark, entering or leaving the house and so on. Costume and make-up also reveal the character's role—hero, villain, adolescent boy, coquette or magistrate. The story will be familiar to the audience, raised on the epics of intrigue and valour, star-crossed love and self-sacrifice that have been woven around China's favourite folk heroes.

Many of the most popular operas have little discernible story, as they are often simply a lengthy elaboration of a single episode from a well-known tale of derring-do, and the newcomer may tend to find them static after a short while. Others, like 'The White Snake' or the 'Journey to the West', have such fast-paced action that the eye cannot keep pace with the frenetic whirling, twirling and somersaulting on stage.

Different parts of China developed their own styles of performance, but nowadays many of the distinctions are blurred. Peking opera is still regarded as the purest and most classical form and a really good performance is an experience to treasure.

China's emperors were reputedly connoisseurs of opera and did much to foster professional troupes. Major festivals and other events became occasions early on for public performances, and to some extent this continues in modern Hong Kong (see Festivals on page 108). The concept of opera-in-a-theatre is relatively recent, and you may be disconcerted to find the audience chatting, eating, drinking tea and soft drinks—seemingly doing anything but paying attention to the stage. Stay long enough, and you will become aware of a distinct pattern, interest waxing as the singing becomes more impassioned, or a particularly well-executed series of movements ending in a graceful pose worthy of an Olympic gymnast.

It is not always possible but it certainly helps to have some notion of the story before you go to a performance, as there is rarely even a synopsis in English. If you can, find a brief explanation of the most important stage conventions. Above all, go with an open mind, prepared to enjoy what is still in any form a unique spectacle, incorporating many different art forms in one clashing, blazing, glorious whole.

Parallel to the tradition of human theatre runs the development of various kinds of puppet troupes performing the same repertoire on a small scale.

Nightlife

Hong Kong's night centres have lost some of the glamour of the 1950s and '60s, when ships full of sailors emptied their human cargo onto the teeming streets of Wanchai, but some of their seediness remains. Today's city has developed into a more cosmopolitan centre with an educated, relatively affluent population, and its nightlife has matured with it. Hong Kong offers a wide variety of bars, nightclubs, karaoke bars and discos, as well as the representatives of the sex industry—massage parlours, escort services and girlie bars—that are still the main form of 'entertainment' in the Philippines and Thailand.

The areas of night entertainment best known to visitors are Wanchai and Causeway Bay on Hong Kong Island and Tsimshatsui in Kowloon. Most of Wanchai's activities centre on the grid of crowded streets of which Lockhart Road is the main thoroughfare. Despite the arrival of several up-market hotels and the influx of office workers to fill the mushrooming glass towers springing up on every corner, the glow of neon lights at night still lends the 'Wanch' a uniquely nostalgic atmosphere. After all, this was the world of Richard Mason's Suzie Wong, and it is even said—albeit not by the management—that the eminently respectable Luk Kwok Hotel was one of the localities that inspired Mason's story. Causeway Bay is known more for its late-night shopping than its cabaret or dancing, but there are several hotel venues and karaoke joints abound.

Across the harbour, Hankow and Nathan roads flank the stately Peninsula Hotel as they head north with their many side-streets and dimly lit alleys. A maze of small bars, karaoke centres and girlie bars line the streets, while the large hotels dotted around the area are home to a number of more up-market nightclubs and bars.

BARS

Hong Kong's selection of bars range from the cheap and cheerful joints of Wanchai to the flashy hi-tech palaces of Canton Road and the ostentatiously elegant outfits of Hong Kong's top hotels. For a spectacular view, try the **Sky Lounge** in Tsimshatsui's Sheraton Hotel, where the 18-floor ascent is via a glass elevator running up outside the building. Others in search of greenery will enjoy the atrium lounge of the **Royal Garden Hotel**. For close-up views of Hong Kong's busy harbour, what could be more magnificent than the sweep of the floor-to-ceiling window of the lobby bar of the **Regent Hotel**. Across the harbour, the **La Ronda** bar atop the Furama Hotel provides an equally fine view back to Kowloon, while those after a touch of graciousness need go no further than the **Captain's Bar** in the Mandarin Oriental or the vantage viewpoint of the elegant **Clipper Lounge** upstairs.

For those in search of excitment or some boisterous fun rather than glamorous exclusivity, head to the notorious Lan Kwai Fong area off Queen's Road Central and try one of the many bars packed into a couple of small streets. Those on Lan Kwai Fong itself include **Club 1997**, a trendy, rather chic bar where most people wear black and look incredibly sophisticated; **The Cactus Club**, a Tex-Mex bar with good beer and a lively atmosphere; and **California**, an expensive opportunity to sip a cocktail with the young and beautiful. On adjacent D'Aguilar Street, you will find **Schnurrbart**, a German drinking house with a selection of unusual beers that take ten minutes to pour correctly; **Graffitti**, a lively bar with paper tablecloths and crayons to encourage budding artists (and an extensive salad bar); **Al's Diner**, an American-style milk bar with a 1950s jukebox and the best milkshakes in town; **Yelts Inn**, a noisy establishment with a generally young clientele and a host of ex-USSR paraphernalia dangling from the walls; and to one side, up the tiny Wing Wah Lane, **Club 64**, a rough-and-ready bar with tables and chairs outside frequented by the arty fraternity.

Wanchai sports fewer regular bars that do not fall into the girlie bar or pub category, but the small and rowdy **The Wanch** on Lockhart Road is always good for a beer, particularly if you like your music live and loud (see page 137). **Joe Bananas**, at 23 Luard Road, is a trendy nightspot with the banker crowd, complete with American-style food and art deco/pop-rock film posters. Several of the nearby hotels have bars, including the luxurious **Champagne Bar** at the Grand Hyatt, fitted out in 1920s-style art deco, and the less pretentious **Nickelby's** at the Wharney Hotel on Lockhart Road, which has a surprisingly cozy atmosphere, reasonably priced drinks and passable music. **Dan Ryan's** in the Mall, Pacific Place, attracts a regular crowd to its American 'Cheers'-like atmosphere, while a recent addition to the out-of-Central crowd is **China Jump**, a vast US-style bar famed for its generous and lethal cocktails, in Causeway Bay Plaza II, 463 Lockhart Road.

PUBS

Moving downmarket, there are several pleasant bars imbued, to some degree, with a traditional British pub atmosphere featuring wooden beams, dart boards, brass and leather. Many serve hearty pub grub to accompany the foaming tankards of draught beer. There is rather more San Miguel and Carlsberg than authentic British bitter, but then most people would not complain. The large **Bull and Bear**, on the ground floor of Hutchison House in Central, is always crowded, as it is one of the few pub-bars in that westerly part of the business centre in Hong Kong. Also popular are **The Jockey**, in Swire House, and **Mad Dogs**, on Wyndham Street and also on Nathan Road in Kowloon. The **Old China Hand**, at 104 Lockhart Road, Wanchai, is one of the smallest and cosiest. For something slick and noisy, try the **Dickens Bar**, in the basement of the Excelsior Hotel in Causeway Bay, especially on Sundays for the live jazz or the regular Filipino pop combo.

On Kowloon side, the **White Stag**, 72 Canton Road, Tsimshatsui, with its coppertopped bar and wooden beams, could be anybody's local country pub—even the menu is traditional. **The Blacksmith's Arms**, 16 Minden Avenue, Tsimshatsui, is more of an urban local and dishes up large servings of food. Most of these bars open around 11 am or noon and serve until 1 am or 2 am with a happy hour (cheaper prices) normally between 5 pm–7 pm.

HOSTESS AND GIRLIE BARS

Wanchai and Tsimshatsui offer numerous examples of the particularly Asian phenomenon of the hostess club and its poorer relation, the rather less elegant girlie bar. They attract tourists and local residents alike; today Japanese tourists seem to be taking the place of the war-weary American servicemen of the late 1960s and early '70s.

As its name implies, the hostess club is strictly for the male visitor who is looking for company for an hour or two with music and a dance floor. He should be willing to pay for it in slots of 15 minutes or so, although the Western visitor may look askance at a dancing partner who fills her time sheet in at the same time. Billing itself as 'the biggest Japanese-style nightclub in the world', **Bboss**, Mandarin Plaza, East Tsimshatsui, is the best-known club of its kind in Hong Kong (if not in Asia). It occupies 6,500 square metres (70,000 square feet) and boasts 1,100 hostesses and even a mock-up vintage car that traverses the gigantic venue. A luxurious and expensive club is the **Dai-ichi Club**, 1st floor, Harbour View Mansion, 257 Gloucester Road, Causeway Bay; two others are **Club Ginza**, 20 Hankow Road, Kowloon, and the **Club Kokusai**, 81 Nathan Road, Tsimshatsui, one of the oldest of these Japanese-style hostess clubs.

Topless and girlie bars are more difficult to classify and can change owners and personality overnight. Many display lurid poster boards and advertisments outside, but few live up to their promises. A great number of Western women are pictured on the neon signs outside, for example, but few materialize inside. Generally customers do not pay for the company of the girls inside, but the girls ask customers to buy them drinks. Although they vary a great deal in cost and seediness, most have inflated drinks prices and bored looking girls in swimsuits who dance—not always to the music—on or behind the usually mirrored bar.

Today, such girls are rarely local, since Hong Kong's standard of living no longer requires its female residents to sell themselves; instead, women (and children) arrive from other Asian countries such as Thailand, the Philippines—and, increasingly, China. One of the best-known of such bars in Hong Kong is **Bottoms Up**, in the basement of 14–16 Hankow Road, Tsimshatsui. This was Hong Kong's first topless bar and is popular with both locals and tourists.

LIVE MUSIC

Although Hong Kong is not known for its soul and tends to rely on Filipino bands churning out covers of Eagles hits, there has been somewhat of a renaissance of live jazz and rock 'n' roll, with the opening of the **Oasis Lounge** in the New World Harbour View, **Gripps Restaurant** in the Omni Hong Kong Hotel and the **Saxophone** in the back of the **Canton Disco**. International jazz artists perform regularly at the **Jazz Club**, on D'Aguilar Street, Central. The **Godown**, in the basement of Sutherland House, Chater Road,

View of Central from Gloucester Road

Hong Kong on $66,000 a Day

You have taken the airport bus into Hong Kong and are settled into the Emerald Hotel in Western with your wife as the muffled sound of the Des Voeux tram filters into the room. At five in the morning, the desk calls with an urgent message: a long lost uncle had died and left you everything in his will. Money is no object all of a sudden. What do you do?

You call the Peninsula Hotel and book the Marco Polo Suite (HK$20,000 per night). The hotel sends a chauffeured Rolls Royce to pick you up, and when you arrive at the hotel, your own private valet helps you unpack and get settled. A quick shower and you are ready to do Hong Kong right.

First, a light breakfast at the Verandah Grill (HK$240—all prices are for two unless otherwise indicated). You grab yourself six Dom Perignon Cuban cigars at the Davidoff Cigar Boutique to last you through the day (HK$1,170) and off you go to the Heliservices pad for a half-hour aerial tour of the harbour and Hong Kong Island (HK$3,240). Now, to see the city at ground level: you rent your own tram for an hour (HK$500/hour, Monday–Thursday, with a minimum charge for two hours, but who cares?). On the way you stop at Remy Nicolas at Swire House for a bottle of champagne, Krug's Clos du Mesnil 1980 (HK$1,030) to toast your good fortune properly.

Next, you motor back to Le Restaurant de France for lunch. You sit in the plush, quiet surroundings enjoying your lobster salad and sautéd duck liver appetizers, the entrées of lobster stew and panfried roedeer medallions in venison sauce, the desserts of pear in puff pastry with raspberry sauce and warm apple tart Burgundy Marc sherbet. The price for the food, only HK$794, is a pleasant surprise, given its exceptional quality. All the more reason to treat yourself to a fine wine, a 1959 Chateau Margaux Premier Cru at HK$5,250.

After lunch, your wife would like to freshen up and heads off to Elizabeth Arden for the works—hair cut and styled (HK$210), facial (HK$380), body massage (HK$350), manicure (HK$75) and pedicure (HK$150); while you wait, you have your neck and shoulders massaged (HK$280) so you can reach more easily for your wallet.

Then it's to the Macau Ferry Terminal and the twenty-minute helicopter ride to Macau (HK$2,000 return). At the Lisboa, you sample all the games of chance. The house comes out ahead, but you have bet conservatively—you are still the plain old folks you have always been, just richer (losses, $25,000).

Back in Hong Kong your sweet tooth is calling, and on the way back to the hotel, you ask the driver to stop at the Mandarin Food Shop to pick up its special chocolate grand piano with assorted chocolates (HK$600). You take a short nap—the best things in life are still free. Refreshed, it's off for an early evening cruise around the harbour on an authentic sailing junk, the Duk Ling (HK$300 for two for a 90-minute tour).

All that fresh air has worked up your appetites. It is time for elegant Chinese dining at the Regent's Lai Ching Heen (the magnificent view of the Hong Kong skyline is yours at no extra charge). Your eyes are bigger than your stomach but so is your bank account. It is difficult to pass up the double-boiled superior shark's fin with bamboo pith, or the steamed pink garoupa; the braised sliced fresh abalone with oyster sauce can't be missed, so too the steamed chicken with Hunan ham and green vegetables. After the cold meats with jelly fish, braised superior vegetables with bamboo pith, and a little fried rice with seafood, you decide to share the dessert of double-boiled imperial bird's nest in whole coconut. You sip your tea, look at the glittering lights and think the HK$2,000 tab a bargain.

It has been a busy day and you decide to leave dancing at JJ's for another night. Instead, you opt for a quiet glass of Louis XIII cognac (HK$676 for two) at the Grand Hyatt's Champagne Bar and listen to some soothing singing. Just before leaving, you say 'what the hell' and impetuously decide on a caviar nightcap of 50 grams of Beluga Malossol Caviar Caspian (HK$530) washed down with a glass of Dom Perignon (HK$446).

Back in the hotel, your wife suddenly realizes that neither of you did any serious shopping. You don't have a thing to show for the HK$65,721 you spent, not one gift to pack away into the suitcases. Not to worry, there is always tomorrow.

Then again, if you hadn't got that early morning call, you still could have had a wonderful day in Hong Kong. You could have seen the city from the sky by walking along the Peak, seen the glories of the harbour on the Star Ferry, wandered free among the stalls of Western Market, window-shopped at the Landmark, had rice and roast pork at a small Chinese noodle shop, gazed at the rainbow colours of birds at the Zoological and Botanical Gardens, had dinner at a *dai pai dong* and still had a bit of change from the HK$100 bill you started the morning with.

Central, has an unashamedly boisterous bistro atmosphere with live jazz and dancing. Another meeting place with live music is **Hardy's Folk Club**, 35 D'Aguilar Street, Central, where guitarists of every style perform and guest artists are welcome. The singalong atmosphere encourages people from the audience to take to the stage, which can be painful on occasion but is usually amusing. On Kowloon side, **Ned Kelly's Last Stand**, 11A Ashley Road, Tsimshatsui, has a rowdy Australian atmosphere of beer drinking without the frills, live jazz and a menu full of interesting-sounding Australian dishes. Another antipodean haven is the **Stoned Crow**, 12 Minden Avenue, Tsimshatsui. **Rick's Café**, at 4 Hart Avenue, Tsimshatsui, is known as a restaurant/bar/live-music/dance club that features some of the best sounds in town. **Beefy's Cabin**, at 70 Canton Road, has a raucous atmosphere with an excellent live band, while **Flannigan's Wine Bar**, nearby at No 76, is open 24 hours a day, 365 days a year, with live blues from Blue Wail on Mondays and quality music from the in-house DJ on other nights.

DANCING

Clubs with dancing spring up and then wither with alarming alacrity in Hong Kong, but there are some tried and tested options. For dancing, listening to great live rock 'n' roll, seeing and being seen the multi-level, always packed **JJ's**, at the Grand Hyatt, is definitely worth a visit. Also try the upmarket **Manhattan** at the New World Harbour View. **Hot Gossip**, in Harbour City, and **No'va Alpha**, in the basement of Chevalier House on Chatham Road, are popular. **Disco Disco** is one of the longest running at 38 D'Aguilar Street, Central, and currently has a ladies' night on Wednesdays. The atmosphere is lively and the music of a high standard. Also popular is the **Talk of the Town**, in the Excelsior Hotel; newly refurbished in art deco pink and black, it enjoys a stunning view across the harbour (ladies' nights are Mondays and Wednesdays, for which there is no cover charge). In a class by itself is **Canton**, Canton Road, Tsimshatsui, one of the smartest discos around, with an atmosphere that seems to capture the spirit of Hong Kong exactly. Other popular nightspots can be found in the upmarket hotels around Tsimshatsui such as the New World Hotel's imaginatively decorated **Faces**, the electronic gadgetry of the **Falcon** in the Royal Garden Hotel or **Hollywood East** (basement, Hotel Regal Meridien) with its hi-tech lighting effects and ultramodern decor. If you are looking for something a bit more rough and ready, try **Scottie's**, in Lan Kwai Fong, where the tartan decor is as loud as the music, or downstairs at **La Bodega**, on Wyndham Street (upstairs is Hong Kong's first Spanish *tapas* bar).

KARAOKE

This is one Japanese import that has taken Hong Kong by storm. No self-respecting person would refuse to take part in a company karaoke evening, and many have their own machines at home to hone their skills before venturing into public. As a result, voices best left alone in the shower now are on public display. Good friends and sufficient alcohol can free the most inhibited to croon along with the music. From the intimate **Song Delight**, at 115 Chatham Road, to the **Karaoke de Patek Philippe**, at the Chinachem Golden Plaza, 77 Mody Road—with its Italian decor, three lobbies and 20 VIP rooms—the halls are alive with music.

NIGHT SHOPPING

If you have children with you or are nursing a hangover and would like to try something new, head for the night market at **Temple Street** near Jordan MTR. From 7 pm to midnight, the streets nearby hum with activity as the foodstalls do a roaring trade, and fashion sellers, bric-a-brac vendors and fortune tellers vie for the custom of passers-by. If you fancy something a little more up-market, a trip to Causeway Bay, where most of the department stores stay open late, can be fun—and you can easily combine it with a meal out. Most shops in Tsimshatsui also stay open late.

OTHER OPTIONS

There are a number of ways that Hong Kong's transport comes into its own to show another and more romantic side of the Territory. These range from the various sunset and night tours organized by **Watertours** (tel 525 4808, 526 3538), tram parties (tel 891 8765) as well as a ride on the Peak Tram to enjoy the million-dollar night view from the top of the Peak. For those of more artistic bent, a whole range of cultural events takes place after nightfall, including plays, recitals, concerts and showcase traditional Chinese performances. For these, you should consult your visitor's newspaper or check with the HKTA, whose leaflets will keep you fully informed.

Some of the enormous Chinese restaurants provide traditional Chinese floor shows with a meal. Although these can be misleadingly advertised as night clubs, they provide one of the easiest ways to come in contact with the Cantonese taste in entertainment. A successful mingling of food with local colour can be experienced at the **Aberdeen floating restaurants**, but you should be prepared to be entertained by the general ambiance rather than any particularly memorable culinary experience.

Sport

Given the shortage of land in Hong Kong, its citizens are surprisingly well provided with sporting facilities. Practically every sport from wheelchair archery to softball is catered to, although given Hong Kong's climate and coastline the emphasis naturally tends to be on water-related activities. The opening of the Queen Elizabeth Stadium in Happy Valley, the Victoria Park exhibition tennis courts and the Hong Kong Coliseum (this HK$115 million project, built over the railway terminus, seats 12,500 spectators under cover) have even made it possible for Hong Kong to stage international sporting events.

JOGGING

Most of Hong Kong's sports stadiums belong to clubs, universities or associations, so it is difficult to find a track to run on. The Jubilee Sports Centre's 'trim trail' in Shatin is open 7 am–7 pm and is one of the few free places to train. Apart from that, a number of Hong Kong's urban and country parks and public housing estates have similar trails, and there are several small roads that make good running circuits in themselves. One of the most popular is Bowen Road, a narrow but well-signposted track that threads its way around the Hong Kong hillsides between Mid-levels and Wanchai. There are excellent views most of the way and usually several people selling water and snacks if you feel the need. Blacks Link off Wong Nai Chung Gap Road is also a good run (if a little more rocky and uphill at times) with stunning views of Aberdeen as well as Victoria harbour.

GYMS

Most major hotels have extensive gym, sauna and jacuzzi services, but there are also several gyms (including Tom Turk's Fitness Club, Clark Hatch Physical Fitness Centre and Nautilus Health Centre) and dance and exercise classes (Arts Centre) readily available in Central District and Kowloon. The Gym in Melbourne Plaza, Queen's Road Central, offers a day's use for HK$150, which covers everything including your kit.

MARTIAL ARTS

The YMCA organizes classes in yoga, judo, *tai chi ch'uan* (shadow boxing) and martial arts. Many of the clubs also offer instruction, but it is usually necessary to be a member. It may be easier to get up early and take a trip to Victoria Park in Causeway Bay and learn some *tai chi ch'uan* from the real experts.

GOLF

For visiting golfers, the Royal Hong Kong Golf Club has three 18-hole courses at Fanling in the New Territories and nine holes at Deep Water Bay, on Hong Kong Island, but they are available to non-members on weekdays only. The Clearwater Bay Golf and Country Club (in Sai Kung, tour by HKTA on weekdays) and the Discovery Bay Golf Club (on Lantau Island, 8 am–8 pm daily) each have an 18-hole course, plus other facilities.

Racquet Sports

Tennis enthusiasts can use any of the public courts, but booking can be difficult as the sport has become increasingly popular since Michael Chang's international success. You can book ten days in advance (by going in person, with your passport). These courts have no equipment for hire, but the Excelsior Hotel Sports Deck—with both tennis courts and golf range—does. The Hong Kong Squash Centre on Cotton Tree Drive is the best bet for squash fiends, while the new sports centre next door has a huge hall of badminton courts. It is best to get there early to book, however, as both these sports are very popular.

Water Sports

Swimming pools can be found in most major hotels and at sports stadiums in Sai Kung, Wanchai, and Shatin. They are crowded in summer but can be empty out of season, even though the weather may still be warm enough to swim. It is possible to hire windsurfers at Tai Po in the New Territories and at Stanley Beach on the island, while Sai Kung also offers a variety of water sports equipment for hire. Ski boats complete with a driver and equipment can be rented by the hour from Deep Water Bay, on the south side of the island. For sports such as water skiing and wind surfing, ring the HKTA, which will provide names and numbers to contact. For underwater sports, contact either the Hong Kong Underwater Federation or the YMCA Scuba Club. All these sports, unfortunately, come with a health warning: Hong Kong's waters are extremely polluted and can be a health hazard, so don't swallow any!

Shopping

It's a fair bet that most tourists to Hong Kong go home with far more than they came with. Shopping is more than a habit in Hong Kong—it's an obssession. Even well-travelled tourists used to the glamour of Madison Avenue, Rodeo Drive or the Ginza are amazed at the wealth of what's on offer: malls boasting a swathe of leading brand-name boutiques; row upon row of small local shops stuffed to bursting with jeans, sportswear and locally designed fashions; a jumble of factory outlets selling overruns and rejects of European and North American labels at reduced prices; and sprawling markets where jade talismans vie for space with electronic gadgets and fake designer watches. Even the most stubborn anti-shopper will end up wandering uncontrollably from store to store.

Malls and Shopping Centres

The largest malls and shopping centres are The Landmark, Prince's Building, Cityplaza, and Pacific Place on Hong Kong Island, New World Shopping Centre, Harbour City, the Peninsula and Regent shopping arcades in Kowloon, and Shatin City One in the New Territories. For even more concentrated consumerism, the Japanese department stores are second to none: Daimaru, Sogo, Matsuzakaya, Mitsukoshi, Isetan, Seibu, Yaohan and Uny. Here is a universe of brand-name boutiques, including Gucci, Dunhill, Sonia Rykiel, Christian Dior and Bally (and that's only on one floor). And if you work up an appetite, simply head for the basement of Sogo, Mitsukoshi and Daimaru Household Square in Causeway Bay, where you will also find snack shops and small restaurants.

Whole areas of Hong Kong's urban centre act more or less like malls—continuous strings of shops to entice, dazzle and loosen your purse strings. Take a stroll down Nathan Road's Golden Mile or Mody Road, or through Whampoa Garden on Kowloon; or try the locals' favourite, Causeway Bay, the backstreets of Wanchai or the newly refurbished Western Market. A myriad small arcades lie hidden within or beneath office buildings. In tiny Wing Kut Street in Central, for example, is the Shung Lee Shopping Arcade, a rabbit warren of coin and stamp sellers and antique and costume jewellery shops on two floors. Here you can find early 20th-century sunglasses at Yeo Yung's; archaic jades, amber beads and court necklaces at Artistic Sources; or neolithic pots, Yixing teaware and Tang figures in a half dozen little shops. Another interesting venue is the refurbished Victorian red-brick Western Market—a spacious building housing a collection of small open-fronted outlets selling silks, linens and Chinese handicrafts, including beautiful hand-painted kites. There is also a café looking down on the central atrium.

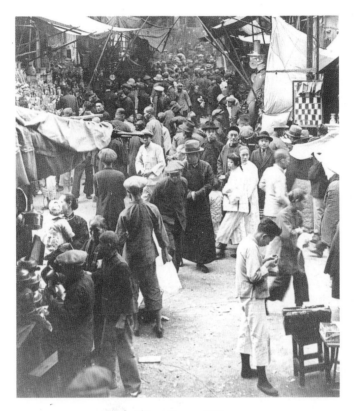

Chinese Bazaar, 1890

One peculiarity of shopping in Hong Kong is that shops selling the same products usually cluster together, so that to buy a particular item you usually need go to only one street and choose among a whole row of competing stores. For shoes, try Leighton Road in Happy Valley; for photographic equipment, Stanley Street in Central; for antiques, Hollywood Road or Cat Street in Central/Western district.

Haggling

Prices in department stores and fashionable hotel arcades are usually fixed, but some shops and all street stalls will expect you to bargain. Much of this is simply a routine, with a standard special price or discount of ten per cent. Persistence may result in a further reduction, but only if you use cash.

Most shops accept the major credit cards, but their attitude tends to be that the handling charge cancels out any discount. This is particularly true at sale time—whether the sale price is a bona fide reduction or not—and you will save time and temper by announcing at the start of the transaction how you intend to pay. Also, shops will often take foreign currency in payment, but do not expect to get the best exchange rate.

ART, ANTIQUES AND CRAFTS

Hong Kong is the centre of the world's Chinese art market, but you don't have to be a millionaire collector to enjoy the wealth of furniture, ceramics, scholars' articles, carpets and paintings you can find browsing through the antique shops of Hollywood Road, Cat Street (Upper Lascar Row) and the Cat Street Galleries on Lok Ku Road. For the serious collector, there are fine dealers who show only by appointment, for example Grace Wu Bruce (845 0840) for furniture and Susan Haworth (541 5779) for ceramics. Don't expect to find overlooked treasures for a song—collectors and dealers walk the streets daily looking at the new arrivals.

For the simple beauty of Ming furniture, you have Schoeni's, Altfield's, and Hobbs and Bishops on Hollywood Road, Chan Shing Kee (228 Queen's Road Central), Martin Fung in the Cat Street Galleries and, in Prince's Building, Peter Lai Antiques. Our favourite is Evelyn Tam & Associates (81 Hollywood Road). In this small, cramped shop (ask to go upstairs) you will find 17th- and 18th-century *huang huali* horseshoe-backed Ming chairs, Ming altar tables, colourful 19th-century Chinese rugs, *huang huali* brush pots and chests, or inexpensive 19th-century redwood food containers that can smarten up any decor. Kit-Fu Tam will take you to their nearby workshop to show you the restoration process and discuss the proper finish for your furniture. At the Ashwood Gallery (40A Upper Lascar Row) you will find more attractive wood, including delicate burlwood boxes.

Among the many reputable dealers in fine Chinese ceramics and works of art are: Peter Lai Antiques, P C Lu & Sons (in the Hong Kong, Peninsula and Mandarin hotels), Charlotte Horstmann & Gerald Godfrey (Ocean Terminal), Ming Gallery (233 Queen's Road Central), Honeychurch Antiques (29 Hollywood Road), Fred Lee Antiques (26 Lyndhurst Terrace) and Chak's Gallery (67 Hollywood Road).

Contemporary Chinese paintings remain an undervalued area where work of first rank artists can be purchased at far lower prices than Western artists of comparable accomplishment. Hanart TZ Gallery (28 Braga Circuit and the old Bank of China Building), Lok Ku Gallery in the Cat Street Galleries, Plum Blossoms in Exchange Square and Alisan Gallery in Prince's Building offer some of the best of today's Chinese painters.

CURIOSITIES

Of course, there are always those special products you never know you want until you see them— an abacus perhaps? Or a jade seal with your name engraved on it in Chinese? One of the best ways to explore Hong Kong's more unusual nooks and crannies in search of something special is simply to take a wander through the streets of areas such as Western District, one of the city's better preserved quarters. Near High Street on Western, just past No 38, is an open-air shop, smaller than a closet, where a man crouches making small wicker chairs, baskets and assorted items in traditional fashion.

Further down Western at No 12 is the Tuck Chong Sum Kee Bamboo Steamer Company, where you can buy steamers in all sizes, good for both steaming and serving food. Fish dry in a vacant lot on Mui Fong Street and dried fish of all kinds are sold in the shops along Des Voeux Road. One that specializes in shark's fin has a macabre window display of delicate—and astronomically expensive—specimens. At the many Chinese medicine shops in this area you can buy ginseng, sliced deer horn and deer tail.

If you are looking for inexpensive but unusual gifts to take back home, the China Products chain can be a goldmine. Owned by China, these stores are not known for their slick service or snappy window displays, but they are crammed with all sorts of everyday items—and a few others besides. Each outlet has ceramics, clothing, linen, stationery, electronics, toys, sports equipment and household goods. The largest stores are next to Victoria Park in Causeway Bay, Hill Road in Western and on Queen's Road Central.

READY-TO-WEAR GARMENTS

Every kind of ready-made garment is available in Hong Kong, from European high fashion to traditional Chinese-made padded jackets, to overruns of designer jeans and sportswear. If your money matches your taste, you could do a lot worse than to make for the World of Joyce at the Galleria, with its excellent selection of designer fashion garments from Europe. Nor should you bypass the talented local designers such as Lily Chao, Joseph Ho or Eddie Lau, or the Japanese boutiques such as Issey Miyake, Matsuda and Paris-based Kenzo. Equally pricey, albeit ever-popular, are the exquisitely made *cheong sam* and sequined and beaded gowns and jackets from Jenny Lewis. Devotees of Diane Freis are more than adequately cared for with shops throughout Central and Tsimshatsui selling her dresses, separates and knitwear.

If you are searching in the moderately priced ranges of silk blouses, dressing gowns and padded jackets, you should make straight for one of the China Arts and Crafts stores. Major branches can be found on Queen's Road Central, the massive China Resources building on Gloucester Road, Wanchai, or in Star House or Silvercord Centre, Tsimshatsui. For fashion sportswear, chains such as Giordano, U2, Esprit and Benetton can be found in almost every shopping street. For children, the Crocodile (Crocokid Wai

Flower vendor

label) and The Children Clothing Company have outlets throughout Hong Kong and Kowloon. For overruns of designer jeans, sports clothes, swimwear, linen—and much, much more—make haste to the south side of the island and the world-famous Stanley Market. Still in Stanley, the long-established Fudo Jeans also has a branch in Spring Garden Lane, Wanchai.

For those looking for a more exotic garment, Eastern Fabric in Ivy House, 18 Wyndham Street, sells *yukata* (cotton kimono housecoats), silk kimono for men, women and children and (more for display than wear) elaborate silk wedding kimono. Here you can buy charming paper wallets or paper glass cases to put in the pockets of your Hong Kong purchases.

The less label-conscious may find the markets in Jardine's Crescent (Causeway Bay) or Granville and Haiphong roads (Tsimshatsui) fruitful, but always check for dyeing faults, tears and crooked seams. The same goes for children's clothes and the overruns that can be found in the markets. Factory outlets are best known for their silk and knit dresses, separates and accessories and, again, those ubiquitous designer overruns. They are located in both Central and Kowloon and particularly at Kaiser Estate, Phases I and II, in Hunghom. Those with outlets on both sides of the harbour include Camberley Enterprises (for Anne Klein II), Four Seasons, Shopper's World and Vica Moda. Browsers in Central should not miss out the cavernous Pedder Building which has been known to yield more than a few pleasant surprises. For the latest and reliable details, look no further than the HKTA's booklet on factory outlets in Hong Kong.

MADE-TO-MEASURE GARMENTS

Hong Kong is famed for its custom-made clothing and—given the skill of local tailors and the availability of reasonably priced fabrics, from Chinese silk brocade to British woollens—it is the ideal place to have clothes made to measure. Good buys in silk (and to a lesser degree wool and corduroy) can be found at China Products and China Arts and Crafts stores. Excellent bargains are also to be found in the lanes snaking off Queen's Road Central and Des Voeux Road, although most of the stall-holders from what was called 'cloth alley' have been relocated in Western Market.

As for tailors, they are absolutely everywhere. You may pay more at the shopping arcades and hotels, but the selection of cloth is greater and the staff speak English and are used to foreigners. Joseph at Kaiwa Tailors, in the Prince's Building, clothes many of the fast-track investment bankers and financiers of Hong Kong in the finest wool from England and Italy; he is not cheap, but he is careful and demanding. James Chan, in the Mandarin, is a top-notch tailor of women's garments and also has some attractive suiting for men. David's Shirts in the Mandarin, Royal Garden and Wing Lee Building in Kowloon, make superb men's and women's shirts. Sam's Tailors at 92–94 Burlington Arcade, Nathan Road, has more pictures displayed of diplomats and dignitaries who shop there than attend the UN. The staff ply customers with soda and beer and can at times push a sale, but they offer a wide selection of fabrics and more than reasonable prices for both

men's and women's garments. With any tailor allow enough time for at least two or three fittings; better yet, give the tailor a garment to copy. Once your measurements are on hand, you can order more clothes after you return home.

SHOES

The range of shoes in Hong Kong is vast in terms of both price and style, but you may have trouble finding larger sizes. Stores specializing in custom-made shoes and boots for foreigners, such as Mayer Shoes in the Mandarin Hotel and Lily Shoes in the Peninsula Hotel, tend to be expensive. However, if you're feeling adventurous, you can try Fun Kee Shoes, 3/F,

Joss sticks burning at a local shrine

Best of Hong Kong

Best Aerobics Beth's Workout comes highly recommended for visitors, as you do not have to be a member to enjoy a good sweat here. 5/F, Wellington House, 14–25 Wellington Street, Central, tel 522 5793.

Best Balcony This goes to Stanley's Restaurant, where you can escape Hong Kong's ubiquitous air-conditioning, but still enjoy a first-class meal in a romantic setting. See Restaurants (page 198) for details.

Best Bakery The Mandarin's in-house store wins hands down on this one. Unbelievably courteous assistants in crisp black and white lace and a daunting array of bread, cake and confectionery. The high-fibre rolls and cheese scones are particularly delicious.

Best Breakfast A double for the Mandarin, as its Grill restaurant offers an unsurpassed breakfast experience if you are after leisure with style. See Restaurants (page 195) for details. For a strictly American taste, try Dan Ryan's at 114 The Mall, Pacific Place, Admiralty, from 7.30 am for piles of pancakes, lashings of maple syrup and heaps of hash browns. And if you are too early or too late for the regular places, Post 97, 1/F, 9 Lan Kwai Fong, Central, serves breakfast 24 hours a day. Their scrambled eggs on brown bread is just the thing at 5 am.

Best Cheesecake The prize for the most mouth-watering offering goes to The American Pie, 4/F, California Entertainment Building, 34–36 D'Aguilar Street, Central. A marvellous consistency, with a taste that explains at last why it is called cheesecake. While there, you could also polish off one of their stunning banana cream pies.

Best Dim Sum There are almost too many to choose from, but the Round Dragon Restaurant at the top of the Hopewell Centre on Queen's Road East (tel 861 1668) offers gracious surroundings, all the old *dim sum* favourites plus some new choices, and the bonus of a panoramic view across the whole of Hong Kong, from the maze of Wanchai to the hills of the New Territories.

Best Gym Head to The Gym at 18/F, Melbourne Plaza, 33 Queen's Road Central (tel 877 8337)—a great way to spend a day after too much travelling, eating and drinking. For just HK$150, you can exhaust yourself in the well-equipped workout room, fit in an aerobics class and then relax with a sauna and steam-room treat. All kit provided.

Best Fish 'n' Chips This British delicacy has reached Hong Kong in the form of the famous Harry Ramsden's fish restaurant on Queen's Road East, next to the Hopewell Centre. Complete with plush red interiors and chandeliers, this vast 560-square-metre (6,000-square-foot) restaurant is the chain's first overseas venture.

Best Haircut Almost every hotel has a hair salon of some description, but the Grand Hyatt's Il Colpo (tel 802 0151), just off the sumptuous marble lobby, is a class apart. The surroundings are stylish, the service is swift and attentive, and the stylists are highly qualified. And, once you have decided to splurge, why not have a manicure and pedicure as well?

Best Ice Cream No problem here—it has to be Haagen-Dazs' on Pedder Street. Once you have tasted their real strawberry ice cream packed full of fruit, rich Swiss almond chocolate, or fresh lemon sorbet, you will be hooked forever.

Best Noodles Take a tranquil break from Chinese food with some Japanese *udon* or *ramon* noodles at Orba, Shop 2, G/F, Shui On Centre, 6–8 Harbour Road, Wanchai, tel 824 2112. Try the vegetarian noodle with beancurd.

Best Salad Bar The Regent's steakhouse-style restaurant gets the award for this one, as their salad bar provides a stupendous choice of fresh fare. The spicy seafood salad is excellent, and there is usually a good selection of vegetarian bean salads. The fresh fruit juices are also impressive.

Best Sandwich Competition is hotting up in this field, but Birley's in the Lippo Centre, Admiralty, comes out top with a great selection of fresh sandwiches without the usual drenching of tasteless mayonnaise. The Italian pizza-like bread is fantastic with avocado salad.

Best Tailor Again, an immense range of contenders, but for a Hong Kong experience, it is worth going to Sam's Tailors at 92–94 Burlington Arcade, Nathan Road, where you can admire his huge photo collection of dignitaries who have submitted to his tape-measure in the past. For women, May at Ricky Bo, 1/F, 24–25 Hilton Arcade, Hilton Hotel provides a very professional service.

Wai Lun Mansion at the junction of Luard and Hennessy roads in Wanchai. For HK$400, you can have your favourite pair of shoes copied, or even design your own with the help of their style catalogue. Little English is spoken here, but it's surprising what you can communicate with pictures and a lot of finger-pointing.

Moderately priced, locally made shoes are found on Hennessy Road, Leighton Road and Wong Nai Chung Road in Happy Valley, where there is a whole string of shops.

BAGS AND BELTS

The bag is like the wristwatch in Hong Kong—a symbol of wealth that speaks its own distinct language. Even heavy-duty paper carrier bags from designer shops are hoarded and paraded around town until they become too scuffed to use. Most local people think nothing of spending a fortune on a handbag, wallet or briefcase, and the television is packed with advertisements encouraging them to do just that.

Central Market

At the top end of the market, most of the designer stores mentioned above have parallel handbag collections. Louis Vuitton and Gucci are such popular brands that every second person seems to be carrying one or the other—largely because the markets are full of imitations. A more mid-range selection can be found in the Japanese department stores, as well as in local shoe shops in Causeway Bay and along Nathan Road.

For cheaper bags, wallets and larger luggage items, there are hundreds of small shops in the lanes between Des Voeux Road and Queen's Road, in Causeway Bay and Wanchai. They are easy to spot by the bunches of suitcases and shoulder-bags dangling outside.

Many bag and shoe shops sell belts in a corresponding price-range. For a cheaper option, try Temple Street night market in Jordan, Kowloon, where you can choose from a huge variety of styles and colours, and have it made-to-measure right there. Chain stores such as Giordano and Esprit also stock a quality range at reasonable prices.

SPORTS EQUIPMENT

The standard Hong Kong outfit is jeans, T-shirt and running shoes, so it's hardly surprising that sportswear is on sale everywhere. For sports shoes, try Stanley Market, along Johnston Road in Wanchai, the side-streets off Nathan Road in Tsimshatsui, or Mongkok further up Kowloon. Sportswear can be found in Stanley, Wanchai and in Mongkok. On Queen's Road East, in Wanchai, the Fame store is dedicated entirely to aerobics, dance and swimwear. It also sells fitness-training equipment.

You can find racquets, balls and other equipment at the local chain store Marathon Sports, as well as at several smaller sports shops in Causeway Bay, Wanchai and Tsimshatsui. Check the *Hong Kong Yellow Pages Buying Guide* for a full listing. If you are willing to pay a bit more, there are several brand-name stores for Nike and Fila located in the major shopping areas.

JEWELLERY, GOLD AND JADE

Hong Kong is packed with all of the above. The only problem will be staying undazzled by the sheer volume on offer and telling the good from the bad. If you're not an expert, the best you can do is to stick to accredited dealers, such as members of the HKTA, whose distinctive junk logo can be seen on windows and doorways.

Gold is imported duty-free and is relatively cheap. At most jewellery stores, the day's price of gold is displayed (so many dollars per tael, the equivalent of 1.2 troy ounces). Even if you count only the side alleys leading off Nathan Road, Hong Kong is home to thousands of jewellery stores, and each one follows its own sales policy and bargaining technique.

All kinds of precious and semi-precious stones can be bought, set or unset, and expert craftsmen can follow individual designs to give you a unique ring or necklace. Hong

Kong is one of the world's major diamond traders and, by and large, dealers are honest and helpful. If in doubt, call the Diamond Importers Association at 523 5497 or the Gemmological Association of Hong Kong at 366 6006. At the same time, it is worth remembering that the most realistic attitude for purchasing is that you are not acquiring an investment; you are buying a gem you can't live without. It is rare to recoup your money except in a private sale.

The Chinese consider jade to be a stone from heaven and a valued talisman. As a result Hong Kong has the world's best selection of jade, but prices tend to be high. For cheap pieces, make a visit to the Jade Market (see Kowloon, page 70), but for more expensive jewellery and figurines be sure you know what you are doing. Jade comes not only in various shades and opaqueness of green but also in white, yellow, orange and lavender. Although it boils down to a question of personal taste, most lovers of jade regard the best pieces as possessing all these colours.

Pearls come in an enormous range, and Hong Kong stocks them all, from the cultured and evenly matched to the baroque, freshwater version and natural black. Colours can vary from cream to a distinct pink.

Although some stores are still selling the remains of their ivory stock, importing ivory is now illegal and many of the expert carvers have turned to new careers creating intricate masterpieces out of ice or chocolate for some of Hong Kong's grander hotels.

If chunky handcrafted silver is your fancy, take a watchful walk along Hollywood Road and Cat Street in Central or visit the department stores or China Arts & Crafts, which sell beaded, semi-precious and porcelain necklaces, some featuring local designer Kai Yin Lo's less expensive line in necklaces and earrings made of amethyst, turquoise, jade and quartz. Her shops in the Mandarin and Peninsula hotels are much pricier.

If you like glitz but don't have the cash for the real thing, there are hundreds of costume jewellery shops dotted around the shopping centres and alleyways. Wing Kut Street in Central is devoted entirely to baubles. Supposedly open only to trade buyers, shops here will in fact sell to anyone—with few questions asked as long as you buy more than one or two items. Most major department stores—particularly the Japanese ones—also have a large range of cheaper jewellery.

Electronics, Computers and Sound Equipment

Hong Kong is 'gadget city' when it comes to electronic wizardry of all types. Offices are highly automated, a digital diary is a must, pagers and portable phones abound—and, everywhere you look, people are attached to Walkmans or portable CD players (a common sight on the MTR or bus is two friends plugged into a single pair of headphones). Stereo enthusiasts and kids of all ages will find all of the remarkable toys of the new electronic age from complex sound systems to pocket-sized electronic games.

This abundance is also reflected in the illegal side of the trade; Hong Kong is full of copies. A word of warning: remember that, though it may be fun to pick up the occasional cheap clone, it is unreasonable to expect an inappropriately robust performance. As anywhere else in the world, you get what you pay for. Bear in mind, too, that salesmen will try to sell you the best brand name because it carries the highest price. Ideally, ask around among your own friends before you buy, and shop around. You may not necessarily find a cheaper deal, but you may find one that is more reliable and offers a worldwide guarantee. Make sure that the shop stamps the guarantee and gives you a legible receipt. Some shops will throw in extras such as bags, straps, batteries, tapes, leads or plugs. The dealers like to keep their stock moving, so it pays to bargain.

The Asia Computer Plaza in Silvercord Building, Canton Road, Tsimshatsui, is a hacker's dream. Under one roof, it houses every type and size of computer, as well as stocklists of the more elusive peripherals and software, and there are even exhibitions and regular displays and seminars to keep the consumer fully up to date. Particularly useful is ACP's own switchboard at 734 6111. It can connect you to an information centre from which you can either collect current product listings or be transferred to any outlet you choose.

The main areas for hi-fi shopping are Tsimshatsui and Causeway Bay, where every street appears to be a succession of audio stores. For more upmarket brands, try Prince's Building in Central, where some of the European name brands also have outlets. These shops tend to be more expensive but offer better service, and they usually allow you to listen to various speakers and amplifiers before making your choice.

If buying electrical items, check the voltage is compatible with your home country. In the case of VCRs and TVs, remember that Hong Kong uses the PAL/SECAM system. If in doubt about your own, ask the sales assistant—most shops have leaflets on world systems and frequencies. Never buy anything unseen, and if you must leave a deposit never go above ten per cent and make sure they give you a detailed receipt. Smaller electronics merchants have been known to shut up shop and disappear overnight.

CAMERAS

Hundreds of stores throughout Hong Kong and on both sides of the harbour sell a bewildering selection of the very latest in photographic equipment. You are likely to find what you want in most parts of Tsimshatsui, including Hankow Road, the Ocean Centre complex, or Nathan Road, and on Hennessy Road in Causeway Bay. Prices tend to be about ten per cent off list price, and you can ask to see the list.

Stanley Street in Central contains a clutch of shops catering to the more serious buyer. On top of the usual range of automatics and big-name Japanese brands, they sell a wide range of second-hand bodies and lenses, as well as film and other paraphernalia.

Twin Cities

When first I visited Hong Kong, I could hardly imagine why anyone would want to go back to New York. For as the Colony threw over its imperial ties, it was coming more than ever to resemble a sweet-and-sour version of the capital of the modern world. Like New York, in its way, the orphan city was full of the street-smart bravado of a strutting young man in a hurry, a rags-to-riches Seventh Avenue shark who takes the world on, but only on his own terms. Like New Yorkers, Hong Kongers seemed to pride themselves on their rudeness, their impatience with the slow or sentimental ('Am I being courteous?' said the badge worn with black irony by the conductor on the Peak train who barked out orders and trampled on children as he kept the turnstiles spinning). Like New York, above all, Hong Kong seemed to prize energy before imagination and movement more than thought. The place had a one-track mind—and it was decidedly the fast track. Hard-driving and fast-talking, it ran on hard cash and quick wit, hard heads and quick kills. In Hong Kong, even Maxim's was a fast-food joint . . .

When first I visited, in 1983, the biggest deal in town and the center of the most furious bartering seemed to be the city itself; Hong Kong's very identity was being placed (as once Manhattan's had been) on the marketplace. And no sooner had China won the bidding than the world's most famous marketplace turned into a wholesale store feverish with the activity of a closing sale (Low prices! Moving soon! All stocks must go!). By the time I returned in 1985, the hottest place for young professionals was called 1997. And in the prime location of the Harbour Ferry departure lounge, the prize novelty of the store called 1997 (where every item sold for exactly HK$19.97) was a lumpy and ill-favored creature named the Rice Paddy Doll, a macabre variation on the Cabbage Patch Kid. This one, however, was not an orphan but an exile, equipped with a Hong Kong British passport and a sign that read: 'I want to Emigrate' or 'Immigration Department' or 'I would love Australia.' Already, so it seemed, the city had undertaken to turn its death to profit; already, it was flogging tickets to its own funeral.

Pico Iyer, *Video Night in Kathmandu*, 1988

The People of Hong Kong

Although Hong Kong is a British colony with a predominantly Chinese population, the demographic picture is not actually quite as simple as it seems. This increasingly cosmopolitan city has always had a sprinkling of residents from other countries, but in recent years, as its Chinese residents flocked to Australia and Canada to earn their overseas passports before 1997, fortune-seekers from Europe, North America and elsewhere in Asia have entered in droves. Hong Kong's buoyant economy and exciting atmosphere have long acted as a magnet to those looking for a better future, but never more so than now, particularly in light of the growing prominance of the Asia Pacific region on the international stage.

The vast majority of local people are Cantonese, in that either they or their recent ancestors came from the area around Canton (Guangzhou) in Guangdong province. Other Chinese people represented are the traditional fisherfolk, the Hakka and Chiu Chow, originally from China's southern coastal area; Taiwanese, who mostly work here as expatriates or as intermediaries between their country's business community and that of the mainland; and east-coast Fujianese and Shanghainese migrants, although more of the former went to Taiwan. For the visitor, perhaps the most obvious result of this *mélange* of people from different regions of China is the stunning variety of Chinese cuisines on offer in Hong Kong.

The second-largest group in Hong Kong is the Philippine community, who number some 90,000, the majority of whom are women employed as domestic helpers. Most are paid no more than the basic wage, their board and perhaps a flight home once every year or two, but many suffer poor treatment at the hands of their employers. Several Philippine support organizations have sprung up to help counsel these workers and give them legal advice, and there is a whole sub-culture that revolves around their weekly Sunday gatherings in Central. Thousands of young women come into town to spend their free day together, usually attending Catholic mass before meeting up for lunch and socializing in the streets. Chater Road is closed to traffic every Sunday and changes character completely from the centre of Hong Kong business to a Manila park, as crowds of chattering people relax with friends, play cards, take photos to send back home, sell T-shirts and trinkets, share home-made food and catch up on the latest news.

The Vietnamese are not strictly part of Hong Kong's population, but over 50,000 live behind bars in the Territory (see Vietnamese Refugees, page 166), while some earlier arrivals who chose to stay now live and work in the community. Many of these remain connected with the camps, however, either because they have friends or loved ones still inside, or because they are the only people capable of carrying out the necessary translation and interpretation work needed for the screening process.

Many other Asians live in Hong Kong, including Thais, Japanese, Malaysians and Singaporeans, but the most influential group is the 18,000-strong Indian community. Prominent in business circles beyond their numbers, they contribute significantly to Hong Kong's economy, particularly in the import/export area, and have established a powerful Indian Chamber of Commerce. Approximately 8,000 of them come originally from Sind, in what is now Pakistan. The community comprises Hindus, Muslims and Sikhs, this last of whom have a particularly splendid temple on the corner of Queen's Road East and Stubb's Road, lit with coloured lights.

The rest of the population is collectively known as *gweilos*, variously translated as 'ghosts' or 'foreign devils', although foreign Asians are also lumped into this bracket by some locals. Mostly from Western Europe, North America, Australia and New Zealand, these people are in turn split into various categories: real expatriates who are paid a phenomenal wage and seemingly endless allowances for housing and travel; 'expat brats', who either attend one of the élite local schools or descend on the Territory at holiday times from their boarding schools abroad; sinophiles who have studied or are studying Chinese and creep off to the mainland or Taiwan whenever possible; young adventurers—often working in research, journalism or sales—who come for some Asian experience and some travel time, perhaps before returning to do yet another degree or MBA back home; and the long-haulers, who have found their niche in the community, often by setting up their own business, and intend to stay.

Unless you are here for some time, it is unlikely you will meet all of these groups of people, as they each tend to have their own distinct circles of friends, neighbourhoods and places they frequent, but you can have some fun trying to spot them.

If you are still confused, a useful booklet is on sale locally, titled *How to Avoid Getting Ripped-Off in Hong Kong Buying Cameras and Photo Accessories* by James Morgan.

Once you have bought your new camera and snapped a whole roll of film, try Robert Lam for developing and printing. There are a huge number of quick-developing shops, but this chain, which has a large outlet in Jaffe Road, Wanchai, gives quality service and—if you decided against the manual camera—can sometimes help rectify your exposure mistakes.

WATCHES AND CLOCKS

Hong Kong is the one of the world's largest manufacturers of watches, mostly of the cheaper (but reliable) variety. For the best prices, try the shops along Queen's Road Central or the side streets of Kowloon, and always bargain. When buying an expensive brand, make sure you get the manufacturer's guarantee and beware of large discounts; there have been cases of inferior workings inserted behind the Rolex or Omega faces. For a wide selection of timepieces of every description, try City Chain stores, whose numerous branches are evenly scattered on both sides of the harbour.

ODDS AND ENDS

• Bath soaps that have the potent fragrance of green apples, strawberries, tangerine and other fruits at the environmentally conscious Body Shop in the Landmark, Pacific Place and Ocean Centre.

• Ultramodern Italian furniture and lighting at Arakis on Wyndham Street, Casa Nova at 62 Leighton Road and many shops along Wong Nai Chung Road.

• Indonesian 'Lombok' picnic baskets at Vincent Sum Collection, 19 Lyndhurst Terrace.

• Sequined evening bags in the stalls of Li Yuen East and West Street.

• A football field of toys from A to Z at the cavernous Toys R Us at Ocean Terminal.

• Decorative ceramic reproductions at Mei Ping's on Wyndham Street.

• For the sportsmen, fishing tackle at Po Kee's in Ocean Terminal, equestrian supplies at Nag Trade Ltd at Star House, Tsimshatsui, and windsurfing equipment at Windsurf Boutique, Rise Commercial Building behind the Park Hotel.

• Copies of furniture from MacIntosh to Memphis—or originals of his own design—made by Andy Tang at Pettie's Furniture in the Hollywood Centre, 223 Hollywood Road.

THE PATH TOWARDS DEMOCRACY

Hong Kong has been governed by diplomat-governors for over twenty years: Sir (now Lord) Murray MacLehose 1971–82, Sir Edward Youde 1982–84, and Sir (now Lord) David Wilson 1984–92. As London came to realize that good relations with China was one of the most important factors for Hong Kong's stability, the appointment of governors with a diplomatic background was deemed desirable.

However, after the Sino-British Joint Declaration was signed in 1984 and a date fixed for the end of British rule in Hong Kong, it was thought that the governor for the final years of British administration should be a politician, a statesman of sufficient stature to handle decision-making on the spot.

This thinking was put into practice in 1992 when Mr Chris Patten, former party chairman of the Conservative Party, was appointed to succeed Lord David Wilson. Patten, the first politician to become Governor of Hong Kong, has brought a thoroughly new style of government to the Territory together with a new set of aims.

In the diplomat-governor days, democracy was not supported by the government since it was considered irksome to China. As people became better educated and more affluent, their aspirations to participate in political decisions also increased. The Government recognized that this had to be accommodated but endeavoured to concede as little, and as slowly, as possible. Pressure for democracy from the public was not overwhelming because people's freedoms were still relatively assured under the British administration, which is responsible to Parliament.

In the face of Hong Kong reverting to China, the situation changed. Suddenly it became a matter of urgency for the British administration to train local officers to replace senior officials who, until recently, were mostly expatriates, and also to develop a democratic government largely elected by the Hong Kong public, in order to give reality to 'Hong Kong people ruling Hong Kong'.

However, with the resumption of sovereignty within view, China's opposition to the development of democracy in Hong Kong also became stronger and more active. To avoid annoying China, Britain acquiesced repeatedly. Despite promises in 1984 to establish a representative government rooted in Hong Kong by 1988, there was still no election by universal suffrage (locally called direct election) in the Legislative Council. The only elections were by functional constituencies, most of which represented the business and professional community, and only a small proportion of the public was entitled to vote.

After the Tiananmen Square tragedy in 1989, the call for democracy in Hong Kong intensified. Newly formed political parties urged the Government to quicken the pace of democracy. The non-civil servant members of the Legislative and Executive Council voted unanimously to urge the government to make half of the Legislative Council seats electable by universal suffrage. However, this recommendation was rejected. In 1990 the Basic Law, Hong Kong's 'mini-constitution' after 1997, was promulgated in Beijing. Only 20 directly elected seats, or one third, were allowed on the 1997 legislature.

In 1991 Hong Kong had its first direct elections. The United Democrats of Hong Kong, the liberal political group which campaigned the most vigorously, won 15 out of the total of 18 seats. Candidates supported by organizations connected with China suffered complete defeat.

China renewed its attempts to halt democracy in Hong Kong by refusing to sanction the Hong Kong Government proposal to build a new airport in Chek Lap Kok. Such a project requires huge funding. Without China's approval, financing would prove most difficult. In the end, to break the impasse, British Prime Minister John Major visited Beijing in September 1991. He thereby became the first Western head of state to visit China after the Tiananmen Square incident.

In spite of a Memorandum of Understanding signed by the two heads of government in which China pledged to support the new airport project, communication again broke down. This may have shown the British Government that former reconciliatory tactics no longer work. In any case, in 1992 shortly before the Chinese New Year, the retirement of Lord David Wilson, the last of the diplomat-governors, was announced. A few weeks after the general election in Britain, Mr Chris Patten was appointed his successor.

Even before Patten arrived to take up his post, there were numerous indications that he would break with tradition. He was the first governor to take up the post without receiving an obligatory knighthood. He was the first governor to abandon the colonial ceremonial dress with its white ostrich plumed hat. He has adopted a much more informal style with people than any governor before him and became instantly popular.

More importantly, he broke with the practice of seeking agreement with the Chinese Government through secret talks before announcing his plans and proposals to the Hong Kong public.

On 7th October 1992, in his first annual address to the Legislative Council, he announced a set of proposals for political reform for 1995, and said he would discuss them with China in his first visit to Beijing.

These proposals were mild. No proposal was made to increase the number of directly-elected seats. Instead, much more broadly-based functional constituencies were introduced. An election committee, to elect another 10 members, was also to be elected on democratic principles. These proposals received instant popular support.

China took great exception to the proposals and particularly to the fact that they were made public before China was consulted. Suspecting the British to be playing games, China launched a series a strong attacks on the Governor and on the British Government in retaliation.

Following an announcement that a government contract to build a new container terminal would not be recognized by China after 1997, the Hong Kong stock market fell 308 points in one day, and continued to fall a further 100 points the following day. Patten's popularity suffered visibly as a result.

Many, particularly from the business sector, blamed the governor for antagonizing China, and called for him to abandon his proposals and return to secret talks as China demanded. It was widely feared that continued lack of co-operation by China would harm Hong Kong's economy. Simultaneously, others feared that if the Governor capitulated, the British Administration would lose all credibility. Hong Kong's autonomy, as promised in the Joint Declaration and the Basic Law, would also be jeopardized.

This experience throws into sharp contrast the basic views of the community regarding Hong Kong's political development. One view sides with the traditional stance of the diplomat-governors and holds that good relations with China far outweigh any other consideration, including the development of democracy. The other view supports the new stance Patten seems to represent. It holds that democracy is Hong Kong's only defence and must be pursued as vigorously as possible, in spite of China's opposition.

Neither of these views will disappear. In fact, they have been, are and will remain the central split in Hong Kong politics, and provide the dynamics of most of Hong Kong's political debates in public and behind the scenes.

Chronology

1841 January 26. The British flag is raised on Hong Kong island following Britain's defeat of the Chinese in the First Anglo-Chinese (Opium) War.

1842 Treaty of Nanjing. Hong Kong Island is ceded to Britain with Sir Henry Pottinger as the first governor. The ports of Xiamen, Guangzhou, Fuzhou, Ningbo and Shanghai open to foreign trade and residence. Population grows to 12,000 Chinese and a few dozen Europeans. Race course and cricket grounds are established.

1845 A major source of income is the sale of 75-year land leases, opium monopoly and licences on alcohol, pawnbrokers and billiard-room operators. However, Britain has to continue its subsidies to balance the budget.

1850s Refugees from the Taiping Rebellion swell the Chinese population to 73,000.

1856 The 'Arrow', a Hong Kong-based trading ship, is captured by the Chinese. Governor Bowring orders warships to bombard Guangzhou, provoking the Second Anglo-Chinese War.

1857 Anti-British feelings lead to a Hong Kong baker selling bread laced with arsenic.

1858 The Treaty of Tianjin opens up 10 more Chinese ports to foreigners and cedes Kowloon Point and Stonecutters Island to Hong Kong. A duty is imposed on opium, thereby legalizing its trade.

1860 Kowloon and Stonecutter's Island are ceded to Britain under the Treaty of Beijing.

1862 The Sanitary Committee is formed to tackle the drainage problem.

1864 Hongkong and Shanghai Bank is founded.

1865 Population stands at 121,825 Chinese, 2,034 Europeans and 1,645 Indians. Gas street lighting is introduced.

1866 A recession causes the failure of many large companies.

1867 Hong Kong is linked to London by electric telegraph.

1886 The Dairy Farm Company is formed.

1887 The College of Medicine is opened to become part of Hong Kong University.

1888 The Peak Tram begins operations.

1889 The Fan Ling Golf Course opens.

1890 Praya reclamation begins(completed 1904), creating Central District.

1892 Sun Yat-sen graduates from Hong Kong College of Medicine.

1894 Plague outbreak leads to hundreds dead, clearing of slums and sanitary reforms.

1899 July 1st. The New Territories (including the islands of Lantau, Cheung Chau and Lamma) are leased from China for 99 years.

1900 Taikoo Docks builds a dry dock to accomodate the biggest ships afloat.

1904 Tram service opens between Kennedy Town and Shaukeiwan.

1906 Hong Kong is devastated by a typhoon that kills 10,000 people and wrecks the waterfront.

1909 Opium trading ban.

1911 Revolution in China leads to a new influx of migrants.

1912 A rail line is opened between Kowloon and Guangzhou.

1918 Fire at Happy Valley racetrack kills 600 people. Tai Tam reservoir is completed.

1919 First full-blown strike by engineers to protest increased rice prices.

1920 Repulse Bay Hotel opens. Roads are built around the island and from Kowloon to Castle Peak.

1922 First General Strike, led by the Communist Party.

1925 Boycott of British goods and trade by China, following confrontation in
–26 Shanghai.

1936 Kai Tak airport opens. Flights from Penang link Hong Kong and Britain.

1937 Pan American begins transpacific service to Hong Kong.

1941 Japanese invasion. After a two-week battle, the governor surrendered Hong Kong on Christmas Day. Europeans are interned in Stanley Prison.

1945 August 14th. The Japanese surrender. Hong Kong's population is now 600,000 (up from one million in 1941). The Hongkong and Shanghai Bank opens letters of credit to traders without guarantees, helping spur a rapid economic recovery.

1950 Britain recognizes the People's Republic of China. People flood into Hong Kong from China, bringing the population to 2,360,000. The influx brings the money, skills and labour force to create a manufacturing economy.

1953 Christmas Day fire destroys squatter settlement leaving 50,000 homeless. The government begins building resettlement estates that will eventually house 2.4 million people.

1967 May–November. Riots and strikes break out, inspired by China's Cultural Revolution.

1968 Plover Cove reservoir is completed.

1972 The first cross-harbour tunnel opens.

1974 The ICAC is set up following the scandal of police corruption.

1975 Work begins on the Mass Transit Railway (completed 1989). The Kowloon–Canton Railway is modernized, and tracks electrified.

1984 The Joint Declaration is signed by Britain and China in Beijing. Hong Kong will revert to Chinese rule in 1997, with 50 years of economic autonomy to follow.

1989 Tiananmen crackdown provokes pre-Democracy demonstrations.

1990 Provisional Airport Authority is set up to oversee the building of Chek Lap Kok Airport and associated projects. Construction is started despite objections by the Chinese government.

1991 The first phase of Kowloon Walled City clearance is begun.

1992 The Eastern Cross-Harbour Tunnel opens. Christopher Patten is appointed Hong Kong's last governor.

1997 At midnight on June 30, Hong Kong will revert to China's sovereignty after 156 years of British government.

Vietnamese Boat People

One of Hong Kong's largest, and most unwelcome, foreign contingents is from Vietnam. Known collectively as 'boat people' because most of them braved the open seas in rickety vessels to flee their country, this community now numbers some 54,700 individuals in 12 camps across the colony.

Their presence in Hong Kong is a bone of contention for all concerned: the Vietnamese themselves want to be given asylum in third countries as bona fide refugees; the United Nations High Commission for Refugees (UNHCR), which oversees the local situation, wants them to volunteer to return to Vietnam as soon as possible; and the Hong Kong government does not mind where they go as long as they leave.

The exodus started soon after the Vietnam War, when groups of ethnic Chinese from the south began to flee in fear of persecution by the incoming northern forces. The first 3,743 arrivals, who were picked up in May 1975 by a Danish ship the Clara Maersk and transported to Hong Kong, were located in open camps and allowed to mingle freely with the local community.

From 1975 to 1978, this relaxed policy continued, with some individuals opting to stay and make their way in the colony and others choosing resettlement overseas. It was not until December 1978 that the government admitted the task of dealing with boat people was beginning to prove irksome and withdrew its welcome mat. A ship carrying 3,383 Vietnamese was given provisions by the Hong Kong government but urged to continue its journey to Taiwan. Not until four weeks later did the authorities finally—and reluctantly—allow it to dock.

The situation deteriorated swiftly in 1979, and Hong Kong received a massive influx of 66,000 Sino-Vietnamese, expelled after Vietnam's border conflict with China. The UN responded to the crisis by calling its first conference on Indochina's refugees, at which it was decided that any individual in flight would automatically be considered a refugee and resettled abroad. The countries of Southeast Asia agreed to function as ports of first asylum, with countries such as the US, Canada and Australia as final resettlement destinations. As a result of this policy, some 38,000 Hong Kong-based refugees were successfully resettled overseas in 1980 alone.

Unfortunately, by 1982, the enthusiasm of both the resettlement countries and the Hong Kong government was starting to flag, and two closed camps were set up as a deterrent to potential refugees: Hei Ling Chau, a custom-built camp, and Chi Ma Wan, a converted facility. The scheme seemed to work, and arrivals remained fairly static for the next four years.

The turning point came in 1988, when thousands of refugees—mostly from northern Vietnam—began to pour into the Territory. The Hong Kong government unilaterally renounced the 1979 agreement assuring automatic refugee status and announced that all arrivals after June 16 would be subject to a screening process to determine whether they were genuine refugees fleeing persecution or simply people seeking better economic opportunities. At the same time, the closed camps were renamed detention centres—a move the UNHCR opposed—and the notorious Whitehead camp was constructed. The plight of the inmates, who live surrounded by high fences ringed with barbed wire in a concrete, treeless mass of tin huts, soon became a target for criticism.

Meanwhile, asylum seekers continued to escape Vietnam throughout 1989—34,000 came to Hong Kong alone—as the economic situation deteriorated, a major famine hit the country and the USSR withdrew its support.

The problems showed no signs of abating, and a second international conference was called in a desperate search for a solution. The result was the Comprehensive Plan of Action, which tried to stop countries ending their first-asylum policy, but a screening process was simultaneously enforced throughout the region, and voluntary repatriation was strongly encouraged. Meanwhile, an 'orderly departure programme' was set up in Vietnam to help those with relatives abroad join them more easily.

The screening process soon attracted criticism, especially after the first forcible repatriations in December 1989. Negotiations continued in 1990 with the Vietnamese government to define the terms under which those screened out could return home. The resulting Hanoi Agreement promised to facilitate the whole process.

This was followed in 1991 by a further agreement on double-backers—those who returned a second time to Hong Kong after repatriation—which stipulated that all arrivals must return within a certain timeframe and reduced the integration allowance to returnees (repatriated individuals had previously received as much as US$300 each to help their reassimilation at home).

Today, ten detention centres operate in Hong Kong, all run by the local authorities and overseen by the UNHCR: Kai Tak, Chi Ma Wan (Upper and Lower), Hei Ling Chau, High Island, Lo Wu, Nei Kwu, Shek Kong, Tai A Chau and Whitehead. There is also a reception centre on Green Island, a departure centre called New Horizons and the one remaining open camp at Pillar Point. Whitehead is by far the largest, housing more that 23,500 individuals, few of whom will gain refugee status. Many of the detainees have been in Hong Kong for several years—some for more than a decade.

Although the camps vary a great deal in their degree of openness, life inside is dominated by overcrowded conditions and sheer boredom. Various local and international organizations operate inside their confines in an attempt to provide basic services. The UNHCR oversees the screening process, encourages and organizes voluntary repatriation and is responsible for the asylum seekers' welfare; Save the Children runs some pre-school education programs; Hong Kong Christian Aid to Refugees provides various skills-teaching services; Garden Streams, a local group, offers creative opportunities to limited numbers of adults and children through their Art in the Camps project; and International Social Services ensures that children under 16 receive some sort of basic schooling.

Resources are scarce, however, and vast numbers of people are left with little to do but while away their time. Within such a large group of people, there are naturally divisions on regional grounds that cause occasional outbreaks of violence and even deaths. Other problems include the care of numerous unaccompanied minors, dealing with growing numbers of pregnant young women and a thriving black market.

Back in Vietnam, the main barrier to economic development is widely acknowledged to be US trade sanctions. A large number of European and Asian companies are already doing business in the country, but Vietnam's access to badly needed aid and loans from the World Bank and the Asian Development Bank remains blocked by the US.

The EC has made some inroads with a program to create jobs by stimulating economic activity within Vietnam. Focused on Haiphong, Quang Ninh and Ho Chi Minh, the scheme has earmarked US$11 million for a three-year period from 1991 for loans to small businesses, 50 per cent of which will go to returnees. Apart from loan funds, the plan also provides vocational training, healthcare and technical assistance.

It remains to be seen whether such programs will change the climate within Vietnam sufficiently to entice the refugees back. Most believe that, despite recent elections, Vietnam's centrally controlled economy holds little hope for the immediate future without financial help from institutions such as the World Bank, the International Monetary Fund and the Asian Development Bank—and that means help from the US.

Tours and Day Trips

Hong Kong

Local entrepreneurial talents have produced an inventive selection of tours within and around Hong Kong. Many of these outings can easily be done independently, but if you decide to opt for a tour, then select with caution or you may find yourself merely on a glorified shopping expedition to spots where your guide is assured a percentage. Most tours offered by HKTA-registered companies should be reliable. It is also worth remembering that touring by coach, especially in the New Territories, can turn out to be half a day of sitting in heavy traffic staring at unsightly, half-constructed new towns. Check the routings and find out exactly how much time has been allocated to each stop—sometimes, the halt is long enough only to take a photo or two.

Probably most worthwhile is Hong Kong Watertours, which has an impressive range of trips of different lengths, some combining sea and land touring, others offering relaxed drinks or meals on board while the boat sails past parts of Hong Kong's varied shoreline—more comfortable, more isolated and much more expensive than just taking the usual public ferry. Two other interesting and well-organized tours are a visit to the Song Dynasty Village (see Kowloon section) and a cruise on the Hong Kong Hilton's Wan Fu—a replica of a 19th-century Royal Navy pirate chaser. Book at your hotel. Helicopter tours are available through Heliservices Hong Kong Ltd; telephone 802 0200 for information and bookings.

The Star Ferry also runs seven special cruises daily: Noon Day Gun Cruise at 11.15 am; Seafarer's *Dim Sum* Cruise at 12.30 pm; Seabreezes Cruise at 2.00 pm; Afternoon Tea Cruise at 3.15 pm; Sundown Cruise at 6.45 pm; Cocktail Cat at 8.00 pm; Harbour Lights Cruise at 9.30 pm. The cruises last from an hour to an hour-and-a-half and cost HK$90–280 for adults and HK$60–200 for children three to 12 years old. All cruises offer full bar, snacks, a souvenir and Chinese calligraphy demonstrations. Departure is from the Star Ferry Kowloon pier and 10 minutes later from the Hong Kong pier. You can buy tickets at the piers or through travel agents, or telephone 845 2324, 366 7024 or 801 7429 for further information.

A number of replicas of the earliest trams are available for private hire. A superb red and gold tram with brass trimmings and an open upstairs balcony makes three daily two-hour *Dim Sum* tours at 10 am, 12.30 pm and 3.00 pm; these two-hour tours, which include unlimited free drinks and a ride on the Star Ferry and in an open-top bus, cost HK$115 (children HK$80) and can be bought at Star Ferry piers or through travel agents. Telephone 845 2324, 366 7024 or 801 7429 for further details.

China

The great majority of those crossing the border into neighbouring **Guangdong Province** are Hong Kong Chinese visiting relatives, but the Territory increasingly acts as the main gateway into China for foreigners. Thousands of tourists and businessmen begin their China travels on a train, plane or hovercraft bound for Guangzhou (Canton).

China Travel Service (HK) Limited (CTS) is the agent in Hong Kong for China International Service, which handles all aspects of foreign travel within China. CTS offers a range of group tours to China. It also offers more pricey individual tours that are a little more flexible than the usual group tour. CTS offices are at 77 Queen's Road Central (tel 525 2284) and 27 Nathan Road (tel 721 1331). Most travel agents in Hong Kong will handle the booking of CTS tours to China (for which they receive a flat commission).

Many Hong Kong tour operators and agents run their own tours to China. Some of these tours may be more expensive, but they may also offer extra facilities that a straight CTS tour does not (an escort from the Hong Kong office, for example, to iron out all problems that inevitably greet travellers in China). It is worth checking carefully on these points before selecting your tour. Competition is keen, especially among operators and agents offering short trips (six days in Beijing, three in Canton, four or five in Shanghai) and cheaper tour prices may indicate only that agents are undercutting each other.

CTS offer two day-trip tours from Hong Kong—one just over the border to **Shenzhen** (spelt Shumchun in Hong Kong) and the other to **Zhongshan** (Chungshan), entering China through Macau. Of the two, the trip via Macau is by far the superior. It takes you by hydrofoil from Hong Kong to Macau (70 minutes) where you cross the border into an attractive landscape of ricefields and traditional Cantonese villages. A tour bus takes you to the birthplace of Dr Sun Yat-Sen (regarded by the Chinese as the founder of modern China) and on to a country town for lunch. On the way back to Macau you visit a commune, fishing village or kindergarten.

The cheaper trip to Shenzhen offers less chance to see anything of Guangdong Province. The town, with 300,000 or so inhabitants, is distinctly untypical since it is the hub of one of China's special economic zones, established to attract foreign (particularly Hong Kong) investment and technology. High-rise residential and commercial blocks abound, industry is growing, and accompanying social problems associated with the town's sudden economic boom are much in evidence. A visit to the Shenzhen Reservoir, which is one of the main suppliers of water to Hong Kong, is included in this visit.

It is also possible to visit the Chinese city of **Zhuhai** directly by ferry from Hong Kong. An otherwise unremarkable new town with several hotels and rows of small factories, Zhuhai is best known for its golf course, frequented largely by Japanese tourists.

Macau

The Portuguese enclave of Macau lies only 60 kilometres (37.3 miles) away from Hong Kong, but it is surprising what a different world awaits you at the end of the one-hour jetfoil journey—a world of cobbled streets, venerable banyans and churches founded soon after the Portuguese arrived in 1557.

It is safe to say that no other place in the world can match Macau's blend of architectural traditions, mostly harmonious, sometimes incongruous, but always interesting. Sino-Iberian is the basic style, with overlays, underlays and sometimes highlights from a dozen traditions incorporated in a single pediment or balcony. Dutch, Moorish, Spanish, Japanese and Italian traders and residents all made distinctive contributions to this ten-square-kilometre (six-mile-square) melting pot of cultures. Very little remains from the earliest days, as most of the sumptuous churches were rebuilt in the last century; the **Leal Senado**, with its magnificent wood-panelled library and council room, dates back little more than 100 years. Art Deco and Art Nouveau were strong influences in the 1920s, when Macau had its first building boom. Looking at some of the charming survivors of this era, it is intriguing to spot where other influences came into play.

In Macau, the pace of everything is slower than in nearby Hong Kong, but in recent years development has been proceeding quickly, as you can see and hear in many parts of the city. Nevertheless, residents have a keen sense of the value of their past and a feeling for conservation has strengthened in recent years. New paint has brought about a blossoming of geranium pink and red, fresh peppermint green, ochre and amber in many formerly dilapidated areas. A limited amount of more ambitious restoration work has been carried out on several prominent government buildings. These spruced-up buildings are by no means empty shells; they form part of Macau's day-to-day fabric. Some serve as government or commercial offices, others are private residences or shops, and a few have been given renewed purpose as museums.

Macau is an easy place to explore at your own pace with the help of some of the excellent leaflets and maps obtainable free from the Macau Department of Tourism. The leaflet called *Walking Tours* is particularly good. You can also pick up most of this material at the Macau Tourist Information Bureau in Hong Kong, Room 305, on the third floor of the Shun Tak Centre where you board your vessel for Macau. You can reserve hotel accommodation and tours here, too.

Try to avoid the weekends or public holidays when you plan a trip to Macau. And it is always a good idea to buy your return ticket before leaving Hong Kong, as you can always join the stand-by queue to travel back earlier if you wish, and you can change to a later sailing provided you do this well ahead of your scheduled departure time. Tickets

can be bought at Ticketmate outlets in many places in Hong Kong or in the Shun Tak Centre.

If you grow tired of walking, taxis are usually easy to find and fares are low. Carry a map to help when dealing with the drivers, most of whom do not understand English. Macau also has pedicabs for short distances. Don't miss the façade of St Paul's, Lin Fong Miu, Kun Iam Tong, Teatro Dom Pedro, Luis de Camões Garden and Museum, Protestant Cemetery, Lou Lim Ieoc Garden, St Joseph's Seminary and Leal Senado (go inside to see the raised garden and the beautiful wood-panelled library). You cannot go far without stumbling upon an intriguing site in this *mélange* of past and present.

Spare time for the two outlying islands, which are relatively unspoiled despite the density of population on peninsular Macau. Use the public buses, charter a taxi for a couple of hours or use an international driving licence to hire a **Macau Moke** (arrange this in Hong Kong or on the spot). It is easy to miss the tiny village behind the government buildings and temple off Taipa's main square. Explore the narrow alleyways, enjoy the warm Iberian colours of the diminutive houses, and stumble on yet another section of the marvellous mosaic that is Macau.

After the museums, monuments and mementoes, complete your Macau experience with the unique flavours of Macanese food. Like everything else about Macau, the cooking has been formed by a host of influences from around the world, successfully combined with the Portuguese-Chinese base from which all its dishes have developed. African chicken, chilli crabs or garlic prawns are distinctive and delicious. So also are the rich stews and soups based on Portuguese sausage. No Macau meal is complete without its complement of Portuguese wines and a brandy to finish. Dine in style surrounded by sparkling crystal and gleaming silver at restaurants in Macau's leading hotels. Or opt for the more homely atmosphere of some of Macau's humbler establishments, where chickens and puppies keep you company.

The majority of Macau's visitors are Hong Kong people in search of gambling. They head straight from the pier to the casinos, the canidrome or the trotting track, leaving the rest of Macau to the enterprising few. If you decide to make your Macau visit more than a day trip, it is worth bearing in mind that the enclave's hotels offer very good value, especially mid-week, when some attractive package deals are available at most seasons of the year.

The **Mandarin Oriental** provides five-star comfort and elegance, with service and facilities to match. Part of an internationally renowed hotel group, it has a guest to staff ratio of 1:1. Outdoor swimming pools, sauna, exercise area, jacuzzi, massage, tennis courts and squash courts are all included in the health centre. There is a small 24-hour casino within the hotel. The **Hyatt Regency**, located in idyllic surroundings on **Taipa Island**, is the ultimate in getting away from it all. Its Resort Centre caters to all tastes,

(preceding pages) Macau historian Father Manuel Teixeira

providing everything from professional tennis coaching and aerobics classes to aromatherapy beauty treatments and poolside sunbathing loungers. Alfonso's prepares outstanding Portuguese and Macanese specialities.

Pousada de São Tiago must be one of the most romantic and luxurious hotels in the world, nestling inside the walls of a 16th century fortress, in an unrivalled location overlooking the South China Sea. It has 23 rooms decorated in traditional Portuguese style—hand-carved mahogany furniture and individually crafted Portuguese tiles and crystal chandeliers.

Hotel Bela Vista dates back to early Victorian days and has recently been renovated to its former glory by Mandarin Oriental Hotels. Unfortunately, the prices have risen to match. It has long been a favourite with savvy Hong Kong visitors on account of its intractably nostalgic atmosphere and romantic verandaed dining area.

The **Lisboa Hotel** seems designed for compulsive gamblers who wish to spend as little time as possible away from the casinos within its confines. Despite the tawdry and noisy surroundings, its restaurants, A Galera and Portas do Sol, are elegant havens of gastronomic delight at affordable prices. Other restaurants providing excellent and distinctive food include Gallo in Taipa Village; 1999 in Coloane Park (adjacent to the walk-through aviary); Fernando's Place at Hac Sa, the black sand beach; Henri's; Solmar; Pinocchio; and Portuguesa.

Colonial Barbarism

When the first mutterings of the coming storm of the Taiping Rebellion, which in the providence of God was destined to re-establish the waning fortunes of Hongkong, were observed by the Cantonese Authorities, they shrewdly availed themselves of the known fact that the Chinese in Hongkong were as much influenced by that secret political propaganda as those of the interior of China to strike another blow at the success of Hongkong as a Colony for Chinese. So they persuaded Sir J. Davis into passing an Ordinance (No 1 of 1845) the effect of which was that the Hongkong Police should search out and arrest political refugees as being members of the Triad and other secret societies, who, after a term of imprisonment, should be branded each on the cheek and then be deported to Chinese territory where of course the Mandarins would forthwith arrest, torture and execute them. That a British Governor should ever have enacted such a monstrously barbaric and un-English law is hardly credible. It is a strange fact that with all his experience of Chinese, philanthropic Sir John Davis allowed himself to be so duped by Chinese diplomatists as to become the unconscious tool of Mandarin oppression in its worst form. It was not merely an unwise disregard of the sound principle formulated by Gladstone, that 'England never makes laws to benefit the internal condition of any other State'; it was not merely a drastic denial of the world-wide assumption that British soil is a safe refuge from political tyranny and oppression; but it was also a positive assertion, in the face of all China, that Hongkong Governors would pledge themselves to co-operate with the Manchu conquerors of China in arresting, imprisoning, branding on the cheek (as the life-long mark of the outlaw) and delivering into the hands of Mandarins for execution any hapless Chinese patriot that should be fool enough to put his foot on British soil. By order of the Home Government this barbaric Ordinance was modified nine months later by substituting, in an amendment, branding under the arm for that mark on the cheek which would have made reform even in the case of a criminal absolutely impossible.

E J Eitel, *Europe in China*, 1895

A Licence to Kill

Before leaving Hong Kong, I accompanied a Missionary friend, on several occasions, to the Chinese portion of the town, walking through the native bazaar and the back streets bordering on the beach, where we distributed tracts in some houses among the few persons capable of reading them. In several houses we witnessed the apparatus for opium-smoking, but saw no one in the act of smoking till we came to the house of a wealthy Chinese, named A-quei. He possesses about fifty houses in the bazaar, and lives on the rent, in a style much above the generality of Chinese settlers, who are commonly composed of the refuse of the population of the neighbouring mainland. During the war, A-quei acted as purveyor of provisions to the British armament, and acquired some wealth. After the peace, he was at first afraid to return to the mainland, lest he should be seized as a traitor by the Mandarins. In the end he settled at Hong Kong, where he is said to encourage disreputable characters by the loan of money, and in various ways to reap the proceeds of profligacy and crime. He introduced us to a partner, named A-tai, whom we saw in the process of smoking opium, inhaling the smoke through the mouth and emitting it through the nose. The thick fluid of prepared opium being held for a few moments over a flame, till it became more solid, was placed in the bowl of the pipe, which was held over a small glass lamp, burning for the purpose; and the smoker, stretched on a kind of couch with a head-pillow, gently reposed himself, in order to enjoy the exciting effects of the fumes. A-tai had just purchased, as the highest bidder, from Government, the exclusive right of selling opium by retail, in any quantity less than a chest, in Hong Kong. For this he said that he had agreed to pay 550 dollars a month. He intended to institute an office, from which he could sell licenses to individual opium-house keepers to retail the drug; and out of these licenses he hoped to make his profits, after paying the 500 dollars monthly to the British Government.

Rev George Smith, MA, *A Narrative of an Exploratory Visit to Each of the Consular Cities of China and to the Islands of Hong Kong and Chusan on Behalf of the Church Missionary Society in the Years 1844, 1845, 1846*

Restaurants

One star means inexpensive (below HK$100 per person), two stars mean moderately expensive (HK$100--HK$200), three stars mean verging on the costly (HK$200--HK$350), and four stars represents HK$350 and over per head, all excluding alcoholic drinks. In the case of Chinese restaurants, prices are per person but calculated for parties of four to six.

CHINESE

American Restaurant**
20 Lockhart Road, Wanchai, tel 527 7277
美利堅飯店　灣仔駱克道20號
Strange name for a Peking-style Chinese restaurant, but despite the occasional huge table of rowdy tourists, the red and green painted areas have an authentic feel—and the food is excellent. Peking duck is of course a favourite, as are some of the warming winter hotpots, mutton with bunches of spring onion, steamed pork-filled dumplings and delicious Tsientsin cabbage in chicken oil. Try the hot-fried shredded beef, which you stuff into small pouches of flatbread before eating by hand. Lunch hours are particularly crowded, so be sure to book ahead.

Bodhi Vegetarian Restaurant*
384–388 Lockhart Road, Wanchai, tel 573 2155
菩提素食　灣仔駱克道384號至388號
This restaurant is considered by many ardent vegetarians to be one of Hong Kong's finest providers of 'green cuisine' in its price range. The variety of dishes is impressive but may seem bewildering to the uninitiated—such as fried bamboo fungus with asparagus or the yellow fungus in coconut soup. The deep fried taro cakes are especially good. There is a chain of Bodhi restaurants in Hong Kong; another branch is at G/F, 56 Cameron Road, Tsimshatsui, Kowloon, tel 739 2222.

The Dumpling Shop*
67 Granville Road, Tsimshatsui, Kowloon, tel 723 6390
餃子店　九龍尖沙咀加連威老道67號
Simple and cheap, a no frills restaurant. If you want dumplings, this is the place. Fifty kinds of dumplings—steamed, fried and even teppanyaki-style—are offered. Dumplings filled with pork and chilli peppers, shrimp and green onions, and minced chicken are among the many varieties available.

Fook Lam Moon***

35–45 Johnston Road, Wanchai, tel 866 0663

福臨門酒家　灣仔莊士敦道35至45號

Almost a tradition in Hong Kong, this prestigious restaurant is known for its élite clientele, as it started as a caterer to the rich and powerful. Expensve specialities such as shark's fin, abalone, and bird's nest soup are all excellent, as is the crispy chicken.

Fung Lam**

Siu Yat Lau, Sai Kung, tel 792 6623/792 1346

楓林小館　西貢兆日樓

This is a Cantonese-style chain extending from the New Territories to California, where the breadth of the menu is such that you can choose from more than 20 varieties of beancurd. Smoked duck will reach you after an intriguingly complicated preparation in which the bird is scalded, wind-dried, smoked over wood chips, tea and charcoal and then steamed. Also try the sliced beef with chilli and bean sauce. The Hakka-style shrimp baked with salt is delicious—as is the chicken with lemon sauce (ask the waiter not to make it too sweet). Fung Lam also manages the Yucca de Lac seafood restaurant (tel 691 2011) at Lot 716 in Ma Liu Shiu village, which has a spectacular view of the harbour, as well as a second Fung Lam restaurant at 45 Tsuen Nam Road, Shatin, New Territories, tel 692 1175/691 1484.

Great Shanghai**

1/F, 26 Prat Avenue, Kowloon, tel 366 8158

大上海飯店　尖沙咀寶勒巷26號2樓

There are some who consider this to be the best Shanghai restaurant anywhere in the city. Certainly the restaurant does not stint on peppers, oils or garlic and has created an imaginative menu using Hong Kong's abundance of fresh ingredients. Specials include chicken in wine sauce, shrimps, braised eels with bamboo shoots and noisette of pork served with vegetable and covered in a heavy soy sauce.

King Bun Restaurant***

158 Queen's Road Central, tel 543 2223/543 4256

敬賓酒家　中環皇后大道中158號

This is considered the best Cantonese restaurant in the city. The whole feel of the place is of serious expertise, and the menu is dauntingly large. This is the place to confirm what sweet and sour pork really should taste like, with green and red peppers and Chinese onion added in just the right balance. The pigeon, Yunnan ham casserole and barbecued duck are also excellent. Come winter, try the deer and other game, or the incomparable snake soup. It is not, however, a place to go on your own or without a Chinese friend; go in a large party with a Cantonese speaker, and you will enjoy a banquet to remember.

Loong Yuen**
Holiday Inn Golden Mile, Nathan Road, tel 739 6268
龍園　尖沙咀金域假日酒店
It is worth visiting this restaurant the day before you intend to eat, as there are a range of specials that take a long time to cook. Apart from beggar's chicken and double-boiled shark's fin, you can even have a whole suckling pig. Booking ahead is advisable, as it is a popular place with tourists and locals.

Luk Yu Teahouse**
24–26 Stanley Street, Central, tel 523 5463/45
陸羽茶室　中環士丹利街24至26號
This marvellous old-style eatery, with its lacquered chairs, marble-topped tables, mirrored cupboards and brass spittoons, was established in 1925. It recently gained some notoriety as the site of a triad shooting, but it remains an extremely popular restaurant and a temple to the morning ritual of drinking tea with *dim sum* (bite-sized savoury

Fresh seafood

snacks). Named after the god of tea, the restaurant has 500 seats on four storeys. It is best to go with a Cantonese speaker, because no English menus are available. Some of the best delicacies on offer are meat dumplings cooked with tangerine peel, minced ham in thousand-layer cake, fried shrimp roll and roasted duck with rice in lily leaves.

Lung Wah Hotel**
Lot 156, 22 Ha Wo Che, Shatin, tel 691 1594
龍華酒店　新界沙田下禾輋22號
This is the restaurant to visit if you like pigeon—or fancy trying it. Several different recipes are listed on the menu, and there are many more available if you know what to ask for. The restaurant serves 2,000 pigeons a day—over 1,000,000 a year. Here is the chance to try everything from satay pigeon to roasted Shek Ki pigeon, baked pigeon, pigeon egg with mushroom, and steamed pigeon heart. In winter, try the marvellous snake soup. To get there, drive past Shatin on Taipo road and stop opposite Shatin Police Station; using the overpass, you will reach the restaurant through a small aviary. Book ahead at weekends.

Man Wah***
The Mandarin Oriental, 5 Connaught Road, Central, tel 522 0111
文華廳　中環干諾道中5號
The decor of the Mandarin Oriental's Chinese restaurant is undeniably spectacular, and its classical Cantonese cuisine is unequalled. Seasonal specialities change, but look for the crispy Loong Kwong chicken with sweet walnut and deep-fried scallops or mashed wintermelon, crabmeat soup or minced pigeon in lettuce.

New Golden Red Chiu Chow Restaurant**
13 Prat Avenue, Tsimshatsui, Kowloon, tel 366 6822
新金紅潮州酒家　尖沙咀寶勒巷13號
Apart from the strong Iron Buddha tea, Chiu Chow food is not usually the favourite of visitors, since it can be rather thick and extreme, placing a strong emphasis on offal and blood gravy. New Golden Red, however, offers an exceptional experience. Recommended dishes includes the soyed goose with fried goose blood and vinegar and garlic on the side, sliced chicken with *chinjew* sauce, and lemon duck soup. Another Chiu Chow dish is fried chicken formed balls—good fleshy chunks of chicken formed together with deep-fried pearl leaves. Count this as an adventure.

One Harbour Road****
Grand Hyatt, 1 Harbour Road, Wanchai, tel 861 1234
港灣一號　香港灣仔港灣道1號君悅酒店

This split-level terraced restaurant with fountain, greenery and panoramic view of the harbour offers a truly elegant dining experience. Delicate and innovative cuisine is matched by impeccable service, and the artfully presented *dim sum* is never over steamed. Scallops sautéed with seasonal vegetables, and steamed garoupa with scallions and ginger, are two dishes prepared to let the ingredients speak with clear, pure voice. A jacket and tie is required for male diners and booking is advisable.

Shang Palace***
Shangri-La Hotel, 64 Mody Road, Tsimshatsui East, tel 721 2111
香宮　尖沙咀麼地道64號香格里拉酒店
You expect Anna Mae Wong in a red silk *cheong sam* to come slithering down the aisle of this opulent, red-lacquered restaurant. The Peking duck is succulent and crispy, the beancurd rich and fresh, the pea shoots sautéed not a moment too long. Reasonably priced for the high quality of the food, and its décor is a nice change of pace from the usual sleekness of marble and polished wood.

Sichuan Garden****
3/F, Gloucester Tower, The Landmark, Central, tel 521 4433
錦江樓　中環置地廣場告士打大廈3號
Certainly the most expensive Sichuan-style restaurant in the city, Sichuan Garden is held in high regard by local Sichuanese themselves as serving dishes unequalled anywhere else in Hong Kong. The sizzling prawns and delicately smoked pigeon are particularly fine, but the management singles out the spiced beef and tripe with pungent sauce, camphor-smoked duck and tea leaves, and shredded beef in garlic sauce.

Spring Deer**
1/F, 42 Mody Road, Kowloon, tel 366 4012
鹿鳴春飯店　尖沙咀麼地道42號2樓
This is a long-time favourite with connoisseurs of Peking duck, so make sure you book ahead. The duck comes nicely browned, has a rich aroma and is served with a minimum of meat on each slab. Try the chicken steamed with chilli and sweet peppers and then fried, or the handmade noodles. Another excellent dish is the roast shad on the hot pan or the prawns cooked with sour/hot red chilli sauce—not as dangerously spicy as it sounds.

Sun Tung Lok***
G/F, 376–382 Lockhart Road, Wanchai, tel 573 8361
新同樂魚翅酒家　灣仔駱克道376至382號地下

Often mentioned in guidebooks and eulogized by food writers, Sun Tung Lok is synonymous with exotic food and, in particular, with shark's fin. The prices are high, and the staff is sometimes disinclined to make allowances for indecisiveness, so go in a group with at least one Chinese-speaking person and treat yourself to a feast. The abalone is delicious and expensive, and the shark's fin supreme is self-explanatory; equally tasty is the sautéd sliced duck with walnuts. And ask for the braised cuttlefish, which is scored, crisp and melting in a chilli-based sauce. Other Sun Tung Lok locations include: 137 Connaught Road West, Hong Kong, tel 549 1137; 25–27 Canton Road, Harbour City, Kowloon, tel 722 0288 (five lines).

Tai Woo Restaurant**
City Garden, Electric Road, North Point, tel 893 9882
太湖海鮮城　北角電器道城市花園
One of a strategically located restaurant chain frequented by locals and visitors alike, the Tai Woo Restaurant serves first-rate Cantonese food. Try the braised brisket of beef simmered for hours, vegetarian hotpot, crisp rolls of beancurd and tasty chicken, and do not forget *dim sum*, served between 11 am and 5 pm (for which no reservations are taken). The Wellington Street branch in Central is particularly good for fish. Other Tai Woo restaurant locations are: 17–19 Wellington Street, Central, Hong Kong, tel 524 5688; Blocks 4&5, Ground Floor, North Point, Hong Kong, tel 571 6263; 20–22A Granville Road, Tsimshatsui, Kowloon, tel 739 8813; 14–16 Hillwood Road, Tsimshatsui, Kowloon, tel 369 9773.

Tien Heung Lau****
18C Austin Avenue, Tsimshatsui, tel 366 2414
天香樓　尖沙咀柯士甸道18C
One of the most expensive Chinese restaurants in Hong Kong, Tien Heung Lau is spoken of in awe for its beggar's chicken and Hangchow cooking. Go with a Chinese friend to help order seasonal specialities; also keep a wary eye on the price column. Recommended is fried white shrimp covered with Hangchow tea and deep-fried eel in fine garlic sauce. A splendid finale is a duck and *wonton* (shrimp and pork dumplings) soup—half a duck is cooked and boiled in clay amidst hundreds of *wonton*.

Yung Kee Restaurant**
32 Wellington Street, Central, Hong Kong, tel 522 1624
鏞記酒家　中環威靈頓街32號
This is another venerable restaurant frequented by locals and serves excellent Cantonese dishes such as roast goose or scallops, and the famed hundred-year-old eggs. In winter ask for snake soup with thinly sliced preserved duck, chicken and abalone; in spring, try

Wait Until Dark

The waterfront was provided with jetties and steps, and Downing naturally supposed that he would be landed at one of them. But the sampan anchored some distance from the shore. On asking the pilot's mate the reason for this, the man told him the water was too shallow. Presently the real reason came out. The Chinese Government maintained in Macao its own officials, for at no time had the Portuguese had undivided control of the city. The pilot's mate was in the bad books of the local mandarin; he dared not bring his sampan right in.

In a moment, however, an egg-boat came up. This was a most singular conveyance, being eight feet long, six feet broad, flat-bottomed and wall-sided, with the gunwale only six inches above water. For cabin it had a mat bent over like an archway. Two Chinese girls were in charge of this tub. They invited Downing to come ashore in it.

Nothing loath, the young man complied and was given a stool under the circular roofing, which apparently had suggested the local name of egg-boat. The girls sat fore and aft, and began to row. They were dressed in blue trousers and smocks; their hair was in two plaits tied with red cotton. Being the first women Downing had seen for a long time, he found them both delightfully attractive. They seemed so good-natured too, as they smiled and showed their splendid teeth. The one at the back was only a foot from him. He noticed now that she had artificial flowers in her hair. While striving to converse in the fantastic patois known as pidgin-English, he took hold of her arm in his efforts to make his meaning clear. This seemed to perturb the young woman, for she drew back and looked nervously at the waterfront. 'Na, na!' said she. 'Mandarin see, he squeegee me.' On Downing expressing astonishment at this remark, she gave him to understand that by port regulations egg-boat girls were not allowed while on duty to dally with passengers, and more particularly with foreign devils, and that if one of the port police had seen her just now he might misconstrue, perhaps wilfully misconstrue, her passenger's gesture and she would have to tip him or else he would report her. Downing waxed indignant over this oppression. So sympathetic was he, that she hastened to reassure him, and smiling demurely murmured: 'Nightee time come, no man see.'

Maurice Collis, Foreign Mud, 1946

An abandoned Vietnamese junk, Kennedy Town (above); the fishing village of Tung Chung, Lantau Island, soon to be the site of the new airport (below)

downing the live fish, lightly steamed, or braised pigeon with bean sauce. In summer there is winter melon soup or braised abalone; autumn and winter call for rice birds. Particular recommendations from the culinary *cognoscenti* are the grilled prawns or scallops, and pomfret with chilli and black bean sauce.

Zen***

LG 1, The Mall, Pacific Place, Hong Kong, tel 845 4555

采碟軒　金鐘太古廣場第1期LG1室

The Hong Kong branch of three London restaurants, this is *nouvelle* Chinese cuisine at its finest in an elegantly minimalist room highlighted by its fountain sculpture. Tastes are pure and simple, the combination of elements complementary rather than combative. The chive-stuffed dumplings melt in your mouth. Highly recommended dishes are the minced beef and egg white soup, and the roast Lung Kong chicken.

INDIAN

Maharajah Restaurant*

222 Wanchai Road, Hong Kong, tel 574 9838

皇室餐廳　香港灣仔道222號

A splendid variety of dishes and specialities are available at this unpretentious restaurant. Try the delicious appetizers such as mutton samosas, Indian breads baked in their own clay oven, nine different tandoor dishes, including the tenderest chicken tikka imaginable, seafood and vegetarian varieties and, the perfect dessert, Indian ice-cream with saffron and nuts. The service is attentive and friendly, and prices make any meal there a bargain. Another Maharajah Restaurant is located at 13A Granville Circuit, Tsimshatsui, Kowloon, tel 366 6671/723 3344.

Johnston Mess*

1/F, 104 Johnston Road, Wanchai, tel 891 6525

灣仔莊士敦道104號2樓

Set up by the youngsters of the family who own the nearby—and equally popular—Maharani Mess on Lockhart Road, this is a surprisingly light and airy restaurant with an unusual choice of Southern Indian dishes. The spicy stuffed peppers are a delight, the simple vegetable curry is excellent, and the range of breads is greater than usual. Service is friendly and you can take your own bottle if you like.

Viceroy of India**

2/F, Sun Hung Kai Centre, 30 Harbour Road, Wanchai, tel 827 7777

華仕萊苑　灣仔港灣道新鴻基中心3樓

A spectacular view of the harbour awaits you at this spacious restaurant with an outside terrace area. It is best known for its lunch buffet (HK$80 per head), which includes a wide choice of curries, plenty of vegetarian choices and some excellent tikkas. Prices are slightly higher than most local Indian restuarants, but the wine list is extensive and the atmosphere pleasant.

JAPANESE

Tomowa Japanese Restaurant***

G/F and 1/F, 17–19 Percival Street, Causeway Bay, tel 891 2898

友和日本料理　香港銅鑼灣波斯富街17至19號地下

The restaurant has separate entrances at street level, so decide if you want to sit at a counter on the ground floor or enjoy a meal in a cosy booth in one of the four rooms on the first floor. The staff are friendly and attentive, and the atmosphere is relaxed and very much the real thing. As for the menu, the cuttlefish with crab eggs cannot be faulted, and the *sushi* and *teppanyaki* set dinners are perfect. Other gems include the seasonal *namaebi* (live prawn) and the *tomowa yosenabe* (lobster, abalone, trough shell and a selection of seafood and seasonal vegetables cooked at the table).

KOREAN

Korea House**

19/F, Korea Centre, 119–121 Connaught Road Central, tel 544 0007

香港干諾道中119至121號韓國中心19字樓

One of a chain within Hong Kong, this restaurant is frequented by resident Koreans. The food is authentic, with individual burners on the tables, and the atmosphere can be extremely lively. The *kimchi* (fermented and pickled vegetable seasoned with garlic, chilli, pepper, ginger, fish and other seafoods) is excellent, as is the beancurd. Other outlets include: Blissful Building, 247 Des Voeux Road, Central, tel 541 6930; Empire Centre, Tsimshatsui East, tel 367 5674; and 8/F, BCC Building, 25–31 Carnarvon Road, Tsimshatsui, tel 722 6505.

Korea Restaurant***

56 Electric Road, Causeway Bay, tel 571 1731

韓國餐廳　香港銅鑼灣電氣道56號

This highly recommended restaurant has good beef and prawn barbecues, serves a variety of *kimchi*, peppers stuffed with beef, and roasted mackerel. It also boasts *bulgogi* (sliced grilled beef) that is unrivalled outside Seoul. A second Korea Restaurant is located at Ming Fai Shopping Centre, City Garden, North Point, Hong Kong, tel 566 0706.

THAI

Thai Delicacy*
44 Henessey Road, Wanchai, tel 527 2591
泰禾美食　灣仔軒尼詩道44號
This little gem of a restaurant has recently gone upmarket, having installed a front door (it used to be open to the street). Despite the basic décor, the food is good and can be very hot indeed, so watch the menu and, if in doubt about how spicy a dish is, ask the waitress. The seafood salad is a refreshing mix of squid, fish and tomato salad sprinkled with fresh lime, and the young papaya salad is always delightfully spicy. The green fish curry is also a good choice. Several Thai beers are available.

Supatra's**
50 D'Aguilar Street, Central, tel 522 5073
美味泰國荣　中環德己立街50號
This pleasant, no-frills, two-storey Thai restaurant in Lan Kwai Fong serves the usual delights: spicy charred beef salad, *pad thai* noodles, spicy shrimp soup with lemon grass, red and green curries of chicken, beef, seafood and beancurd. Good, dependable Thai food when you tire of the purity and delicacy of Cantonese cuisine. The upstairs is quieter and less frenetic than downstairs.

VIETNAMESE

Saigon Beach*
66 Lockhart Road, Wanchai, tel 529 7823
邊海　灣仔駱克道66號
An extremely popular and very cheap restaurant that is quickly full, so try to get there early. Run by Chinese-speaking Vietnamese, this place serves some of the best bread in Hong Kong, along with a mass of seafood, noodles and soup dishes. The spicy shrimp noodle soup is recommended, as are the prawns wrapped around sugar cane and the crab cooked in beer. Serves 333 brand beer.

FRENCH

Au Trou Normand**
6 Carnarvon Road, Tsimshatsui, Kowloon, tel 366 8754
諾曼第法國餐廳　九龍尖沙咀加拿芬道6號
Opened in 1964 and still thriving under the stalwart Bernard Vigneau, this homely basement bistro with gingham tablecloths and erratic service is one of the quirkier candidates

Ten Thousand Buddha Monastery, Shatin

for Hong Kong's restaurant roll-call of honour. It remains a firm favourite for the simple reason that it serves French food and, despite the almost Gallic insouciance of the waiters, is still one of the nicest places in which to meet friends and relax. Recommended is the liver mousse flavoured with armagnac; after that, fillet of sole, white wine and courgette sauce. For dessert, try the *crêpes normandes* flambéd with calvados.

La Rose Noire***

8–13 Wo On Lane, Central, Hong Kong, tel 526 5965

黑玫瑰餐廳　香港中環和安里8至13號

So much has been made of its dark cul-de-sac location and jumbled signposting that La Rose Noire is now probably a more familiar site than some of its more brightly lit cousins in nearby Lan Kwai Fong. This is an old-fashioned bistro complete with a drinker's bar and intimate tables, each sporting a black silk rose. The food is unobtrusively Gallic: starters include deep-fried camembert and snails in puff pastry, and main dishes range from pan-fried goose liver with sour cream gravy to steak tartare and grilled king prawns with garlic butter sauce. The wine list is varied, as is the repertoire of Michel, *le patron*, when he settles himself at the piano and takes you musically into the midnight hour.

Sabatini****

Royal Garden Hotel, 69 Mody Road, Tsimshatsui East, tel 721 5215

尖沙咀東部麼地道69號帝苑酒店

The former Restaurant Lalique has been redecorated and transformed into an elegant Italian restaurant specializing in 'Roman food'. Two native Italian chefs offer a traditional menu including *antipasta*, sea bass, roast lamb, veal and scampi.

Margaux****

Shangri-La Hotel, 64 Mody Road, Tsimshatsui East, tel 721 2111

馬高餐廳　九龍尖沙咀東部麼地道64號香格里拉酒店

This elegant restaurant has a million-dollar view across the harbour and is clearly the pride and joy of the Shangri-La, Kowloon. The menu hints at *nouvelle cuisine* (sauces are light and delicate) and the preparations are finely crafted. Specialties include dill-marinated salmon, crab meat ravioli in a light shell with basil sauce, and grilled guinea fowl breast with a truffle cream sauce. Naturally, Margaux has the usual entrées of beef (American), veal (Dutch) and garoupa (Hong Kong), not to mention the 28 vintages of Château Margaux on the wine list.

GERMAN AND AUSTRIAN

Baron's Table***
1/F, Holiday Inn Golden Mile, 50 Nathan Road, Kowloon, tel 369 3111 ext 291
男爵扒房　九龍尖沙咀彌敦道54號金域假日酒店1字樓
One of the most highly respected of hotel restaurants, the Baron's Table offers a sumptuous helping of hearty German, Austrian and Swiss specialties in rustic European surroundings. Also included is a Gourmet Health Menu for those able to resist the regular fare or one of the seasonal promotions.

Chesa***
Peninsula Hotel, Salisbury Road, Tsimshatsui, Kowloon, tel 366 6251
瑞樵閣　九龍尖沙咀梳士巴利道半島酒店
A delightfully cosy haven of warm and punctilious service. All the favourite Swiss specials, from air-dried beef to Swiss barley soup, schnitzel, veal sausages and fondues. There are only 16 tables, and you can watch closely the expression of fellow diners as they agonize over some of the miracles wrought in chocolate and listed in cruel detail on the dessert list. Expensive, but it is essential to book one or two days in advance.

Mozart Stub'n***
8 Glenealy, Central, tel 522 1763
中環己連拿利8號地下
Excellent Austrian cuisine with a traditional flavour in a cosy farmhouse-type environment. The veal goulash is a must, and if you think you have tasted good apple strudel, wait until you have tried their hearty home-made version. The wine selection is extensive, with a daily selection chalked up on the blackboard. Book early, as it is always full.

ITALIAN

Grappa's**
Shop No 132, Pacific Place, 88 Queensway, Central, tel 868 0086; Shop No 105–8, Harbour City, Tsimshatsui, tel 317 0288
金鐘太古廣場
The best way to start in this cheerful, American-style Italian restaurant is with a hunk of their homemade bread served with olive oil and black pepper. The *penne putanseca* is the best in town—spicy, rich, but not oily, and generously endowed with sun-dried tomatoes. Pizzas are thoughtfully prepared, and the squid ink pasta is excellent. The wine list is well balanced, and there is, of course, a vast selection of grappas. The serving staff are

Cheung Chau Bun Festival

not only snappily dressed (long white aprons, black trousers, white shirt and braces),
they are also helpful, swift and attentive. A great evening out for a reasonable price.

Il Mercato*
126 Stanley Main Street, Lower Ground Floor, Stanley, tel 813 9090 (Pizzeria tel 813
9239)
赤柱赤柱大街126號
Il Mercato and its accompanying Pizzeria filled a long-felt gap in the local market and
started a local craze for pizza. On offer are traditional Italian dishes and such specialties
as *risotto alla crema di scampi, lombato di vitello con burro e salvia* (veal) and, for devotees
of pasta, *penne con peperoni freschi*. No less enticing are the various desserts and the list
of Italian wines and liqueurs that completes this authentic menu. The Pizzeria maintains
the high standard: the dough is freshly made and hand-stretched, the finest ingredients
available are placed on top, and the whole thing is baked directly on the tiles of an oven.
The menu includes Italian sandwiches and ice cream. A delivery service to the south side
of Hong Kong Island operates seven days a week. A second major Mercato outlet is at

34–36 D'Aguilar Street (tel 868 3068), where the delicatessen counter sells an excellent salami and a stunning *tirami su*.

La Bohème***

2/F, 151 Lockhart Road, Wanchai, tel 891 7717
香港灣仔駱克道151號3樓
Surprising location for such an upmarket restaurant, but a welcome change from the glitz of hotels. A quiet, secluded place with a romantic feel, La Bohème specializes in northern Italian food. The salads are varied and tasty, and the seafood risotto is unusually good. This is the place to try a real lasagne and see what you have been missing. Service is discreet but helpful, and there is also a varied set lunch that provides good value for money.

Nicholini's****

Hotel Conrad, Pacific Place, 88 Queensway, Admiralty, tel 521 3838
意寧谷　金鐘太古廣場港麗酒店
An excellent selection of dishes, but you'll pay for it. Decorated in modern pastel shades (with matching upholstery on the plush seating) and subdued lighting. The angel-hair pasta with smoked salmon and cream sauce is exquisite, and the seafood *penne* is a treat. The finale is definitely worth waiting for—after all those cardboard-like *tirami su* imitations, Nicholini's version is a real experience to savour.

SPANISH

Café Adriatico***

89 Kimberley Road, Tsimshatsui, Kowloon, tel 368 8554
九龍尖沙咀金巴利道89號
This is a genuinely charming restaurant in a pleasantly quaint setting, and the staff are friendly and expert. Part of an international chain that stems from Manila's most-celebrated bistro, Café Adriatico is rightly popular for its Spanish/Filipino cuisine. Appetizers include spiced Spanish *gambas* and *salpicao* (tenderloin cubes stir-fried with garlic and chopped celery). The main dishes embrace a selection of seafood, including *calamares* Biscayne and mushroom-baked sole, and grills such as a steak section devoted to 'great peasant fare'. For dessert, make for the *baklava*.

La Bodega**

31C/D Wyndham Street, Central, tel 877 3101
中環雲咸街31號 C/D

Hong Kong's first *tapas* bar, this restaurant—with its window frontage, checked table-cloths and blackboard menu—is a cosy way to start the evening. They serve a very tasty *paella*, and the spicy potatoes, *calamares* with chilli sauce, and prawns with chilli and garlic are favourites. The service can be erratic, but the ambience is good and the prices reasonable. The wine list has an unusual selection of Spanish and South American wines.

AMERICAN AND GRILLS

Beverly Hills Deli**

2 Lan Kwai Fong, Central, Hong Kong, tel 526 5800

百富利餐廳　香港中環蘭桂坊2號

Hong Kong's first New York-style delicatessen, the Beverly Hills Deli serves Kosher food; they even do take-outs and telephoned deliveries. The Lan Kwai Fong branch gets it right all down the line with specials galore: Texas chilli, salads, waist-watcher platters (daily Scarsdale on request), burgers, 15 spaghettis, 11 pizzas, Dr Brown's soda, root beer—the lot. Another Beverly Hills Deli is located at L2, 55 New World Centre, Tsim-shatsui, Kowloon, tel 369 8695/6.

Bocarinos Grill****

Victoria Hotel, Shun Tak Centre, Central, Hong Kong, tel 540 7228

百樂軒　香港中環干諾道中200號信德中心海港酒店

This restaurant has acquired a fine reputation for international cuisine and courteous service. The décor leans towards genteel hacienda and has a feeling of space and privacy. Black caviar served with a shot of vodka makes a good starter, followed by delicacies such as smoked duck breast, lobster *tartelette* or grilled lamb and juniper berries; particularly recommended is their pigeon flavoured with mango, kiwi, papaya and wild rice. The pride of the restaurant is its grills—beef, lamb, veal and vension, as well as sea-food—which are cooked on a mesquite wood broiler. Cheese *aficionados* will be delighted to note that the Bocarinos board offers no fewer than 30 varieties. There is also a splendid business lunch at the bargain price of HK$95.

JW's California Grill***

Marriot Hotel, Pacific Place, Queensway, Admiralty, tel 841 3899

JW'S 加州扒房　香港金鐘道88號太古廣場萬豪酒店

Starve yourself for a day before eating here, as the American-style portions are huge. The restaurant boasts that if you fail to receive your main course within ten minutes of finishing your starter, your bill will be thrown away. The grills are excellent, and remember to check the special of the day. The wine list is extensive and the waiters helpful if you have problems choosing.

The Mandarin Grill****

Mandarin Oriental Hotel, 5 Connaught Road, Central, tel 522 0111

香港干諾道中5號文華酒店

The management of the Mandarin tends to push their Pierrot restaurant on the top floor, but many still prefer the warm elegance of the Grill, with its burnished copper, roast beef trolley, pan-fried escalopes of Hong Kong, truffled sweetbread, fresh *agnellotti* pasta with spinach and ricotta cheese, lobsters from the tank prepared any of six ways, broiled English farm sausages with bacon and lamb kidneys, and, of course, sizzling steaks. Very expensive and wholly worthwhile. It is essential to book if you are thinking of a weekday luncheon. The Grill also offers a breakfast fit for a king, with everything from fresh fruit and yoghurt and eggs benedict to black pudding and kippers. Worth spending several hours over.

The Steak House**

The Regent Hotel, 18 Salisbury Road, Tsimshatsui, tel 721 1211

牛扒屋　尖沙咀梳士巴利道18號麗晶酒店

The Steak House is an all-American treat: American charcoal-grilled steaks (nine choices), an all-American salad bar (about 20 ingredients of the freshest kind), even American desserts like grasshopper pie, plus one of the finest selections of American wines in Asia. Very tasty and filling, and the salad buffet is an innovative treat for weight-watchers. It is a shame that one must order the steak to qualify for the salad. The view across the harbour is as distracting as ever and the service punctilious.

OTHERS

Club Sri Lanka*

Basement, 17 Hollywood Road, Central, tel 526 6559

斯里蘭卡會所　中環荷里活道17號地庫

This popular restaurant, particularly among the working population in the area, serves vegetarian and non-vegetarian Sri Lankan fare. Though the menu is not extensive, the food is consistently good and the service friendly. For a reasonably priced meal in unpretentious surroundings, the buffet lunch or dinner is recommended.

Hugo's***

Hyatt Regency Hotel, 67 Nathan Road, Tsimshatsui, Kowloon, tel 311 1234

希戈餐廳　九龍尖沙咀彌敦道67號凱悅酒店

Hugo's is named after the Bavarian Baron Hugo Ludwig Wilhelm von Gluckenstein, whose fame as a host stemmed from his extravagance in serving only the best food and wine. The menu is varied to suit all tastes, with dishes that combine Western cuisine with an Eastern flavour. For soup, try the artichoke bisque with three caviars: for appetizer, sliced raw Kobe beef fillet served with a choice of hot and spicy tomato-pepper sauce or cold mustard dressing. Seafood being one of their strengths, test the tiger prawns braised in subtle pepper sauce with brown rice, or poached turbot with shark's fin enhanced by madeira champagne sauce.

Gaddi's****

Peninsula Hotel, Salisbury Road, Tsimshatsui, Kowloon, tel 366 6251
九龍尖沙咀梳士巴利道半島酒店

A stalwart favourite of most tourists and residents who can afford it, Gaddi's specializes in gourmet cooking. The beauty of the place rivals any Parisian restaurant. Not a single dish can be faulted, and it is worth scrutinizing the 'Gaddi's favourites' before giving way to temptation in the form of beluga caviar and lobster or the *salade d'homard*, roast rack of lamb or *entrecôte deux*. Some find the atmosphere of hauteur and genial disdain a little too brittle for honest enjoyment of a meal, but others aspire to no other life. The fact remains that no visitor who can afford the prices should miss Gaddi's, as it is as much a Hong Kong institution as the 'Pen' itself.

Landau's Restaurant**

257 Gloucester Road, Causeway Bay, tel 891 2901
蘭度餐廳　香港銅鑼灣告士打道257號

'Nostalgic atmosphere, gastronomic delights and superb service' is how the place itself summarizes its appeal. Oaken décor, genially deferential service and specials that range from medallion pork 'Lucullus' and breaded pork cutlet 'Romano' to Macau sole, baked avocado with snails and calf's liver sautéd with rosemary. Comfortable and dependable.

M at the Fringe**

2 Lower Albert Road, Central, tel 877 4000
香港中環下亞厘畢道2號 藝穗會

With its unique décor—cello-shaped chairs and walls painted with Mannerist figures—and excellent, imaginative cuisine, this restaurant is always full. Serving lunch, dinner and late-night supper, this is an especially good place for a leisurely lunch, with the sun streaming through the second-storey windows. The menu has a Mediterranean accent, with a filo tart of goat cheese and sun-dried tomatoes, *meza*, and onion and fennel soup among the appetizers. Pumpkin and almond tortellini tastes as rich as in the restaurants of Mantua. Other dishes include barbecued calves' livers with onion *confit* and crisp *polenta*, sirloin steak rolled in Sichuan peppercorns and steamed salmon fillets with balsamic butter sauce. Save room for the hot raspberry soufflé, the *tarte tatin* or the homemade ice creams.

The Lippo Centre towers over Hong Kong Park

Pierrot****

Mandarin Oriental Hotel, 5 Connaught Road, Central, tel 522 0111

香港干諾道中5號文華酒店

Everything about the Pierrot smacks of quiet elegance in this much-vaunted élite restaurant. Highly recommended are the lobster medallions with Perigord truffles, tomato mousseline, crab soup flavoured with tarragon and mango, *filet au gratin* of Welsh lamb with herbs in a red bellpepper sauce, and the roast *magret* of Barbarie duck in a mustard seed sauce. The smoked seabass is served with steamed celery and a light Beluga caviar sauce, the roast pigeon arrives on a parsley sauce with trumpet mushrooms, and the supreme of Bresse chicken is baked in a salt dough with fresh rosemary.

Satay Hut**

Houston Centre, Mody Road, Tsimshatsui, tel 723 3628

沙爹屋　九龍尖沙咀麼地道好時中心1樓

Not at all a hut, but a pleasant, small restaurant hidden away in a corner of the Houston Centre serves good Singaporean/Malay food. The menu contains old favourites from the Straits: tender chicken and beef satay, spicy beef *rendang*, chicken rice, *gado-gado*, an *ikan bilis* with peanuts (too sweet for our taste), and the full range of fried noodle dishes. The batik-clad staff are courteous and helpful and will answer your questions if you are not familiar with this wonderful Asian cooking.

Spices**

109 Repulse Bay Road, Repulse Bay, tel 812 2711

香港淺水灣淺水灣道109號

Some lament the old Repulse Bay Hotel, but *carpe diem* and let us be grateful that a place as nice as Spices came out of the renovation. Decorated with taste and featuring a pan-Asian menu of the best of spicy dishes, this is a clever idea that works well. Order a cooling *lhassi meethi* (yoghurt blended with milk and rose water) as you await your spicy prawn soup with lemon grass, followed by *tabouleh* (cracked wheat, tomato and parsley salad) or perhaps a *fritada baboy* from the Philippines. Everything pleases here, from the friendly staff to the colonial ambiance evoked by high ceilings—not to mention the convenience of a spacious car park on the premises.

Stanley's Restaurant***

86–88 Stanley Main Street, Stanley, tel 813 8873

赤柱法國餐廳　香港赤柱赤柱大街86至88號

Stanley has the honour of having been one of the very few settlements on Hong Kong before the British arrived in 1842, but it took some years to get a Western restaurant.

The wait was worth it: Stanley's serves excellent food, looks like the private home it once was, and is owned by three Europeans. There are seven separate dining areas on three floors, including two balconies and a private room; the fresh air and sound of the surf complete the idyll. There are à la carte menus, an inexpensive set lunch menu and a menu *de dégustation* for dinner. Specialities shown on the blackboard change daily.

Stanley's is open from morning to night 364 days a year and is deservedly popular enough to require booking for weekends and public holidays. What could be more pleasant than to follow a successful foray in the market with a delicious meal or tea and then ride back to Central, watching the view from the upper deck of a No 6 bus. For those who drive, there is a parking service.

The Belvedere****
Holiday Inn Crowne Plaza Harbour View, 70 Mody Road, Tsimshatsui East, Kowloon, tel 721 5161
海景假日酒店　九龍尖沙咀東部麼地道70號
A favourite place of many, this gourmet restaurant features seafood such as crabmeat cocktail with a brandy cream sauce or pan-fried sirloin steak with a spicy black pepper sauce. Also recommended are the whole range of *flambés* and prime cuts of beef. A huge plus is their weekday business lunch and Sunday buffet, which take place to the strains of a hearteningly proficient jazz combo.

The Time is Always Now**
UG/F, Wilson House, 19–27 Wyndham Street, Central, tel 877 1100
時間永遠是現在　香港中環雲咸街19至27號威信大廈閣樓
If you are a hungry culture vulture, then come to this art gallery café, the first in Asia. The concept, inspired by the passionate and prolific artist Victor IV, is to create an atmosphere where the exclusivity of conventional art galleries is broken down. The setting is spacious and sophisticated, and the walls are adorned with an awesome display of large modern paintings. Relax in the large, comfortable chairs and cast your eye over the cosmopolitan menu. The speciality is chicken in *filou* pastry stuffed with garlic cheese mousse, and the *tirami su* is reputedly the best in town. A select wine list and a full coffee bar make this trendy establishment an aesthete's delight.

High and Low

There are two kinds of street in Hongkong. The smooth level main streets parallel to the shore, lined with shops, crowded with the newest cars; and the narrow, staircased climbing streets which cut across them. In the large level streets can be found all the world's finished goods in profusion, for everything comes to or goes through Hongkong, and the harbour is full of ships unloading more. 'You can buy anything here', is the Colony's motto. Anything from a fighter airplane to the latest perfume. There are no restrictions. And now that the rich have come from Shanghai there is plenty of free capital floating about, and there is a boom on.

There is a boom on. Superficially, Hongkong is dazzling with prosperity. The rich have brought their money, and they build and banquet and buy. The shops are crammed full with everything that the rich can desire, and what do the rich like best but American things, slick and streamlined and colourful? Cameras, bathing suits, lipsticks, perfumes, watches, shoes, nylons, silks and brocades, perfumes and stockings, all in great heaps on the shop counters. Hongkong is a shopping paradise.

Like battalions of seagulls, the idle rich Chinese women walk from shop to shop, their voices raised above the din of the street, their bracelets tinkling on their wrists. Their scarlet-taloned hands dig into the silks and velvets, the brocades and the satins. Cantonese shopgirls and Indian salesmen unfold roll after roll of iridescent satin, drape shimmering silks round themselves for the inspection of their clients. The rich women crowd into the jade and gold shops, congregate at beauty counters, eddy among the lipsticks glistening in their gold cases, the strapless bathing suits, the Chanel perfumes, the 'falsies' spread on the counters. They buy and buy, noisy, rapacious and bored.

Around the Hongkong Hotel, in the English business section of the city, American sailors amble, hail taxis, have their shoes shined by little boys. On their arms hang shrill Chinese prostitutes. Tourist women in off-the-shoulder dresses gaze at embroidered silk underwear and ornate Chinese coats. Shanghai bankers and businessmen in twos and threes, all in natty sharkskin suits, flamboyant American ties, with Parker 51s in their coat pockets, talk business in earnest sibilant tones. Wounded lost soldiers of the Kuomintang, dirty and ragged, some on crutches, stand against the walls of the shops, and watch the street with an angry scowl on their dark faces. Under the covered archways of the sidewalk glide, flow, rattle and clatter the anonymous common men of Hongkong. Each man, despite his air of belonging, a transient, claiming as his origin a village back in South China, refusing to belong to the Colony, maintaining his status of passer-by even when he works here all his life, even when his children are born here, sometimes even when he is born here. This is the most permanent fact about the Colony: with few exceptions, those who come regard themselves as on the way to somewhere else.

In the narrow, vertical, staircased streets of the Chinese district abide the poor, and few go to look at them. The streets are dirty, the houses smell. The tenements are four-storeyed. Their insecure rotting wood balconies are draped with washing. These structures have no bathrooms, no latrines, no courtyards, and only one communal kitchen for anything up to twenty families. The floors are divided into cubicles. Each cubicle is eight by eight feet and houses a family of five or upwards. The beds in these cubicles are in tiers. At night the pails of human excreta are placed outside the door for collection. Up and down the staircase of the street the innumerable children of the poor play in the dust. Here are the street sleepers, the human scavengers that live off refuse from the hotels. Here a family spreads a mat between a cobbler's stall and a congee man's table and calls it a home. Here between the feet of the passer-by the offal of the markets—two rotting tomatoes, a handful of beans, one broken egg—is offered for sale by the poor to those poorer than they.

As beings from different planets, invisible to each other, unconscious and indifferent, these people move, walk side by side, jostle each other, sidle to avoid contact. Their glances skid over each other and rest nowhere. Absorbed in their preoccupation, aware only of their own perils and opportunities, riveted to their individual search for safety and survival, each is filled with the illusion of entireness, moves in his world and denies the others, for to acknowledge others would breach his own tenacity in the struggle for existence.

Han Suyin, *A Many-Splendoured Thing*, 1952

Hotels: A Selected List

Hong Kong has some of the best hotels in Asia—perhaps in the world—featuring comfortable, well-equipped guest rooms, efficient and friendly service, imaginative décor, marvellous views and topnotch facilities for wining, dining, meeting and relaxing.

Despite the effects of 4 June 1989 on tourism—occupancy rates in that summer plummeted to less than 60 per cent at many of the major hotels—more and more hotels are being built. Occupancy rates have risen again, and it is difficult to book rooms at the finer hotels at short notice.

Whichever hotel you choose in the top categories, it will be a modern high-rise building with air-conditioned rooms. All have private bathroom, telephone and colour television, and most have a refrigerator and minibar. Odds are that the views will be spectacular. Keen competition keeps the standard of service very high and most hotels have round-the-clock room service.

Hotels in the moderately priced category (standard) are clean, comfortable and efficiently staffed. They tend to be a little farther from the tourist hubs but are well served by taxis and public transport.

All hotels have good restaurants. The smaller ones may have one dining room serving European and Chinese food. The large hotels contain some of the best restaurants in town (see Restaurants, page 178), where a great deal of local expense-account entertaining takes place. The hotels are also used extensively for business meetings, conferences, art exhibitions, trade promotions and special events such as antique auctions.

The following list offers a brief description of some of Hong Kong's hotels. All add ten per cent service charge and five per cent tax to the bill. Listing is in alphabetical order. Price categories are based on the price of a standard double room. Note that in many cases single and double rooms are charged at the same rate.

SUPERIOR (MORE THAN US$200 PER NIGHT)

■ HONG KONG ISLAND

Conrad
Pacific Place, Admiralty, tel 521 3838
港麗酒店　金鐘道88號太古廣場
Opened in 1990. 513 rooms, many with striking views of the city, Peak and harbour. Bar, lobby lounge, 4 restaurants (French, Chinese, Italian and buffet) and 24 hour business centre. Outdoor pool (heated in winter) and jacuzzi.

Grand Hyatt
1 Harbour Road, Wanchai, tel 588 1234
君悅酒店　灣仔港灣道1號
Opened in 1989, this 575 room hotel is well designed and appointed with excellent harbour views. 3 restaurants, 2 bars, disco, business centre, rooftop pool, jogging track, golf driving range and health club.

Hilton
2A Queen's Rd, Central, tel 523 3111
希爾頓酒店　中環皇后大道中2號A
Centrally located with 750 rooms, popular restaurants (including Chinese, American, grill and buffet), 2 bars, coffee shop and business centre. Outdoor swimming pool terrace. Brigantine cruises and regular dinner-theatre presentations. Features a Grand Ballroom, accommodating 1,200 guests.

Island Shangri-La
Pacific Place, 88 Queensway, Admiralty, tel 877 3838
港島香格里拉大酒店　金鐘道88號太古廣場
565 rooms. Fully equipped, with all the facilities of a super-luxury class hotel; excellent restaurants (Japanese, French, Cantonese) seafood bar, delicatessen, café, bars, etc. Health club and large outdoor swimming pool.

Mandarin Oriental
5 Connaught Road, Central, tel 522 0111
文華東方酒店　中環干諾道中5號
In easy reach of Central offices, a hub for local and visiting businessmen. Famed for its pool, service, restaurants and Roman-baths. 542 rooms, 5 restaurants, 3 bars, popular coffee shop, newly renovated lobby, health and business centres. Also features bakery, well-known shopping arcade and even its own art gallery.

Marriott Hotel
Pacific Place, 88 Queensway, Admiralty, tel 810 8366
萬豪酒店　金鐘道88號太古廣場
This elegant hotel sits above the up-market Pacific Place shopping complex and is within walking distance of Central district. It has 605 rooms including 42 suites, 3 restaurants, 2 bars, health centre, pool and a business centre.

Waterworld, Ocean Park (above); Ocean Terminal, Tsimshatsui (below)

■ KOWLOON

Nikko

72 Mody Road, Tsimshatsui East, tel 739 1111
日航酒店　尖沙咀麼地道72號
The Nikko features a superb view of the Hong Kong skyline, and is situated adjacent to the shopping and nightlife of Tsimshatsui East. 461 rooms, comprehensive facilities including 4 restaurants, 3 bars, open air pool, fitness centre and business centre.

The Peninsula

Salisbury Road, Tsimshatsui, tel 366 6251
半島酒店　尖沙咀梳士巴利道
The grande dame of Hong Kong hotels with its fleet of Rolls-Royces, famous lobby and fabled restaurants, the Peninsula retains its old-fashioned opulence and grace whilst providing comprehensive modern facilities. 152 rooms. New tower to open in early 1994, providing more rooms and a new gym, swimming pool and business centre.

Ramada Renaissance

9 Peking Road, Tsimshatsui, tel 375 1133
華美達麗新酒店　尖沙咀北京道9號
This, the star of the HK Ramada Renaissance Hotels, has 496 rooms, 4 restaurants, bar/lobby lounge, plus excellent sports facilities including squash court and outdoor pool.

The Regent

18 Salisbury Road, Tsimshatsui, tel 721 1211
麗晶酒店　尖沙咀梳士巴利道18號
602 rooms. Top luxury hotel, with 4 restaurants (including Chinese, European, and a steak house), 2 lobby lounges, health club, outdoor pool and jacuzzi, fax line in every room and well-known shopping arcade.

Kowloon Shangri-La

64 Mody Road, Tsimshatsui East, tel 721 2111
九龍香格里拉大酒店　尖沙咀麼地道64號
719 rooms. Very grand and well-appointed, featuring a Grand Ballroom, wide choice of restaurants, coffee garden and 4 lounges. Good location, with harbour views.

Sheraton Towers

20 Nathan Road, Tsimshatsui, tel 369 1111
香港喜來登酒店　尖沙咀彌敦道20號

A Conventioneer's Guide

The Hong Kong Convention and Exhibition Centre is a state-of-the-art jewel expressing all that is right about Hong Kong: style, convenience, service and magnificent views of the harbour. Many convention centres seem to be huddled in the decaying heart of a city or on its outskirts, among railroad tracks and freight terminals, a long uninviting cab ride to the safety of a hotel. Hong Kong's Convention Centre, the largest in Asia, is at One Harbour Road in the centre of Wanchai, only 15 minutes' drive to the airport, next to the ferries to Tsimshatsui and a five-minute cab ride to Central and Causeway Bay.

In October 1986, Queen Elizabeth II laid the first stone, and two years later the centre was completed. The entire centre complex of 4.4 million square feet includes the Grand Hyatt to the west and the New World Harbour View Hotel to the east. This complex, all under one roof and connected by walkways to the neighbouring Great Eagle Centre and the China Resources Building, has such a wealth of services and facilities that if a conventioneer cannot find what he wants here, he probably doesn't need it.

In the centre itself are two exhibition halls of 9,000 square metres (97,000 square feet) each, big enough for a football field or a Pavarotti concert for 8,000 people; a ballroom type convention hall capable of holding a Chinese banquet for 1,500 or a Western one for 3,000; two theatres; and 26 flexible meeting rooms, all with harbour views. The theatres and Convention Hall are equipped for simultaneous translation in eight languages, and the centre offers word processing in Chinese, English and Japanese, accounting and notary services, and, of course in Hong Kong, mobile phones and pagers. The centre's shopping arcade has banks, a film processor, print shop, a Thomas Cook's travel agency and an International Call Office of Hong Kong Telephone for phone and fax messages.

But conventioneers do not live on meetings alone. On Level One there is the Harbour Lounge with piano music from happy hour to closing time at midnight. On Level Six is the Gallery Café with a magnificent view of the harbour through what is supposedly the largest glass wall in the world. Dusk in the café is lovely, as the colours of the sky change and the harbour sparkles with lights. The premier restaurant in the centre is the spacious Congress Restaurant, on the seventh level, whose Friday and Saturday night buffet requires reservations over a week in advance. At very short notice you can arrange a private Chinese dinner for a minimum of 12 in one of the meeting rooms—they all have harbour views—that includes complimentary champagne and floral arrangements at a cost from HK$3,500 to HK$5,000 per table.

The Grand Hyatt is the most beautiful of all Hong Kong hotels and from the centre's Arrival Plaza is a short walk through the hotel's shopping arcade to its Tiffin Lounge and the grandeur of the lobby. At the other end of the convention complex is the New World Harbour View, not in the Hyatt's five star league but no slouch when it comes to eating, drinking and music. You can walk from the New World via covered walkway to the China Resources Building, with its Chinese Garden, or to the Great Eagle Centre, with its many restaurants, including the highly rated Tao Yuan. If it's a nice day, you can stroll along the landscaped promenade in front of the Convention Centre and relax in the garden directly west of the Hyatt.

At the Hong Kong Arts Centre down the block there is usually an exhibition on at the Pao Galleries, or ask one of the helpful staff at Track One on the second floor to put on a CD of your choice and sit and listen. There is an URBTIX ticket outlet in the lobby where you can purchase tickets for most cultural events, some of which are held at the Performing Arts Centre across the street. Check the bulletin boards and flyers found in the lobby of the Arts Centre for current attractions.

When you return to your home office, you can say with a straight face that you barely left the Convention Centre. What the boss doesn't know won't hurt!

805 rooms. Luxury hotel, featuring a wide choice of restaurants (Japanese and Indian as well as Chinese and European) lounges, bars, coffee shop, health club with gym and saunas, rooftop swimming pool and sun deck.

FIRST CLASS (US$150–200 PER NIGHT)

■ HONG KONG ISLAND

Furama Kempinski
1 Connaught Road, Central, tel 525 5111
富麗華酒店　中環干諾道中1號
An elegant high-rise with 517 rooms overlooking the harbour, close to the Star Ferry and MTR. It has comfortable meeting areas and a spectacular revolving restaurant. 2 other restaurants, 2 bars, disco.

New World Harbour View
1 Harbour Road, Wanchai, tel 802 8888
新世界海景酒店　灣仔港灣道1號
In the Convention Centre complex near business districts, offering superb harbour views and exceptionally comprehensive facilities: good choice of restaurants, large outdoor pool. Sports facilities shared with Grand Hyatt (which is part of the same complex).

Park Lane Radisson
310 Gloucester Road, Causeway Bay, tel 890 3355
栢寧酒店　銅鑼灣告士打道310號
Opposite Victoria Park and close to a busy shopping district. 850 rooms, 2 restaurants, disco, gallery lounge and coffee shop.

Victoria
Shun Tak Centre, 200 Gloucester Road, Central, tel 540 7228
海港酒店　中環干諾道中200號信德中心
Harbour views for 75 per cent of the 536 rooms and 330 apartments. 3 restaurants, lobby lounge, music room, pool, health club and business centre.

■ KOWLOON

Holiday Inn Golden Mile
46–52 Nathan Road, Tsimshatsui, tel 369 3111
金域假日酒店　尖沙咀彌敦道46至52號

597 rooms. Situated on the shoppers' Golden Mile, this is a well run hotel with a good choice of restaurants, including the Baron's Table offering German cuisine. Also features rooftop pool and health centre.

Hyatt Regency

67 Nathan Road, Tsimshatsui, tel 311 1234

香港凱悅酒店　尖沙咀彌敦道67號

723 rooms. Located right in the centre of Tsimshatsui. Usual luxury facilities. Chinese and European (Hugo's) restaurants, bar and coffee shop.

Miramar

130 Nathan Road, Tsimshatsui, tel 368 1111

美麗華酒店　尖沙咀彌敦道130號

500 rooms. Well-equipped, with a good choice of restaurants, plus bar, coffee shop, convention centre, gym and swimming pool.

Omni Hong Kong Hotel

Harbour City, Canton Road, Tsimshatsui, tel 736 1888

奧麗香港酒店　尖沙咀廣東道3號海港城

Next to the Ocean Terminal and the Star Ferry, with good restaurants, a bar and jazz lounge plus usual luxury facilities, including open-air pool. Other Omni hotels in Kowloon, also in Canton Road, are the Omni Marco Polo and the Omni Prince.

Regal Airport Hotel

Sa Po Road, Kowloon City, tel 718 0333

富豪機場酒店　九龍城沙埔道

Situated beside Kai Tak airport. 385 rooms, 4 popular restaurants, bar and a host of other facilities ranging from a business centre to babysitters.

STANDARD (US$75–150 PER NIGHT)

■ HONG KONG ISLAND

China Harbour View

189 Gloucester Road, Wanchai, tel 838 2222

中華海景酒店　灣仔告士打道189號

Opened in 1988 with 325 modern, well-appointed but small rooms. 2 restaurants, lounge, business centre. Good location.

China Merchants

160 Connaught Road West, Central, tel 559 6888

華喬酒店　西環干諾道西160號

A conveniently located high-rise with 3 restaurants, 2 bars and conference room. Good value for money.

Eastin Valley

1A Wang Tak Street, Happy Valley, tel 574 9922

東豪酒店　跑馬地宏德街1A

111 rooms. Small hotel with good facilities: Cantonese restaurant, coffee shop, business centre, and a health club featuring sauna, gym and outside pool.

Excelsior

281 Gloucester Road, Causeway Bay, tel 894 8888

怡東酒店　銅鑼灣告士打道281號

Next to the cross-harbour tunnel and Causeway Bay nightlife, close to shops, 3 restaurants/bars. Famous for its nightclub, tennis courts and sports/health facilities. 923 rooms.

Harbour

116–122 Gloucester Road, Wanchai, tel 511 8211

華國酒店　灣仔告士打道116至122號

On the waterfront, close to nightclubs and restaurants. 200 rooms, nightclub, 2 restaurants (Chinese and Western). A friendly and reasonably priced hotel.

Lee Gardens

33–37 Hysan Avenue, Causeway Bay, tel 895 3311

利園酒店　銅鑼灣希慎道33至37號

Close to the nightlife and shops of Causeway Bay, the hotel has extensive public areas and 788 rooms. 3 restaurants, 3 bars.

New Cathay

17 Tung Lo Wan Rd, Causeway Bay, tel 577 8211

新國泰酒店　香港銅鑼灣銅鑼灣道17號

A quiet, comfortable hotel with 230 rooms. Restaurants, lobby bar and coffee shop. Moderately priced.

New Harbour

41–49 Hennessy Road, Wanchai, tel 861 1166

星港酒店　灣仔軒尼詩道41至49號

Situated in the heart of Wanchai with 173 rooms, known for good food and atmosphere. Competitively priced.

■ KOWLOON

Ambassador
26 Nathan Road, Tsimshatsui, tel 366 6321
國賓酒店　尖沙咀彌敦道26號
A friendly hotel with 313 rooms. Convenient for downtown Kowloon. Coffee shop, bar, 2 restaurants.

International
33 Cameron Road, Tsimshatsui, tel 366 3381
國際酒店　尖沙咀金馬倫道33號
Convenient and comfortable, a hotel long known for moderate prices, it has 89 rooms, a restaurant and bar.

Kowloon
19–21 Nathan Road, Tsimshatsui, tel 369 8698
九龍酒店　尖沙咀彌敦道19至21號
707 rooms. Opened in January 1986, and part of the Peninsula Group of hotels, this hotel features 2 restaurants, a bar, and a coffee shop.

Kowloon Panda
3 Tsuen Wah St, Tsuen Wan, New Territories, tel 409 1111
九龍悅來酒店　新界荃灣荃華街3號
The New Territories' first and only international-style hotel has a full range of facilities, including Chinese and Italian restaurants, coffee shop, lobby lounge, outdoor swimming pool, gym, sauna, banquet room, and a whole floor devoted to karaoke.

Metropole
75 Waterloo Road, Yaumatei, tel 761 1711
京華國際酒店　油麻地窩打老道75號
487 rooms. Well appointed hotel with 4 restaurants, bar, coffee shop and rooftop swimming pool.

Nathan
378 Nathan Road, Homantin, tel 388 5141
彌敦酒店　油麻地彌敦道378號

An unpretentious and convenient hotel at the top of the Golden Mile. 186 rooms.

New World

New World Centre 22 Salisbury Road, Tsimshatsui, tel 369 4111

新世界酒店 尖沙咀梳士巴利道22號

On the edge of Kowloon Bay next to a vast shopping and entertainment complex, the hotel has 716 rooms, 2 restaurants, coffee shop, bar, and swimming pool.

Park

61–65 Chatham Road, Tsimshatsui, tel 366 1371

百樂大酒店 尖沙咀漆咸道61至65號

An old favourite for its large rooms and comfortable bar-lounge. The hotel is well located, and has 410 rooms, 2 restaurants and a coffee shop.

Windsor

39–43A Kimberley Road, Tsimshatsui, tel 739 5665

溫莎酒店 尖沙咀金巴利道39至43A號

166 rooms. Comfortable hotel featuring a Chinese restaurant, plus a bar and coffee shop.

BUDGET (UP TO US$75 PER NIGHT)

■ KOWLOON

The Salisbury YMCA

41 Salisbury Road, Tsimshatsui, tel 369 2211

香港基督教青年會 尖沙咀梳士巴利道41號

Recently renovated, with health centre, swimming pool, badminton and squash courts. 360 rooms. Advance booking is recommended, as the YMCA is a rare commodity in Hong Kong—both moderately priced and well located.

STB Hostel

2/F, Great Eastern Mansion, 255–261 Reclamation Road, Mongkok, tel 332 1073

學聯旅舍有限公司 九龍新填地街255至261號東鴻大廈3樓

Clean and well-organised hostel with double rooms, dormitories and cafeteria. Advance booking is recommended.

Gilded wood carving

Recommended Reading

A wealth of literature and information has been published about Hong Kong. For authoritative historical background, Maurice Collis' *Foreign Mud* (Faber & Faber, 1964) and G B Endacott's *A History of Hong Kong* (Oxford University Press, 1973) are excellent. The standard history of 19th-century Hong Kong is *Europe in China* (Oxford University Press, 1983) by E J Eitel. First published in 1895, it remains an essential source for historians of Hong Kong; it is also a delight for the general reader, as Eitel's wry, acerbic narrative celebrates the fractious and eccentric character of life in the colony in the years 1841–82.

Hong Kong's strange genesis and stranger survival is described in *Borrowed Place, Borrowed Time* by Richard Hughes (Andre Deutsch, 1968). Hughes was a veteran reporter who lived in Hong Kong for almost 30 years and his book offers an intriguing and highly readable account of the place.

Austin Coates is one of Hong Kong's leading historians with a lucid and attractive style. Among his books are *Myself a Mandarin* (Fredrick Muller, 1968; Heinemann [Asia], 1975) which describes his years as a magistrate; *Whampoa* (South China Morning Post, 1980), the history of local shipping; and *The Road* (Harper Collins, 1949), a novel about a clash of vision and values between rural Hong Kong villagers and the colonial government.

For history, anecdote and some magnificent photographs try *Hong Kong: The Cultured Pearl* by Nigel Cameron (Oxford University Press, 1978). Hugh Baker's two-volume *Ancestral Images* (South China Morning Post, 1979) gives some fascinating insights into the traditional life of rural China.

For an overview of life in the Colony today, Jan Morris' *Hong Kong* (Viking Penguin, 1988) provides the lively narrative and authoritative research her readers have come to expect. Kevin Rafferty's *Hong Kong: City on the Rocks* (Viking Penguin, 1990) is more chaotic but is currently the most thorough consideration of the events that precipitated the coming Chinese takeover in 1997.

The Hong Kong government has published many excellent books dealing with different aspects of the Territory. Of special note are *This is Hong Kong: Temples* (1977) with detailed descriptions of 12 Chinese temples, and *Rural Architecture of Hong Kong*, which illustrates in words and pictures some of the historic buildings still surviving in the New Territories.

For an indispensable reference book, the government publishes an *Annual Review*, packed with statistics, analysis and superb picture essays on just about every aspect of Hong Kong—all official, up-beat and reliable.

For an uncommonly healthy perspective, try *Another Hong Kong: An Explorer's Guide* (Emphasis Hong Kong Ltd, 1989), an affectionate tour of over 50 walks that emphasize the persistently rural quality of life beyond Central and Tsimshatsui.

James Clavell has fictionalized the leading characters and machinations of the great hongs, or trading companies, in *Taipan* (Dell, 1966) and *Noble House* (Hodder & Stoughton, 1981). Both required exhaustive research, but the facts have not been allowed to spoil a good adventure story.

The same applies to two other books with a Hong Kong setting. John Le Carré's *The Honourable Schoolboy* (Hodder and Stoughton, 1977) is a spy thriller featuring some recognizable local residents. Robert Elegant's *Dynasty* (Collins, 1977) is an exciting and highly fanciful saga of a Eurasian family very loosely based on a local clan.

Easily the most lyrical evocation of Hong Kong between the wars is *A Many-Splendoured Thing* by Han Suyin (Jonathan Cape, 1952), which describes the prolific Eurasian writer's love affair with a British war correspondent and is one of the greatest love stories ever told.

The Anglo-Chinese author Timothy Mo was born in Hong Kong and has three times been nominated for the Booker Prize, Britain's premier literary award. His first novel, the *Monkey King* (Andre Deutsch, 1978) is one of the few books to portray the inner workings of a Cantonese family accurately, whilst *An Insular Possession* (Picador, 1986) is an epic historical account of Hong Kong's formative years.

Hong Kong-based Odyssey Guides offer a broad range of books about the Territory. Alan Birch in *Hong Kong: The Colony that Never Was* (The Guidebook Company, 1991) records the present for posterity in his account of this extraordinary political anomaly. *A Visitor's Guide to Historic Hong Kong* (The Guidebook Company, 1991) by Sally Rodwell is an immensely readable account of Hong Kong's history from the stone age through 150 years of British rule, while *Over Hong Kong* (Odyssey Productions, 1992), with an introduction by Nury Vittachi, is a photographic record of the Territory from the air, updated annually. On a more practical note are *Hong Kong in Depth A–Z Guide* (The Guidebook Company, 1993) and Odyssey Illustrated Guides to Macau, China, Guangzhou and other destinations in China. Also packed with practical tips is Moon's *Hong Kong Handbook* by Laurie Fullerton.

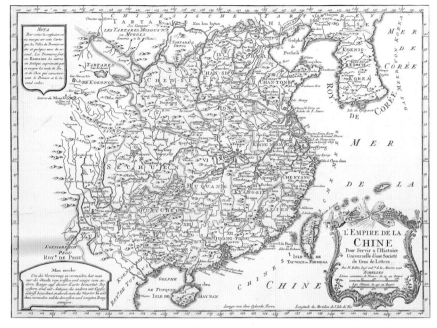

Jacques Nicolas Bellin, L'Empire de la Chine, 1748 *(above);* Sea fight between government gunboats and pirates, *oil painting, artist unknown, Hong Kong Museum of Art (below)*

INDEX